A JOURNEY THROUGH THE BIBLE

A JOURNEY THROUGH THE BIBLE

Volume 1
Genesis to Esther

DENIS LYLE

Christian Year Publications

ISBN-13: 978 1 872734 55 2

Typeset by John Ritchie Ltd., Kilmarnock
Printed by Bell & Bain Ltd., Glasgow

"But continue thou in the things which thou hast learned and hast been assured of, knowing of whom thou hast learned them; And that from a child thou hast known the holy scriptures, which are able to make thee wise unto salvation through faith which is in Christ Jesus. All scripture is given by inspiration of God, and is profitable for doctrine, for reproof, for correction, for instruction in righteousness: That the man of God may be perfect, thoroughly furnished unto all good works."

2 Timothy 3:14-17

Contents

Foreword

Denis and I have been close friends for over 20 years. I have been blessed and encouraged many times by his teaching and preaching ministry and I was thrilled to be asked to write this *Foreword* for Denis' latest writing. When I first learned of Denis' Bible Study at Lurgan Baptist: *'A Journey Through the Bible'*, it was my hope and prayer that the series would appear in print. I am so thankful that this great body of work is now becoming available.

I have thoroughly enjoyed all of Denis' writings and these latest volumes will be a welcome addition to any believer's collection. In the opening Chapter, Denis explains that his method of study is telescopic and not microscopic. With such a vast subject matter, this method is very understandable. However, Denis' detailed, thorough examination and explanation of each book make this an invaluable resource for every child of God, regardless of their Biblical knowledge.

As you read these Volumes, your attention will be drawn to the necessary historical and chronological background. You will be made aware of the typical and devotional application. You will find informative and accurate biographical information about the authors and some of the main characters. Prophetical subjects are examined as they arise and the reader will find evangelical truths explained. Denis does not gloss over important doctrinal teaching. You will find instruction on many of the major doctrines from the Creation in Genesis to the Glorious Return of Christ in Revelation.

Denis explains the Bible is a 'Him-book'. It is all about Christ. Therefore, Denis seeks to bring the reader's attention to Christ throughout these writings.

I am sure that these Volumes will prove to be very helpful to the Bible student and to all who love God and His precious Word.

Thank you, Denis, for putting this work into print.

Ian Wilson
Pastor of Rathfriland Baptist Church, Northern Ireland

'Study to shew thyself approved unto God, a workman that needeth not to be ashamed, rightly dividing the word of truth' (2 Timothy 2:15).

Preface

George Washington, the first President of the United States of America, said: **"It is impossible to rightly govern the world without God and the Bible"**. Abraham Lincoln, the 16th President of the United States, said: **"I believe the Bible to be the best gift God has ever given to man. All the good from the Saviour of the world is communicated to us through this book"**. From as early as I can remember, like Timothy I have **'known the holy scriptures'** (2 Timothy 3:15). Brought up in a godly home where the Word of God was practised, and sent to a local church where the Bible was faithfully preached, I have always had a tremendous interest in and respect for the Word of the Lord. My prayer is that we all as Christian believers may be like the man in Psalm 1 of whom it is said: **"His delight in the law of the Lord; and in His law doth he meditate day and night"** (Psalm 1:2).

These Volumes on **'A Journey Through the Bible'** were the outcome of a series of studies conducted in Lurgan Baptist Church on Tuesday evenings. They began in the autumn of 2013 and concluded in the spring of 2017. On this journey, I took one book of the Bible each night and sought to give an overview of that whole book.

During the series, I drew widely from all sorts of writers. Their books on the Bible enlightened me, enriched me and encouraged me and some of their content is found in these volumes. That is my disclaimer to plagiarism.

The Psalmist in that Psalm which is all about the Word of God says: **"Oh how I love Thy law! it is my meditation all the day"** (Psalm 119:97). I trust that as you ponder the pages

11

of 'A Journey Through the Bible' that you will have a new appreciation of the written Word and a fresh appreciation of our wonderful Saviour, of whom this Book so eloquently speaks.

Denis Lyle
Lurgan Baptist Church
Northern Ireland
June 2017

Bibliography

Unlocking the Bible: J. David Pawson - Collins

Willmington's Guide to the Bible: H.L. Willmington - Tyndale House, Wheaton, Illinois

Wiersbe's Expository Outlines on the New Testament: Warren Wiersbe - Victor Books

The Bible Exposition Commentary: Warren Wiersbe - Victor Books

The Message of the Old Testament: Mark Dever - Crossway Books

The Message of the New Testament: Mark Dever - Crossway Books

The McArthur Bible Handbook: John McArthur - Thomas Nelson

Adventuring Through the Bible: Ray Steadman - Discovery House Publishers

God's Wonderful Word: Trevor Knight - Young Life

A Sure Foundation: Alan Cairns - Ambassador

Bible Survey Outlines: Roland V. Hudson - Eerdmans Publishing Company

Explore The Book: J. Sidlow Baxter - Zondervan Publishing House

The Bible Book by Book: Raymond Brown - Collins

Know your Bible: Graham Scroggie - Pickering & Inglis

From Cover to Cover: Brian Harbour - Broadman Press

Exploring the Old Testament Book by Book: John Phillips - Kregel

Exploring the New Testament Book by Book: John Phillips - Kregel

The Old Testament: Gareth Crossley - Evangelical Press

Jensen's Survey of the Old Testament: Irving Jensen - Moody Press

A Survey of the New Testament: Robert H. Gundry - The Paternoster Press

The Collected Writings of J.B. Hewitt: Gospel Tract Publications

Basic Bible Study Notes: Ian Brown (Martyrs Memorial Free Presbyterian Church, Belfast)

An Introduction to the New Testament: Lamoyne Sharpe - Printed in U.S.A.

CHAPTER 1
God's Wonderful Word

A high school teacher taught a course entitled: *"The Bible as Literature"*. Only seniors in the top 10 per cent of the class could take this course. A pre-test was given to evaluate the students' biblical knowledge. One student, asked to define the Epistles, gave as his answer: *"The wives of the Apostles"*. A pastor was so humoured by this answer that he shared it during his next sermon. One of the church members approached him afterwards and asked: *"If the Epistles were not the wives of the Apostles, whose wives were they?"*

That may be a humorous story, but it begs the questions of each of us:
What do we know?
What do we believe?

In this Book, I want to take the reader on: **"A Journey Through The Bible"**. Our business, our purpose, is: *"An overall view of each book which will lead to a better understanding of the whole book which will lead to an increasing knowledge of its Author"*.

Our method of Bible study will be *telescopic* and not *microscopic.* In other words, we will try to give a bird's eye view of each book, thus promoting a better understanding of the whole book.

However, we cannot embark on **"A Journey Through the Bible"** without first examining what the Bible has to say about itself. So let us explore *"God's Wonderful Word"*.

G. Campbell Morgan had grown up in a Christian home, never questioning that the Bible was the Word of God. In college, however, his faith was severely challenged and he began to entertain doubts. *"The whole intellectual world was under the mastery of the physical scientists",* he later said, *"and of a materialistic and rationalistic philosophy. There came a moment when I was sure of nothing".* In those days, opponents of the Bible appeared every Sunday in great lecture and concert halls across England, attacking Christianity and the Bible, and these atheists and agnostics troubled the young student. He read every book he could find, both for and against the Bible, both for and against Christianity, until he was so confused, so riddled with doubt, that he felt he could not go on.

In desperation he closed his books, put them in his cupboard and turned the lock. Going down to a bookshop, he bought a new Bible, returned to his room, sat down at his desk, and opened it. He said: *"I am no longer sure that this is what my father claims it to be .... the Word of God. But of this I am sure - If it be the Word of God and if I come to it with an unprejudiced and open mind, it will bring assurance to my soul of itself".* As he looked into the book before him, studying its form and structure, its unity and message, he was amazed. He later said: *"That Bible found me. I began to read and study it then, in 1883, and I have been a student ever since".*

What about you? Have you doubts about the Bible? Are you asking the question: *"Is the Bible the Word of God?"*

I believe we hold in our hands: ***"The Holy Bible".*** The word "Bible" comes from the Greek word for "book". Therefore, *"The Holy Bible"* simply means *"The Holy Book".* It is the Book that stands alone, unapproachable in grandeur, solitary in splendour, mysterious in ascendancy. As Thomas Carlyle said: *"There never was any other book like the Bible, and there never will be such another".* According to Dr. Stephen Olford: *"The Bible contains 3,566,480 letters, 810,697 words, 31,175 verses, 1189 chapters and 66 books".*

God used three wonderful methods as He carefully carved out that most blessed of all books, the Bible, and these *"tools of the Trinity"* are ***Revelation, Inspiration and Illumination.***

How did we receive our Bible? Well, around 1400 B.C., God began to quietly call some 40 people into His presence. Oh, He did not call them all at once. In fact, it took Him nearly 16 centuries to complete the task. But God spoke the burden of His heart in simple but sublime language to those chosen forty. With a holy hush they heard Him tell of creation, corruption, condemnation, justification, sanctification and glorification. These were weighty words indeed. But when God had finished, the first tool in carving out the Bible was set aside. *Revelation* had occurred.

Now we see this Almighty Author as He quickly but carefully guides each chosen vessel in his assigned writing task. The human instruments are dealt with individually. Job, a rich farmer, will write differently from Amos, a poor farmer. The words of the educated Paul will be more complicated on occasion than those of the uneducated John or Peter. But behind every word in this book is the Divine Author, God Himself. Finally, the last penman lays down his pen. The angels watch as their Creator lays aside the second tool in the making of the Bible. *Inspiration* has taken place.

Soon many thousands of men and women join the ranks of those original forty and begin their assigned task of taking God's glory story to the uttermost parts of the earth. As they do, untold multitudes are stopped in their tracks, convicted in their hearts and saved from their sins. By what secret power did all this take place? The answer is simple, the Divine Author of the Bible is using the third and final tool. *Illumination* - and illumination continues to take place.

So the Scriptures are shaped. Think of these three tools like this:

1. Revelation: From God to man, man hears that which God wants written;

2. Inspiration: From man to paper, man writes that which God wants written;

3. Illumination: From paper to heart, man receives the light of that which God has written.

One of the classic passages on "God's Wonderful Word" is the passage in 2 Timothy 3:

"But continue thou in the things which thou hast learned and hast been assured of, knowing of whom thou hast learned them; And that from a child thou hast known the holy scriptures, which are able to make thee wise unto salvation through faith which is in Christ Jesus. All scripture is given by inspiration of God, and is profitable for doctrine, for reproof, for correction, for instruction in righteousness: That the man of God may be perfect, thoroughly furnished unto all good works."

Here is brought before us:

(1) THE ORIGIN OF THE BIBLE

Where did this Book come from? You might say it came from the local book shop or perhaps it was given to you by a friend or family member as a gift for Christmas. But in reality your Bible has come to you from God Himself. Is this not exactly what Paul says? *"All Scripture is given by inspiration of God."* Literally this verse says: *"All Scripture is God-breathed."* God-breathed! This means:

(a) SUPERNATURAL INSPIRATION.

"All Scripture is God-breathed." Do you know something? The ultimate worth of any work depends on the one who wrote it. Who is its author?

Some years ago there appeared in an American magazine a cartoon purporting to portray a scene at the counter of a public library. Someone had just asked for a Bible. *"Bible?"* asks the attendant. *"Bible. Never heard of it. Do you know the author's name?"* To that inquiry the Bible itself supplies the answer: *"All Scripture is given by inspiration of God."* What does inspiration mean? Our word *"inspiration"* comes from a Latin word meaning *"to breathe into"*. But the concept of *"breathing in"* is not found in this passage. Some have assumed that God breathed some kind of divine life into the words of those who penned the original documents of Scripture. But the Greek term for inspiration here (*theopneustos*) means *"God-breathed"*. That is, Scripture is not the words of men into which God puffed divine life. It is the very breath of God. Scripture is God Himself speaking.

Inspiration does not mean men wrote God's truth in their own words. It does not mean God merely assisted the writers. It means that the words of the Bible are the words of God Himself. Every Scripture was breathed out by God. Indeed sometimes the phrase *"the Scripture"* is used in place of God – for example, Galatians 3:8. Look at Exodus 9:16 and then at Romans 9:17. You see, when the Scripture speaks, God speaks and when God speaks, the Scripture speaks.

In every sense, when you pick up the Word and read it, you are hearing God's voice. That is exciting! Why do we believe the Bible to be the Word of God? Because God is the Author of this book. The Bible is the very Word of God. *"God-breathed"* also means:

(b) VERBAL INSPIRATION.

"All Scripture." The word Paul uses here – *'Scripture'* – means *"writing"* (*graphe*). Now did Paul mean that all kinds of writing were inspired? Obviously not. Paul is talking here about the Holy Scriptures. It is the Holy Scriptures that are God-breathed. The words of the Bible are God-breathed.

Some say that the words are not necessarily inspired, but only the thoughts. But did you ever think a thought without words? What kind of thought did you think? Were no words involved? You see, words reveal what we are thinking. Did the Lord Jesus believe in verbal inspiration? Well, listen to His words: *"Man shall not live by bread alone, but by every word that proceedeth out of the mouth of God"* (Matthew 4:4). Not some of the words, not part of the words, but every word. In fact Christ goes further. He says this: *"For verily I say unto you, Till heaven and earth pass, one jot or one tittle shall in no wise pass from the law, till all be fulfilled"* (Matthew 5:18).

Do you know what a jot is? It is the smallest letter in the Hebrew alphabet. Do you know what a tittle is? It is a little horn on a Hebrew letter. It is only about 1/32nd of an inch. Do you see what Christ is saying? *"Until Heaven and earth pass away, the smallest letter of the Hebrew alphabet and the smallest part of a letter shall under no circumstance pass from the law till all be fulfilled."* That is our Lord's view of inspiration.

We love the words of the Bible. Salvation, justification, grace, faith, hope, and love. We sing:

> *"Sing them over again to me,*
> *Wonderful words of life,*
> *Let me more of their beauty see,*
> *Wonderful words of life."*

"God-breathed" means supernatural inspiration and verbal inspiration, but it also means:

(c) TOTAL INSPIRATION.

Do you see what Paul says? *"All Scripture is given by inspiration of God."* The word *"all"* can be translated *"every"*. So we see that all Scripture and every Scripture is inspired. How much of Scripture is God-breathed? Some of it? Most of it? Or all of it? All Scripture and every Scripture is God-breathed. I tell you, I may not understand all the Bible, but I believe it all. I believe all of it from Genesis to Revelation to be the Word of God. Theologians call this the *Plenary Verbal Inspiration of Scripture.* "Plenary" means "all". Nothing is missing. "Verbal" means "every word". So every word in the Bible is God-breathed.

1. The Old Testament is Inspired by the Holy Spirit.

Look at 2 Peter 1 verses 19 to 21:

"We have also a more sure word of prophecy; whereunto ye do well that ye take heed, as unto a light that shineth in a dark place, until the day dawn, and the day star arise in your hearts; Knowing this first, that

no prophecy of the scripture is of any private interpretation. For the prophecy came not in old time by the will of man: but holy men of God spake as they were moved by the Holy Ghost."

Notice here:

(a) The Source of Scripture.

Scripture does not come from man (verse 20). Now, Peter was not prohibiting the private study of the Bible. Some religious groups have taught that only *"spiritual leaders"* may interpret Scripture and they have used this verse as their defence. However, Peter is not referring here to the interpretation of Scripture but to the origin of Scripture. The Bible did not come by the will of man, rather Scripture comes from God. The most important word here is *"moved"* which speaks of being carried along by the Holy Spirit, as a ship is carried by the wind.

Mr. Thomas says:

"The writers of Scripture were carried along, borne along, under the control and direction of the Holy Spirit of God. They wrote as the Holy Spirit directed them to write. They were borne along by Him so that what they wrote was exactly what the Holy Spirit intended should be there. What they wrote was, in a very real sense, not their words, it was the very Word of God."

(b) The Style in Scripture.

"Holy men of God spake" (verse 21). You see, while God is the true source of Scripture, He employed human instruments to write it down. That is why the various books bear the stamp of individuality in their style. The pathos of Jeremiah, the logic of Paul, and the love of John. You see, as you read you become aware of a Divine Author who inspired the writers to say what He wanted said.

2. The New Testament is Inspired by the Holy Spirit.

The same infallible Holy Spirit who inspired the writing of the Old Testament, which bears all the hallmarks of plenary and verbal inspiration, inspired the writing of the New Testament, which also bears all the hallmarks of plenary and verbal inspiration. The Holy Spirit:

(a) Inspired the Gospels.

Look at John 14 verse 26: *"But the Comforter, which is the Holy Ghost, whom the Father will send in My name, He shall teach you all things, and bring all things to your remembrance, whatsoever I have said unto you".* How is it that the Gospel writers could remember everything Christ said and then record it in the Scriptures? The Lord said the Holy Spirit would bring it all to their remembrance. So the Gospels were inspired by the Holy Spirit.

(b) Inspired the Book of Acts.

Look at John 15 verses 26 and 27: *"But when the Comforter is come, whom I will send unto you from the Father, even the Spirit of truth, which proceedeth from the Father, He shall testify of Me: And ye also shall bear witness, because ye have been with Me from the beginning".* So Acts was inspired.

(c) Inspired the Epistles.

Look at John 16 verses 12 and 13: *"I have yet many things to say unto you, but ye cannot bear them now. Howbeit when He, the Spirit of truth, is come, He will guide you into all truth: for He shall not speak of Himself; but whatsoever He shall hear, that shall He speak ..."* So the Epistles were inspired.

(d) Inspired the Book of Revelation.

Look at John 16 verse 13: *"He will shew you things to come".* So the Revelation was inspired.

Let me affirm where we need to stand. When we speak of the Bible as "the Word of God", we do not mean only that it *contains* the Word of God, but that it *is* the Word of God.

No better testimony to the extent of inspiration could be borne than that by Dean Burgon:

"The Bible is none other than the voice of Him that sitteth on the throne. Every book of it, every chapter of it, every verse of it, every syllable of it, every letter of it, is the direct utterance of the Most High".

(2) THE OBJECT OF THE BIBLE

Why did God give us a Bible? Well, the Word of God is written for the glorification of the Saviour, the salvation of the sinner and the sanctification of the saint.

The Bible is vital in:

(a) OUR GROWING UP: EDUCATION.

What a heritage of faith Timothy had! *"From a child"*, he had *"known the holy scriptures"* which were able to make him *"wise unto salvation through faith which is in Christ Jesus"* (2 Timothy 3:15). Each day his godly mother, Eunice, and his godly grandmother, Lois, would take the sacred Scriptures and prepare the day's Bible lesson for "tiny Tim".

You see, they were preparing his little heart. Then one day Paul preached at Lystra and young Timothy came to saving faith in Christ. Paul refers to him as *"Timothy, my own son in the faith"*. (1 Timothy 1:2). He gave his hand to Paul and his heart to Christ. What a testimony was his, from his mother's knee to his Master's knee.

I can imagine a Christian going home that day and someone asking: *"Did anything special happen today?"* *"Not much. We had a long-winded preacher named Paul. Oh, yes, Eunice's boy Timothy trusted the Lord."* (See Acts 14:7) Not much? Paul's future travelling companion was saved. Not much? The recipient of two Bible letters was born again. Not much? The angels in heaven were rejoicing because another sinner had come home.

Do we not need to get them when they are young? When the heart is tender, the will is compliant, the mind is open? Does every church not need to invest more in the lives of little children? More time, more money, more energy, in the spiritual education of our children?

(b) OUR GOING ON: SANCTIFICATION.

In 2 Timothy 3 verse 17, we learn that Scripture was given that *"the man of God may be perfect"*. The word *"perfect"* means mature, complete. The Scriptures are here not only for our salvation, but for our sanctification.

God gave us the Scriptures to <u>know what is right.</u> The word *"doctrine"* means teaching, to know what is right. But Scripture is also profitable to <u>show us what is wrong.</u> It also says for *"reproof"*. It shows us what is right, it shows us what is wrong, but that is not enough. It goes on to tell us <u>how to get right when we are wrong.</u> It is for *"correction"*. Then the Bible is here to tell us <u>how to stay right.</u> It is *"for instruction in righteousness: That the man of God may be perfect, thoroughly furnished unto all good works"*. That is, enabled to meet all the demands of godly ministry and righteous living. Do you know something? The measure of your growth is measured to a great degree by your feeding on the Word of God. Are you going on? Are you growing in grace and in the knowledge of our Lord and Saviour Jesus Christ?

(c) OUR GIVING OUT: PROCLAMATION.

To this young man who had a godly heritage and a great mentor, Paul says: *"Preach the word"* (2 Timothy 4:2). Preach it *faithfully*, as a herald declares the message of his king; preach it *incessantly*, in season and out of season; preach it *effectively*, reprove, rebuke, exhort; preach it *persistently*, even though folk may not endure sound doctrine; preach it *evangelistically*, *"Do the work of an evangelist"* (2 Timothy 4:5). The old, old story of redeeming love! What kind of preaching do we need today? We need the same kind we have always needed. We do not need a new Bible. We do not need a new preacher. Preach the old Book. *"Preach the Word."*

(d) OUR GETTING HOME: CONSOLATION.

Here is the old warrior facing certain death. He says: *"The time of my departure is at hand"* (2 Timothy 4:6). What did Paul want in his last days? He wanted his *"cloak"*, something warm for **his body,** his *"books"*, something stimulating for **his mind,** *"but especially the parchments"*, he wanted the Word of God for **his soul.** I wonder what Old Testament portions he wanted as soft pillows on his deathbed? Was it Psalm 23 verse 4: *"Yea, though I walk through the valley of the shadow of death, I will fear no evil: for Thou art with me; Thy rod and Thy staff they comfort me."* How often I have whispered the promises of God into the ears of dying saints. When Sir Walter Scott was dying he said to his secretary: *"Bring me the book"*. The secretary said: *"But there are thousands of books in your library - which book do you mean?"* He said: *"There is but one book, bring me the Bible"*.

> *There is just one Book for the dying,*
> *One Book for the starting tears,*
> *And one for the soul that is going home,*
> *For the numberless years.*
> *There is just one Book.*

Hold on to your Bible. It will see you home.

(3) THE ORDER OF THE BIBLE

When we turn to what Paul calls *"the holy scriptures"* (2 Timothy 3:15), there is an arrangement, an order. The Bible is a collection of 66 books inspired by God. These books are gathered into two testaments - the Old which has 39 books and the New which has 27 books. Prophets, priests, kings and leaders from the nation of Israel wrote the Old Testament book in Hebrew (with two passages in Aramaic). The apostles and their associates wrote the New Testament books in Greek. God did not arrange the Bible topically so that we could study themes individually. Instead, the Lord arranged it so that we could read one book at a time. Let us look at:

(a) THE OLD TESTAMENT

1. Consider the Old Testament Books:

The 39 books of the Old Testament are divided into 5 categories.

1. The Law or Pentateuch: Genesis to Deuteronomy;
2. History: Joshua to Esther;
3. Wisdom: Job to the Song of Solomon;
4. The Major Prophets: Isaiah to Daniel; and
5. The Minor Prophets: Hosea to Malachi. (They are called 'minor' because of their size.)

The Hebrew Old Testament is divided differently. It groups all of the Old Testament books into three major sections: *The Law, the Prophets and the Writings.* This division is what the Risen Christ had in mind when He appeared to the two on the road to Emmaus. We read how He took them through the law, the prophets and the writings and showed them everything concerning Himself (Luke 24: 27 & 44). So much for the Old Testament books.

2. Consider the Old Testament Period:

The Old Testament covers over 2,000 years of history, before the time of Christ. This can be divided into 4 equal parts of roughly 500 years each. Each period has a key event, a prominent person and a type of leadership.

In 2000 B.C. the key event is *Election;* the prominent person is *Abraham,* and the type of leadership is *Patriarchs* - Abraham, Isaac, Jacob and Joseph.

In 1500 B.C. the key event is **Exodus;** the prominent person is *Moses,* and the type of leadership is *Prophets,* for Israel was led by prophets from Moses to Samuel.

In 1000 B.C. the key event is *Empire;* the prominent person is *David,* and the type of leadership is *Princes* or kings from Saul and onwards.

In 500 B.C. the key event is *Exile;* the prominent person is *Isaiah*, and the type of leadership is *Priests*, from Joshua a priest who returned to Judah from Exile under Zerubbabel's rule to Caiaphas in the time of Christ.

Now, none of these leader types was ideal and each person brought his own flaws to the task. *You see, the nation needed a leader who was prophet, priest and king and they found Him in the Lord Jesus.* Each stage, therefore, was a foreshadowing of the ideal leader who was to come. Someone has well said: *"The Bible is a Him-book. It's all about Him".* Indeed the Lord Jesus Himself said: *"Search the scriptures; for in them ye think ye have eternal life: and they are they which testify of Me"* (John 5:39). You see, the controlling thought for the whole of the Old Testament is a preparation for the coming of the Messiah, the Son of God. In other words, in the Bible we are face to face with the Son of God, the Lord Jesus Christ. Woven into all of Scripture is the perfect portrait of God's beloved Son.

In Genesis, He's the Seed of a Woman.
In Exodus, He's the Passover Lamb.
In Leviticus, He's the Great High Priest.
In Numbers, He's the Cloud by Day and Fire by Night.
In Deuteronomy, He's a Prophet like Moses.
In Joshua, He's the Captain of our Salvation.
In Judges, He's the Judge and Lawgiver.
In Ruth, He's our Kinsman Redeemer.
In 1 and 2 Samuel, He's our Trusted Prophet.
In Kings and Chronicles, He's our Reigning King.
In Ezra, He's our Faithful Scribe.
In Nehemiah, He's the Rebuilder of Broken Walls.
In Esther, He's our Mordecai.
In Job, He's our Dayspring.
In Psalms, He's the Lord our Shepherd.
In Proverbs and Ecclesiastes, He's our Wisdom.
In Song of Solomon, He's the Lover and Bridegroom.
In Isaiah, He's the Prince of Peace.
In Jeremiah, He's the Righteous Branch.
In Lamentations, He's the Weeping Prophet.
In Ezekiel, He's a Wheel within a Wheel.

In Daniel, He's the Fourth Man in the Fiery Furnace.
In Hosea, He's the Bridegroom married to the Backslider.
In Joel, He's the Baptizer of Fire by Holy Spirit.
In Amos, He's our Burden Bearer.
In Obadiah, He's our Mighty Saviour.
In Jonah, He's a Great Foreign Missionary.
In Micah, He's the Messenger with Beautiful Feet.
In Nahum, He's the Avenger of God's Elect.
In Habakkuk, He's an Evangelist Crying for Revival.
In Zephaniah, He's the Restorer of God's Lost Heritage.
In Haggai, He's our Cleansing Fountain.
In Zechariah, He's our Merciful Father.
In Malachi, He's the Sun of Righteousness with Healing in His Wings.
In Matthew, He's the Messiah.
In Mark, He's the Wonder Worker.
In Luke, He's the Son of Man.
In John, He's the Son of God.
In Acts, He's the Ascended Lord.
In Romans, He's our Justifier.
In Corinthians, He's the last Adam.
In Galatians, He's the God that Sets Us Free.
In Ephesians, He's the Christ of our Riches.
In Philippians, He's the One who meets our Need.
In Colossians, He's the Fullness of the Godhead bodily.
In Thessalonians, He's our Soon Coming King.
In Timothy, He's our Mediator between God and man.
In Titus, He's a Faithful Pastor.
In Philemon, He's a Friend who sticks closer than a Brother.
In Hebrews, He's the Sacrifice that Cleanses from all Sin.
In James, He's the Great Physician.
In Peter, He's the Chief Shepherd.
In John, He's Everlasting Love.
In Jude, He's the Lord Descending with thousands of His saints.
In Revelation, He's the King of Kings, and the Lord of Lords.

Well might we say: *"Hallelujah! What a Saviour!"* The Word of the Lord reveals the Lord of the Word from cover to cover. But notice also:

(b) THE NEW TESTAMENT

While the 39 Old Testament books major on the history of Israel and the promise of the coming Saviour, the 27 New Testament books major on the person of Christ and the establishment of the church.

1. The Gospels

They give us a record of Christ's birth, life, death, resurrection and ascension. Each of the four Gospel writers views the coming of the Lord Jesus from a different perspective. Matthew sets before us *His Royalty:* speaking of His kingdom. Mark sets before us *His Humility:* speaking of His servanthood. Luke sets before us *His Humanity:* speaking of His perfect humanness. John sets before us *His Deity:* speaking of Christ as the Son of God.

2. The Acts

Acts tells the story of the early church. It takes us from Christ's ascension, to the coming of the Holy Spirit, the birth of the church, the early preaching of the apostles, and the establishment of the church in Judea, Samaria and into the Roman Empire.

3. The Epistles

Twenty one in all, written to churches and individuals to explain the significance of the person and work of Jesus Christ, with its implications for life and witness until He returns.

4. The Revelation

Revelation starts by picturing the current church age, and culminates with Christ's return to establish His earthly kingdom, bringing judgment on the ungodly and joy for the believers.

What a book we hold in our hands! This is God's Wonderful Word. Its doctrines are holy, its precepts are binding, its histories are true and its decisions are immutable. Read it to be wise, believe it to be saved and practise it to be holy.

I supposed I knew my Bible,
Reading piecemeal, hit or miss,
Now a bit of John or Matthew,
Now a snatch of Genesis.

Certain chapters of Isaiah,
Certain Psalms - the twenty third,
Twelfth of Romans, first of Proverbs,
Yes, I thought I knew The Word.

But I found that thorough reading,
Was a different thing to do,
And the way was unfamiliar,
When I read the Bible through.

You who like to play at Bible,
Dip and dabble, here and there,
Just before you kneel a-weary,
And yawn through a hurried prayer.

You who treat the crown of writing,
As you treat no other book,
Just a paragraph disjointed,
Just a crude, impatient look.

Try a worthier procedure,
Try a broad and steady view,
You will kneel in very rapture,
When you read the Bible through.

The late Bible teacher, H. A. Ironside, told of visiting a godly Ulsterman, Andrew Frazer, who had come to California to recover from tuberculosis. The old man could barely speak because his lungs were almost gone. But he opened his well-worn Bible and, until his strength was gone, he simply, sweetly opened up truth after truth in a way that Ironside had never heard before. Before he knew it, Ironside had tears running down his cheeks. He asked

Frazer: *"Where did you get all these things? Could you tell me where I could find a book that would open them up to me? Did you learn these things in some seminary or college?"*

Frazer answered: *"My dear young man, I learned these things on my knees on the mud floor of a little cottage in the north of Ireland. There with my Bible open before me, I used to kneel for hours at a time, and ask the Spirit of God to reveal Christ to my soul and to open the Word to my heart. He taught me more on my knees on that mud floor than I ever could have learned in all the seminaries or colleges in the world."*

God may be missing in our society, in our government, in our schools and universities but one thing is for certain - God is not missing from His Word, the Bible. The Bible is but a collection of pages that bear His imprint upon every line. On each page of His Word, we see the breath-taking portraits of His Son, the Lord Jesus Christ.

CHAPTER 2
Genesis

As we begin our journey, book by book, we come to the book of beginnings, the book of Genesis. Genesis is the seed plot of the Bible. Every subject of major importance can be traced back to its *"first mention"* in the book of Genesis.

W. H. Griffith Thomas said:

"If we were to approach the Old Testament as though we had never read it before, and were to take note of all the remarkable predictions of Someone who is coming afterward, we would find that this series of predictions begins in the early, unfolding chapters of Genesis".

"Genesis" is a Greek word meaning *"beginning"* or *"generation"*. In fact, in the New Testament, the word *"genesis"* is translated *"generation"* in Matthew 1 verse 1. Genesis is the book of generations or beginnings. It is a very appropriate title as the book includes the origin of so much - our universe, the sun, moon and stars, the earth. Here we have the origin of plants, birds, fish, animals and humans. We have the beginning of marriage, family life, the origin of civilization, government, culture, nations, music, sin, death, murder and war. In fact, Genesis tells us about the beginning of almost everything - except God.

But it not only deals with origins, Genesis also deals with the ultimate questions of life. *Where did our universe come from? Why are we here? Why do we have to die?* Genesis is one of the five books which form a unit in the Jewish Scriptures known either as the Pentateuch (*'penta'* means five) or the Torah which means "instruction". The Jews believe that these five books together form *"the Maker's instructions"* for the world and so they read through them every year taking a portion each week. Most agree that Moses is the author of these first five Old Testament books. (Deuteronomy 31:24 & 26; Numbers 33:1 & 2 and John 1:45)

The Lord Jesus Himself settles all questions concerning the historicity of Genesis by His frequent references to the characters of Genesis as real people and the events of Genesis as real history. Christ clearly regarded the account of Noah and the Flood as an historical event. Do you recall the Saviour's words? *"But as the days of Noah were, so shall also the coming of the Son of Man be. For as in the days that were before the flood …"* (Matthew 24:37 & 38). Do you remember what Christ said about Abraham? He said: *"Before Abraham was, I am"* (John 8:58). When the Lord was asked about divorce and remarriage, He referred His questioners to Genesis Chapter 2 and told them that they would find the answer there. If Christ believed that the book of Genesis was true, we have no reason to do otherwise. You see, if Genesis is not true, neither is the rest of the Bible. If we do not accept that Genesis is true, it follows that we cannot rely on the rest of the Word of God. As David Pawson says: *"If Genesis is not true then 'chance' is our creator and the brute beasts are our ancestors"*. Does it surprise you, therefore, that this book has been under more attack than any other book in the Bible? You see, the devil hates most the two books which describe his entrance and exit, Genesis and Revelation. He, therefore, likes to keep people from believing the early chapters of Genesis and the later chapters of Revelation. If he can persuade us that Genesis is a myth and Revelation is a mystery, then he can go a long way in destroying our faith.

As you read Genesis, you cannot help but note that the first eleven chapters are general and not too detailed, while in the rest of the book, starting with Chapter 12, the lives of four men are given in great detail. The first section - Chapters 1 to 11 - deal with mankind in general, and explains the origin of man and sin, while the last section - Chapters 12 to 50 - deals with Israel in particular, especially the lives of Abraham, Isaac, Jacob and Joseph. So we have divided this book into two sections.

(1) PRIMEVAL HISTORY: THE PRELIMINARIES

Primeval or primitive history. Do you see how the Bible begins? It begins with amazing words: *"In the beginning God"*.

A young woman teacher shared with her class of small children that she was an atheist. She asked her class how many of them were atheists. Not really knowing what atheism was, and wanting to be like their teacher, their hands shot up into the air, that is all hands but one. Lucy did not raise her hand. The teacher asked why she did not raise her hand like the rest of the class and she replied: *"Because I am not an atheist"*. *"What are you?"* the teacher asked. Lucy answered: *"I am a Christian"*. The teacher then asked Lucy why she was a Christian. Lucy quickly answered: *"Because my mummy and daddy are Christians"*. The teacher then said: *"That is no reason to be a Christian. What if your mummy and daddy had been fools, stupid people? What would you be then?"* After a pause, Lucy answered: *"I'd be an atheist!"*

The Bible makes no attempt to prove that there is a God. It takes this fact as self-evident. Thirty two times in thirty one verses in Genesis Chapter 1, God is mentioned by name and a further eleven times by use of personal pronouns. The expression *"And God said"* occurs ten times. Do you know something? This is the most God-centred chapter in the Bible. It may come as a surprise to you to discover that the subject of Genesis Chapter 1 is not creation but the **Creator.** It is not primarily about how our world came to be, but about who made it come to be. It is not so much the story of creation as a picture of the Creator: *"In the beginning God."* You see:

1. God is Self-Existent.

That is how the scholars would put it. In other words, nobody made Him. God is independent of all else than Himself for the continuity and perpetuity of His being.

"In the beginning God created the heaven and the earth." He is not dependent on anyone, not on you, not on me. Indeed, *all* that we have is His.

2. God is Personal.

Does this Chapter not depict a personal God? He has a heart that feels, a mind that thinks. He has a will and makes decisions and sticks to them. All this forms what we know as a personality. God is not an **"it"**. God is a **He**. He is a full person with feelings, thoughts and motives.

3. God is Powerful.

It is evident that if He can speak things into being by His word, He must be powerful. Do you notice that in this opening chapter God gives *"10 commandments"* and every one is fulfilled just as He desires. Look at this phrase *"And God said"* and connect it with *"And it was so"*. The Psalmist says: *"For He spake, and it was done; He commanded, and it stood fast"* (Psalm 33:9).

4. God is Creative.

What an imagination God must have! What an artist! Six thousand varieties of beetle. No two blades of grass are the same. No two snowflakes. No two clouds. No two grains of sand. No two stars. No two faces. No two sets of fingerprints are the same. What an astonishing variety and yet in harmony for it is a uni-verse.

5. God is Triune

In Spurgeon's Catechism we have this question: *"How many persons are there in the Godhead?"* The Answer is: **"There are three persons in the Godhead, the Father, the Son, and the Holy Ghost, and these three are one God, the same in essence, equal in power and glory"**.

Now the Trinity is plainly implied in this Chapter. Look at Genesis 1 verse 26. The Hebrew word for God here is *"Elohim"* and notice God refers to Himself in the plural: *"Let us make man in our image"*, but then in the very next verse we read: *"So God (Elohim) created man in His own image"*. Do you see that the plural *"our"* in verse 26 equals the singular *"His"* in verse 27?

"In the beginning God created the heaven and the earth." Now, if you believe that then the following philosophies are out:

1. Atheism: Atheists believe that there is no God. This Chapter confirms there is.

2. Agnosticism: They say they do not know whether there is a God or not. This Chapter says there is.

3. Animism: This is the belief that many spirits control the world, spirits of rivers, spirits of mountains and so on. This Chapter declares that God created and controls the world.

4. Polytheism: Polytheists believe that there are many gods. Hindus would be in this category. This Chapter states that there is just one God.

5. Humanism: Humanists reject the concept of a god outside the created world. Although this Chapter states that man is created by God, humanists believe that man is God. Yet the Bible says: *"In the beginning God ...."*

Elohim is the name of God which links Him with creation. The basic root of the name is *"El"* which means *"mighty, strong, prominent"*.

Now in these opening 11 chapters there is brought before us:

(a) THE CREATION OF ALL THINGS. (Chapters 1 and 2)

In these opening two chapters, we have fifty six simple but sublime verses that bring before us the concise and complete account of creation. We could look at verse 1 of Chapter 1 as a summary statement. God here tells us just what He did. The remaining fifty five verses then become detailed statements informing us just how He went about doing all He said He did.

Day One: Light

Day Two: Firmament

Day Three: Separation of Land and Water, and Plant life

Day Four: Sun, Moon, and Stars

Day Five: Fish (Sea Life) and Birds (Sky Life)

Day Six: Domestic Animals and Man

Day Seven: God rested from His work

Now when we come to Chapter 2, there is a notable difference. In Chapter 1, God is at the centre. In Chapter 2, man is at the centre, and he is at the centre of a network of relationships, and these relationships define the meaning of life. Do you see here:

1. Our Relationship to that which is Below Us: Nature

Animals are given to serve mankind. Look at Chapter 2 verse 19. In Chapter 9, we read that animals were given to provide food after the Flood (verse 3). Now we are not to be cruel to animals, but animals are further down the scale of value than human beings. We live in an age where more value seems to be placed on the protection of certain animals than preserving the sanctity of the human foetus.

2. Our Relationship to that which is Above Us: God

Man was not only put to work in the garden - he was put on probation. Look at Chapter 2 verses 16 and 17. Man was told: *"Of every tree of the garden thou mayest freely eat: But of the tree of the knowledge of good and evil, thou shalt not eat of it".*

3. Our Relationship to that which is Beside Us: our Wife

"It is not good that the man should be alone; I will make him an help meet for him" (Genesis 2:18). Notice that Adam had a job before he had a wife. You see, man is made primarily for his work, while a woman is made primarily for relationships.

So there was the Creation of All Things, but then came:

(b) THE CORRUPTION OF ALL THINGS. (Chapters 3 to 5)

Martin Luther called Genesis 3: *"The darkest page of all human history"*. This Chapter is the earthquake of the Bible. It forever changed the history of humanity. Is it not significant that Satan went for Eve? *Adam's rib* gave in to *Satan's fib* and it became *Women's Lib*. Eve gives the fruit to Adam, instead of Adam giving fruit to Eve.

Do you see what Satan was doing? He was subverting God's order? *He was treating Eve as if she were the head of the house.* The Bible tells us that the husband is the head of the home, the wife is the heart of the home and the children are the hub of the home. Do you see the tactics the devil adopts? He encourages doubt in the mind, desire in the heart and disobedience in the will. Is this the strategy that he is using with you? Has he been inciting you to doubt God's Word? Has he been enticing you to desire evil in your heart? To disobey with your will?

Do you see the outcome of the Fall? Birth is painful, life is hard and death is certain (verses 16-19). Sin, sorrow, suffering and death flowed from the Fall. Adam's children were now born in his own fallen image (Genesis 5:3). Man's first sin separated man from God. The second sin, as told in the story of Cain and Abel, separated man from man. So God's perfect world is now a place where goodness is hated and the evil people excuse their wickedness.

Genesis goes on to trace the line of Cain in Chapter 4 and the line of Seth in Chapter 5. Cain's line lived for this world. Seth's line lived for the world to come. Chapter 4 takes us into the market-place. Chapter 5 takes us into the morgue. The history of Cain's line climaxed in the wickedness of Lamech, the seventh from Adam. The history of Seth's line climaxed in the godliness of Enoch, the seventh from Adam. Man had now become corrupt, the earth was filled with violence and God had to destroy all things. The Bible says: *"And it repented the Lord that He had made man on the earth, and it grieved Him at His heart"* (Chapter 6:6). There was now:

(c) THE CONDEMNATION OF ALL THINGS. (Chapters 6 to 9)

The Flood was God's answer to man's unrepentant sin. Sin must be punished - and salvation must be provided and it was through the ark. Is the ark not a wonderful picture of our salvation in Christ? It was planned by God, not invented by man. There was only way of salvation - there was only door in the ark. The ark saved them from judgment and Christ saves us from the wrath to come.

Are we not living *"in the days of Noah"*? (Luke 17:26) The days of: spiritual decline (Genesis 4:3); social dilemma (Genesis 6:1); shameful depravity (Genesis 6:5); scientific development (Genesis 4:21); strong delusion (Matthew 24:39). Christ says: *"As it was in the days of Noah, so shall it be also in the days of the Son of man"* (Luke 17:26). The signs are abundant that the end is approaching. But are you ready? Like Enoch, like Noah, are you walking with God? (Genesis 6:9)

Something else affected God deeply in these early chapters of Genesis and that was:

(d) THE CONFUSION OF ALL THINGS. (Chapters 10 and 11)

In Genesis Chapter 10, God sent confusion into the midst of a foolish people. The building of the Tower of Babel was an attempt by man to build a united world society with God left out. It ended in judgment for the Lord confounded the language of the workers, making it impossible for them to work together. The human race was now divided into 3 great racial families, speaking different languages. These 3 families were the descendants of the sons of Noah - Shem, Ham and Japheth.

<u>Shem:</u> Semitic tribes who settled in the Middle East;

<u>Ham:</u> Canaanites and dark-skinned tribes who settled in Africa;

<u>Japheth:</u> Tribes who settled in Europe

Genesis Chapter 11 ends with a sharp contrast. On the one hand we see wilfulness at Babel, on the other hand we see willingness in Abram. We see man's sin in going contrary to God and then we see a man's willingness to do the will of God - and this brings us to the second section of the book.

(2) PATRIARCHAL HISTORY: THE PATRIARCHS

Here in this second section, there is brought before us, the patriarchs (or fathers) of the Hebrew race. You see, if in Chapters 1 to 11 events are predominant, then in Chapters 12 to 50 persons are predominant. These chapters are basically the stories of just four men. First of all there is:

(a) THE STORY OF ABRAHAM. (Chapters 12 to 24)

In Genesis Chapter 12, God raised up a man, Abram, who would become the father of the Hebrew nation. The Hebrew race was chosen by God to be His instrument to bring the Word of God and the Son of God.

William Norman Ewer wrote:

> How odd of God
> To choose the Jews!

Cecil Browne then decided to add a second verse in reply:

> But not so odd
> As those who choose
> A Jewish God
> But spurn the Jews!

God chose the Jews, with the intention that all other peoples might know His blessing through them. Look at Chapter 12 verses 1 to 3 and notice:

1. A Promised LAW.

Do you see what God says? *"I will make of thee a great nation, and*

I will bless thee, and make thy name great; and thou shalt be a blessing: And I will bless them that bless thee, and curse him that curseth thee: and in thee shall all families of the earth be blessed."

Those words comprise the Abrahamic Covenant that is irreplaceable, irrevocable and irreversible. This race was not chosen because of any distinctive qualities they possessed. They were not chosen because they were a choice people. They are a choice people because they were chosen.

2. A Promised LAND.

God promises Abraham the land of Canaan. According to verse 7 of Chapter 12: *"Unto thy seed will I give this land"*. In the very next chapter, we have the duration of Israel's tenure in the land. (See Genesis 13:14-15) God has put a reservation mark and has preserved the land for Israel. God said in effect: *"This is the place I am going to give you forever"*. They hold the title deeds to that place, whatever anybody else says, because God gave the title deeds to them, to Abraham and his descendants for ever. There have been, and still are, battles fought over the land of Israel; but, the land does not belong to anyone else. It belongs to the Jewish people. They have rights of exclusivity to the land. Israel are the rightful heirs!

3. A Promised LAD.

God's initial promise of a son and seed to Abraham came when Abram was 75 years old (Chapter 12:4). Abraham was 86 years old when Hagar conceived Ishmael, the father of the Arab nation. (Chapter 16:16) Do you recall how the Lord describes him? *"And he will be a wild man; his hand will be against every man, and every man's hand against him"* (Chapter 16:12). The battle between the Jews and the Muslims began in Genesis 16. It has been a battle between Ishmael (Muslims) and Isaac (Jews) ever since, and there will be no peace until the Prince of Peace, our Lord Jesus Christ, comes and establishes His Kingdom in the city of Jerusalem. Twenty five years after God's initial promise to Abraham, Isaac, the promised seed arrived, when Abraham was 100 years old and Sarah was 90 years of age. (Genesis 21:5)

"Is any thing too hard for the Lord?"(Chapter 18:14)

> *Got any rivers you think are uncrossable?*
> *Got any mountains you can't tunnel through?*
> *God specializes in things thought impossible,*
> *He can do just what no others can do.*

Paul says: Abraham *"staggered not at the promise of God through unbelief"* (Romans 4:20).

4. A Promised LORD.

Life is a series of tests, is it not? Abraham had his share of tests from the beginning. In Chapter 12, God give Abraham the *Family Test:* He called on Abraham to leave his home, his father and mother and move out of Ur to go to the land of Canaan. In Chapter 12, he was also given the *Famine Test*. He failed this test because he doubted God and went down to Egypt for help. In Chapter 13, he was given the *Fellowship Test:* for when a conflict arose between him and Lot, he gave Lot his choice of land.

In Chapter 14, he was given the *Fight Test:* when he defeated the kings who had kidnapped Lot. He was also given in that chapter the *Fortune Test:* because he was offered all the wealth of Sodom, but he turned it down. In Chapters 15 and 16, he was given the *Fatherhood Test:* when Sarah got impatient with God, could not wait His timing, and suggested they have a child by Hagar. But when we get to Chapter 22, the Lord has reserved for Abraham the greatest of all, the *Faith Test. "Take now thy son* (that was bad), *thine only son Isaac* (that was worse), *whom thou lovest* (that was worse still)... *and offer him ... for a burnt offering* (that was the worst of all)"* (verse 2). Why did the Lord do this? To see if his all was on the altar. God did not want Isaac's life - He wanted Abraham's loyalty. God did not want Abraham's son - He wanted Abraham's heart.

Has the Lord got your heart? He does not want your Isaac - He wants you. Does He have you? Does He have all of you?

Here is Abraham on his way to the top of Mount Moriah about to sacrifice the promised seed, Isaac:

"And Isaac spake unto Abraham his father, and said, My father: and he said, Here am I, my son. And he said, Behold the fire and the wood: but where is the lamb for a burnt offering? And Abraham said, My son, God will provide Himself a lamb for a burnt offering."

Some people misquote this verse and say: "God Himself will provide a lamb", but what it says is this: *"God will provide Himself a lamb"*. Do you know what Christ said? *"Your father Abraham rejoiced to see My day: and he saw it, and was glad."* (John 8:56) Mount Moriah in the Old Testament is Mount Calvary in the New Testament. A Promised Lord – and the Lord demands the same loyalty from every believer. Paul exhorts us, in Romans 12, to present our bodies as living sacrifices unto God.

(b) THE STORY OF ISAAC. (Chapters 24 to 27)

Isaac became the heir of the promises of God to Abraham (Genesis 26:2-4). Now although Isaac lived until he was 180 years of age (Chapter 35:28), very little is said about him. Perhaps his life is best summarized in three phrases which are associated with him. *"And Isaac .... pitched his tent ...., and he digged another well ...., and he builded an altar there"* (Genesis 26:17, 22 & 25). The tent speaks of the pilgrim, the man who trusts God a day at a time and is always ready to move on with God. The well speaks of the resources of God. The altar speaks of the worshipper, who brings his sacrifice and offers it to God. Sadly, Isaac's loss of sight in old age led to deception by his own family.

(d) THE STORY OF JACOB. (Chapters 28 to 36)

This man's story is colourful. He is a most interesting character. John Phillips summed up the life of Jacob in 3 words: *Supplanter, servant, and saint.* The life of Jacob is a picture of the glorious work of God in the life of a believer. He takes a supplanter, makes him a saint, and breaks him to be a servant. The name "Jacob" means *"guile, deceiver, cheat, con artist, twister, and crook"*. That is exactly what Jacob was and yet he was saved. Then, once saved, he had so much of this old man in him. He had so many of the old ways in him that God needed to deal with him. _How did God do it?_ There was a crisis in his life and then there was a process. The crisis took place at Jabbok or Peniel (Genesis 32:30); the process took the rest of his life - for there are no shortcuts to holiness.

All of his life Jacob had been seeking the blessing of God, but he had gone about it the wrong way. All of his life Jacob had been singing: _"I did it my way"_, but now the Lord is going to tell Jacob: _"We're going to do it My way"_. So God breaks Jacob. _"He touched the hollow of his thigh; and the hollow of Jacob's thigh was out of joint"_ (Chapter 32:25). Do you see what the Lord did? The Lord disabled him. He brings him to the place of absolute dependence on God. God wants to do that with every believer. Too often, we are disobedient.

We are so different from God. We cannot use things that are broken. God cannot use things till He breaks them. It is the broken box that gives the perfume (Mark 14:3). It is the broken food that gives the strength (Matthew 14:19). David says: _"The sacrifices of God are a broken spirit: a broken and a contrite heart, O God, Thou wilt not despise"_ (Psalm 51:17). _Brokenness._ Do you know anything about it?

We read: _"And he halted on his thigh"_. He limped. Someone says: _"Jacob, what in the world has happened to you?"_ He says: _"I just got blessed. I met God last night and I shall never walk the same again."_ Do you know what Jacob learned? He learned to lean. He could say, he could sing:

> _"Learning to lean, learning to lean,_
> _I'm learning to lean on Jesus,_
> _I'm finding more power than I ever dreamed,_
> _I'm learning to lean on Jesus."_

(d) THE STORY OF JOSEPH. (Chapters 37 to 50)

It is interesting that one quarter of the book of Genesis - from Chapter 37 to Chapter 50 - is made up of the account of Joseph's life. More of Genesis is given over to Joseph than is given to any of the other main characters. Joseph represents the link between the family and the nation. Up until Joseph, it is a family - the family of Abraham, Isaac and Jacob. Seventy people are found at the end of the book of Genesis constituting the family of Jacob, but the moment we open the book of Exodus, it is no longer a family. It is a nation.

What is the overriding lesson in the life of Joseph? Is it not the providence of God? Providence *"is the hand of God in the glove of history"*. God is active in all that happens in the world. Joseph's life was a demonstration of the providence of God. He could say with Paul: *"And we know that all things work together for good to them that love God"* (Romans 8:28). Oh, think of <u>the trials that Joseph had experienced.</u> He had been forsaken by his brothers; he had been framed by Potiphar's wife; he had been forgotten by the butler. But think of <u>the trust that Joseph had expressed.</u> He tells his brothers: *"God did send me before you to preserve life"* (Genesis 45:5). He says: *"But as for you, ye thought evil against me; but God meant it unto good"* (Genesis 50:20). Joseph saw the big picture of what God had done. He saw that God could take a bad thing and turn it into a good thing. He never questioned what God was doing. *"Why, Lord?"* never passed through Joseph's lips.

Joseph believed that God's hand was at work in every event in his life. Do you? Perhaps his life is a mirror of yours. Have you been forsaken by your family? Have you been falsely accused? Have you been betrayed by those whom you thought would stand by you? Are you in some pit of despair where escape seems impossible? Do you realize that God has a purpose even in the bad things that happen to you? So much so that we can say with the hymn writer:

> *"With mercy and with judgment,*
> *My web of time He wove,*
> *And aye the dews of sorrow,*
> *Were lustred with His love,*
> *I'll bless the hand that guided,*
> *I'll bless the heart that planned,*
> *When throned where glory dwelleth,*
> *In Immanuel's land."*

CHAPTER 3
Exodus

In 1963, President John Kennedy was assassinated in Dallas in the state of Texas. Mrs Kennedy was in the car with him when he was shot. His wounded head fell on her lap. The blood splattered all over her dress and clothes. *That night she flew home on Air Force One.* An attendant came and asked her if she would not like to change her clothes. She refused. Someone else came to her and asked if she would not like to put on something clean. They told her about the reporters who would be in Washington when she arrived. Surely she wanted to put on something more presentable for the press and for the public. She looked up angrily and replied: *"I want them to see the blood. I want the whole world to see the blood. I want them to see what they did to my Jack."*

We should want the world to see the blood. We should want them to see the price that Christ paid when He died for our sins. The sin of the human race demanded the precious blood of Calvary. Is this not what redemption is all about? Redemption means *"release as the result of the payment of a price".* ('Lutroo' - 1 Peter 1:18 and Titus 2:14)

Genesis is the book of beginnings - and Exodus is the book of redemption. The title of the book is a Greek word meaning *"Way out"* or *"Departure".* In the book of Hebrews we read about *"the departing (exodus) of the children of Israel"* (Hebrews 11:22). The word *"exodus"* is used in two other places in the New Testament. Do you recall that on the Mount of Transfiguration there appeared, with the Lord Jesus, Moses and Elijah. Do you recall what they spoke of? They *"spake of His decease"* (Luke 9:31) - that is, Christ's redeeming work on the Cross. Peter uses the same word in the opening chapter of his second epistle for he talks about *"my decease"* (2 Peter 1:15). He means his death. So we can see there are three exodus experiences in the Bible. Israel's deliverance from Egypt. Christ's deliverance of the sinner through the Cross. The Christian's deliverance from the bondage of this world through physical death.

Exodus is the story of the biggest escape in history. Over two million slaves from one of the most highly fortified nations in the entire world. It is a humanly impossible and extraordinary story, and it features a series of miracles including some of the best known in the whole Bible.

After the book of Genesis, the remaining books of the Pentateuch begin with a conjunction. This makes the Pentateuch one single book, written by one single author, Moses. Moses followed God's instructions and *"wrote all the words of the Lord"* (Exodus 24:4). Exodus 1 verse 1 begins with the word *"Now"*, Do you see that? The word connects the book of Exodus with the book of Genesis. In other words, Exodus is but a continuing story of Genesis.

Dr. Graham Scroggie writes:

"The connection between Genesis and Exodus is intimate. In the one the divine purpose is revealed, and in the other the divine purpose is exhibited. In the one are human effort and failure, and in the other are divine power and triumph. In the one is a word of promise, and in the other is a work of fulfilment. In the one is a people chosen, and in the other is a people called. In the one is God's electing mercy, and in the other is God's electing manner."

Dr. R. G. Lee says:

"This book commences by telling how God came down in grace to deliver an enslaved people and ends by telling how God came down in glory to dwell in the midst of a redeemed people."

Is that not beautiful? This book opens in gloom and ends in glory.

Now the whole event of the Exodus has great significance in a number of ways:

1. Nationally

As David Pawson reminds us: *"Nobody can dispute that there is a nation called Israel in the world today. So where did they come from? How did they get started? How did they become a nation if they were originally a bunch of slaves?"* Something big is needed to explain the nation of Israel. That something big is the exodus. Through the events of the exodus, this nation was born. Now they did not have a land yet, but they were a nation with a name of their own: *"Israel"*. The exodus was so big that it is written into the Jewish calendar. So what do we find every Spring? The Jewish people celebrating the Passover and recalling the mighty acts of God. Exodus marked the start of their national history.

2. Spiritually

The Israelites discovered that their God was more powerful than all the gods of Egypt put together. In Exodus, we are confronted with the truth that the Creator of everything becomes the Redeemer of Israel.

3. Biographically

Just as Joseph was raised up by God as the deliverer of His people on their entry into Egypt, so Moses was the man raised up by God four centuries later as the deliverer of His people on their exit from Egypt.

I want us to divide the book into 3 geographical sections. Firstly, Israel in Egypt; secondly, Israel to Sinai and, lastly, Israel at Sinai.

(1) ISRAEL IN EGYPT: SUBJECTION (Chapter 1 to Chapter 12:36)

This takes in a period from 1875 to 1445 B.C. Jacob and his extended family came to Egypt about 1875 B.C. which was 430 years before the exodus (Exodus 12:40). Now, why were they there? Well, do you recall Joseph? Sold into slavery into Egypt and eventually through a series of God-led events he rose from slavery to the position of prime minister. In that position, he saved the nation from famine. That is why Jacob's sons first arrived in Egypt - because of the famine in Canaan. Egypt was the bread-basket of the Middle East thanks to Joseph's wise storing of grain during the seven years of plenty. Joseph saved the nation from famine and because he was respected by Pharaoh, his whole family, consisting of 70 people, were brought down to Egypt. They were given a fertile piece of the Nile delta called Goshen to live on together.

But why did they stay in Egypt? *They went down for 7 years and they stayed for over 400 years? Why?* Well there was a **Human Element** to their stay: They were comfortable. And why not? They had traded a land of famine for a land of fruitfulness. They exchanged a land of pain for a land of plenty. They had found the good life in Egypt. As Douglas White says: *"That which was designed to be temporary was beginning to be looked upon as permanent"*. You see, Egypt being a land of ease and luxury would encourage spiritual and moral decay. Is this not exactly what happened?

Do you recall what Joshua told the Israelites after they had arrived in Canaan? *"Put away the gods which your fathers served on the other side of the flood (the Euphrates), and in Egypt; and serve ye the Lord"* (Joshua 24:14). The phrase *"And in Egypt"* means that idolatry was practised by at least some of the Israelites in Egypt. (See Ezekiel 20:7) You see, <u>Israel not only needed to be taken out of Egypt, but Egypt needed to be taken out of Israel.</u> They had so much in their hands they did not realise the great need of their hearts. As they explained later, they *"sat by the flesh pots and .... did eat bread to the full"* (Exodus 16:3). Is that how it is that materialism seems to sap the very lifeblood of the church? Materially rich, but spiritually poor! Is that you? Like those in the church at Laodicea? James Merritt says: *"Never measure your success by what you own; you always measure your success by what owns you"*.

There was also a **Divine Element** to their stay: Do you recall God's Word to Abram? *"Know of a surety that thy seed shall be a stranger in a land that is not theirs, and shall serve them; and they shall* *afflict them four hundred years …. But in the fourth generation they shall come hither again: for the iniquity of the Amorites is not yet full"* (Genesis 15:13 & 16). You see, had they returned when the famine was over, they would have been only a few people, far too small in number to accomplish what God intended. It was God's intention to remove the people of Canaan from the land and let the Hebrew slaves in. Is God's timing not always perfect? Do you see them now? Look at Exodus 1 verse 7. They numbered about 2.5 million.

This multiplication leads to murder. There was:

(a) THE PERSECUTION GOD SEES.

The Lord saw their *bondage* (Exodus 1:14); their *burdens* (Exodus 1:11) and their *babies* (Exodus 1:16) for all the baby boys born to the Hebrew slaves had to be thrown to the crocodiles in the River Nile. What a situation this was! Life was hard. The hours were long. The workload was heavy. Children were being killed. You say: *"What is God doing? What is going on down there?"* I will tell you what is going on. God is stirring up the nest to get these people to desire something better than old Egypt. God is turning up the heat of the furnace to get them miserable down there in Egypt. I wonder, are you in the crucible right now? Are you experiencing the heat of the furnace? Do you think that your hard moments and tests escape the Lord's notice? Well, look at Exodus 3 verses 7 and 8: *"I have surely seen the affliction of My people … and have heard their cry … I know their sorrows; And I am come down to deliver them"*.

What does the hymnwriter say?

> *"Jesus knows all about our struggles,*
> *He will guide till the day is done,*
> *There's not a friend like the lowly Jesus,*
> *No, not one, no, not one."*

The Egyptians resorted to genocide and the baby Moses should have died this way but then we see he was:

(b) THE PERSON GOD SELECTS.

He was *"drawn out"* of the water to *"draw out"* God's people from the world – Egypt. It has been said that Moses spent 40 years in the court of Pharaoh learning to be something. Then he spent 40 years in the desert of Midian learning to be nothing. Then he spent 40 years on the road to Canaan proving God to be everything. (See Acts 7:23, 30 & 36) Think of it:

1. Moses was Forty Years as a Student.

Stephen says he *"was learned in all the wisdom of the Egyptians, and was mighty in words and in deeds"* (Acts 7:22). Like Joseph, Moses was brought up at court and given the best education at the Egyptian university. This made him far better educated than any of the Hebrew slaves and this enabled him to write the first five books of the Bible. Has God endowed you with a great intellect? Have you placed this at His feet?

2. Moses was Forty Years as a Shepherd.

If you are going to be a leader, the Lord says: *"I've got to teach you how to do a little job. I have got to see if you'll be faithful with a few sheep. How can I trust you with My people until I know you'll be faithful with a few sheep?"* Faithfulness in little things is God's appointed way to bigger things. (See Matthew 25:23) Do you know what? Very often when God is going to use somebody, He will give them the experience of isolation. God always uses the solitude, the isolation experience. There are two interesting phrases concerning Elijah in 1 Kings 17 and 18. God said to the prophet: *"Hide thyself!"* Then, three years later, He said to Elijah: *"Show thyself!"* There is a private ministry and then a public ministry. Are you wondering if the Lord knows where you are? Are you wondering what the Lord has in store for your life? Just be faithful, you just trust God and learn the lessons of isolation, and in God's time He'll do something.

3. Moses was Forty Years as a Servant.

He is described as *"Moses the servant of the Lord"* (Deuteronomy 34:5). Do you realise that you are the Lord's servant?

(c) THE PLAGUES GOD SENDS.

The plagues come through Moses. In the book of Exodus these ten calamities are designed as *"signs"* (Exodus 4:17 and 10:1) or *"signs and wonders"* (Exodus 7:3). They were displays of God's power over all creation.

The Lord is going to do battle with the gods of Egypt and reveal His power. Look at Exodus 12 verse 12: *"I will pass through the land of Egypt this night ... and against all the gods of Egypt I will execute judgment"*. It was God against the gods of Egypt. Every plague that God sent upon the Egyptians involved the destruction of one of their gods. Through these plagues Israel was shown their true God and Egypt was shown their false gods. These plagues are the greatest testimony in the Old Testament to the futility of idolatry. (See Deuteronomy 4:35) The tenth plague was that every firstborn boy in every Egyptian family would die. This would also happen to the Jews unless they followed God's instructions, so note:

(d) THE PASSOVER GOD SPECIFIES.

The Passover is established. Indeed from that significant day to this present day, the Jewish people remember the Passover. It was a *"memorial"* to be celebrated to keep alive in Israel the story of the exodus. (See Exodus 12:14 and Chapter 13:8-10) Indeed, look at Exodus 12:25-27. You see, this Feast commemorated the deliverance of Israel from Egypt. This Passover is also a true type of Christ, for: *"Christ our Passover is sacrificed for us"* (1 Corinthians 5:7). When God sees us through the blood-stained Cross at Calvary, He sees us as white as the driven snow.

Do you see the result of the Passover? Pharaoh *"called for Moses and Aaron by night, and said, Rise up, and get you forth from among my people ... and go"* (Exodus 12:31). Israel were now on their way. So we see now:

(2) ISRAEL TO SINAI: LIBERATION (Chapter 12:37 to Chapter 18:27)

Most scholars date the time of the exodus as 1445 B.C. This was the moment when Israel came out of Egypt by the blood of the Lamb. Notice what it says in Exodus 12 verse 40. The period of sojourning of the children of Israel in Egypt was four hundred and thirty years. Abraham had been told that his descendants would be aliens mistreated in a foreign land for 400 years, using a figure rounded to hundreds (See Genesis 15:13). Now here is God fulfilling His promise and bringing them out. Israel's exodus from Egypt was not the end of their experience with God. It was the new beginning. *"It took one night to take Israel out of Egypt, but forty years to take Egypt out of Israel"*, said George Morrison.

Here we see Israel in three geographical positions. Notice as the children of Israel make their way:

(a) To the Red Sea: Through the Provision of God

Look at Exodus 13 verses 17 to 22. There is a bit of controversy concerning the route which the Israelites took when they left Egypt. There are three possibilities to consider: a route to the north; a route through the middle, or a route to the south. This third possibility - the southern route down to Mount Sinai is the most likely. Here is where Moses had been a shepherd for 40 years and he knew this country well. Everything God does concerning our background He uses at a future date. Moses had spent 40 years in the Sinai desert and now God is leading the Children of Israel through this southern route.

The Israelites left Goshen and came south. Think of it. Over two million people in a waste-howling wilderness with no guide book to direct them, or track to follow. Ahead is the unknown. *What did Israel have going for her?* Well, the nation had a vivid memory of what God had done in Egypt. What else had they going for them? Well, they had a reminder of God's promises in the bones of Joseph? What else? Well, *"the Lord went before them by day in a pillar of a cloud, to lead them the way"* (Exodus 13:21 and see Numbers 9:17-18). From Rameses, the starting point of the exodus (see Chapter 12:37), they went to Succoth, about 15 to 20 miles south east, and then from Succoth to Etham and so on. (See Exodus 13:20) You see, the pillar was given primarily to guide Israel through their wilderness journey. It meant that they were never left to their own devices. All that was required of them was a simple and candid obedience.

Do we also not need an unerring guide as we go through our earthly pilgrimage? God has given to us the Holy Spirit and the Holy Scriptures and these are to be our pillar of cloud and fire until the journey is over. Do you recall what the Lord Jesus said about the Holy Spirit? *"He will guide you"* (John 16:13). It was while the leaders of the fellowship at Antioch were fasting that the Holy Ghost said: *"Separate Me Barnabas and Saul for the work whereunto I have called them"* (Acts 13:2). Sometimes, the Holy Spirit *restrains* (Acts 16:6-7). Other times, the Holy Spirit *constrains* (Acts 16:10). Do we know what it is to be led by the Spirit of God? (Romans 8:14) Are we learning to listen to His voice? (1 Kings 19:12) Are we sensitive to His promptings and leadings?

Of course, the Spirit of God leads us by the Word of God and this is typified in the pillar when the Psalmist says: *"He (God) spake unto them in the cloudy pillar"* (Psalm 99:7). The Holy Spirit will never lead us in contradiction to the Scriptures. Of the Holy Scriptures it is written: *"Thy Word is a lamp unto my feet, and a light unto my path"* (Psalm 119:105). The Scriptures show us the steps we should take. Now have you grasped this? *Nothing forbidden in the Word of God can be the will of God. The will of God is the Word of God, and the Word of God is the will of God.* Therefore if we want to know God's leading, the most important thing is to get to know God's Word. Do you know why so many of us are ignorant of God's will? It is because we do not know God's Word. (See Acts 17:11) Are you sensitive to the Spirit of God? Are you subject to the Word of God?

But then, the children of Israel make their way:

(b) Through the Red Sea: Through the Power of God

Here is how the Psalmist celebrates what God did: *"He rebuked the Red Sea also, and it was dried up: So He led them through the depths,*

53

as through the wilderness. And He saved them from the hand of him that hated them, and redeemed them from the hand of the enemy. And the waters covered their enemies: there was not one of them left. Then believed they His words; they sang His praise." (Psalm 106:9-12)

The Red Sea was divided **Miraculously** (Exodus 14:21) and **Instrumentally** (Exodus 14:16). Moses used the rod. Philip Ryken says: *"The traditional view is that on their way to the Sinai and the south, the Israelites crossed the Gulf of Suez, the north-west arm of the Red Sea"*. The impossible became possible and the sea was divided. No matter how one looks at it, crossing the Red Sea was a miracle. Steve Wagers says: *"To get through the Red Sea in one night the Israelites would have needed a space of at least three miles, so they could walk 5,000 abreast. If they walked double file, it would have been 800 miles long and it would have taken them 35 days and nights to get through. It took God only one night."*

Like Israel, does a Red Sea of trial and trouble confront you? What about the impossible thing that now faces you? Is the God who divided the Red Sea able to deal with your problem? Yes! Listen to the heartening Word of God: *"There hath no temptation (or trial) taken you but such as is common to man: but God is faithful, who will not suffer you to be tempted above that ye are able; but will with the temptation also make a way of escape, that ye may be able to bear it"* (1 Corinthians 10:13).

Can you see Israel coming to the Red Sea, going through the Red Sea and moving:

(c) From the Red Sea: Through the Providence of God

Let us not forget that the desert region over which the Israelites travelled was unable to support human life. It was not the ideal place to take 2.5 million people plus animals. Can you think of:

1. The External Problems.

There was the Problem of <u>Warfare</u>: *"Then came Amalek, and fought with Israel"* (Exodus 17:8).

There was the Problem of <u>Water and Food</u>: Steve Wagers says: *"Just the amount needed to keep them from starving would have added up to 1500 tons a day but to feed them the way we eat would take 4,000 tons. Just to have it hauled would take 2 freight trains, each one a mile long. At today's prices it would cost $4 million a day. Then consider the amount of water required for the barest necessities of drinking and washing dishes each day. It has been calculated you would have to have 11 million gallons every single day. Think of the gigantic task of hauling water. It would have taken a freight train with tank cars 1800 miles long. Yet God supplied them one day at a time for a total of 14,600 days."* That is our God!

During the Yom Kippur War of 1973, the Egyptian army was unable to last more than three days in the desert, yet in Exodus 2.5 million people survived there for 40 years. Is that not amazing? Yet like us, in spite of God's provision and power, they doubted that God could meet their need. *"Yea, they spake against God; they said, Can God furnish a table in the wilderness?"* (Psalm 78:19) Is that what you are asking? Is God asking you to step out in faith and trust Him, but you don't believe He will meet your need?

2. The Internal Problems.

Given the enormous numbers, one of the biggest problems Moses had was judging disputes between the people. Do you recall what old Jethro said to Moses: *"This thing is too heavy for thee; thou art not able to perform it thyself alone"* (Exodus 18:18). *"Distribute the load, Moses."*

One of the famous chaplains of World War One was G. A. Studdart-Kennedy, known familiarly as Woodbine Willie. When you read the story of his life, you will be surprised to find how young he was when he died, just thirty six. It was said of him: "He was worn out but not worked out". Sadly in God's work there are men who die young. Is it necessary? Well, from a divine perspective no doubt the answer is – Yes! But what about the human perspective? As an elder, a deacon, a believer - are you adding to the burden or are you under the burden? Can you take from the leaders the things that you can do, and leave with them the things that they can do?

This brings us to the last section of the book of Exodus which is:

(3) ISRAEL AT SINAI: REVELATION (Chapters 19 to 40)

In the year 1445 B.C. Israel arrived at Mount Sinai. They would be there for almost a year. (See Numbers 10:11) Three major events took place at this time. There was:

(a) THE COMMANDMENT OF THE LAW.

Now when we think of the Law we usually think of the Ten Commandments, but we need to understand that there were three basic sections of the Mosaic Law. There was:

1. The Moral Code.

This section is commonly known as the Ten Commandments. (See Exodus 20:3-17 and Deuteronomy 5:7-21)

2. The Ceremonial Code.

This section dealt with those special ordinances which foreshadowed Christ and His redemption. It included the seven Levitical feasts and the five Levitical offerings. (See Chapters 35-40 and Leviticus 1:1)

3. The Social Code.

This section included rules governing Israel's diet, sanitation, quarantine, soil conservation, taxation, military service, marriage, childbirth and divorce. Indeed there were seventy basic regulations in the Social Code. Some of these went like this: _"Eye for eye, tooth for tooth, hand for hand, foot for foot"_ (Exodus 21:24); _"And he that curseth his father, or his mother, shall surely be put to death"_ (Exodus 21:17) and _"He that sacrificeth unto any god, save unto the Lord only, he shall be utterly destroyed"_ (Exodus 22:20).

Harold Willmington helps us understand these sections of Moses law. He says that _the Moral Code was the Revelation from Christ_ (See

1 Corinthians 10:4); *the Ceremonial Code was the Realisation in Christ* (See Matthew 5:17; Romans 10:4 and 1 Corinthians 5:7) and *the Social Code was the Regulation until Christ* (Galatians 3:24). So the Jewish ceremonial system presented in Exodus and Leviticus was fulfilled by Christ, but the moral content of God's law still remains and nine of the Ten Commandments are repeated in the New Testament epistles for the church to honour and obey.

The first four commandments are directed to man's relationship with God and the last six to man's relationship with man. Maybe you are saying: *"Those commandments are archaic."* Do you think so? Listen to this one: *"Thou shalt not commit adultery".* The book of Hebrews says: *"Marriage is honourable in all, and the bed undefiled: but whoremongers and adulterers God will judge."* (Hebrews 13:4) You say: *"Why are you plucking that one out of the air?"* I will tell you why. Because marriages between professing Christians are falling apart. Will you listen? Marriage is an *exclusive relationship: "Keep thee only unto her".* Marriage is an *enduring relationship: "Till death us do part".* God has given us His law to guard not only the heart but the home. How quickly Israel broke it in:

(b) THE CORRUPTION OF THE CALF.

"And when the people saw that Moses delayed to come down out of the mount, the people gathered themselves together unto Aaron, and said unto him, Up, make us gods, which shall go before us; for as for this Moses, the man that brought us up out of the land of Egypt, we wot not what is become of him." (Exodus 32:1)

Do you see the stages of sin here? Impatience led to idolatry and idolatry led to immorality. (See verse 25) When we begin to be impatient with God, because He is not acting *'as'* and *'when'* we want, the next stage is to turn to 'other gods' and finally, having left the Lord, we forget His standards for our lives. What stage are you at?

The book concludes with:

(c) THE CONSTRUCTION OF THE TABERNACLE.

What an amazing thing! God wants to dwell among His people. (See Exodus 25:8) The tabernacle points to Christ. Indeed Christ is the perfect tabernacle. (See Hebrews 9:8, 11-12) The tabernacle was to provide for Israel a visible centre of worship and to preview the work of the Lord Jesus.

Moses describes the brazen altar: John describes the Lamb of God (John 1:29). Moses speaks of the brazen laver: John speaks of the water of life (John 4:14). Moses writes of the table of shewbread: John writes of the bread of life (John 6:35). Moses talks of the lampstand: John talks of the light of the world (John 9:5). Moses presents the altar of incense: John presents the great high priestly prayer of Christ (John 17:1). Moses witnesses of the mercy seat: John witnesses of Christ our mercy seat (1 John 2:2).

The tabernacle previews the work of the Lord Jesus, but it also testifies to the holiness of God. The root meaning of the word *"tabernacle"* or *"sanctuary"* carries with it the thought of *"holiness"* and describes not only the place but the purpose of the tabernacle. An interesting study is to take a concordance and follow *"holy"* as it relates to the tabernacle in the book of Exodus. Do you know what you will discover? That over 30 times you will find the word *"holy"* as it relates to the tabernacle. Why, the engraving on the plate of pure gold attached to the mitre and worn by Aaron the high priest sums up this testimony to the holiness of God. The words were to read: *"Holiness to the Lord"* (Exodus 28:36).

The whole tabernacle was carefully guarded from anything that might defile the sanctity of God's dwelling place. Everything about the tabernacle witnessed to the holiness of God. Do you recall what they called the first section? *"The holy place"* (Exodus 26:33). Do you know what they called the second section? *"The most holy place"* (Exodus 26:34). Everything about the tabernacle testified to the absolute holiness of God. That is why their approach to God had to be through sacrifice (the brazen altar) and cleansing (the brazen laver).

God is holy, therefore we need to be careful about <u>our worship</u>. Will you remember that as you come on a Lord's day morning?

"God is greatly to be feared in the assembly of the saints, and to be had in reverence of all them that are about Him" (Psalm 89:7).

God is holy, therefore we need to careful about <u>our walk</u>. *"So be ye holy in all manner of conversation"* (1 Peter 1:15).

Perhaps Robert Murray McCheyne's prayer should be often on our lips: **"Lord, make me as holy as it is possible for a saved sinner to be."**

CHAPTER 4

Leviticus

I wonder, what do you think of when you hear the name *"Leviticus"*? Maybe you think of Levi's blue jeans. Or maybe you think of nothing, it just sounds obscure. If you have read this book, maybe you think of priests or sacrifices or lots of rules, and still it sounds obscure. That is the way Leviticus is. Mind you, it does have some famous parts. *For example, did you know that America's Liberty Bell takes its name from this book?* If you have seen the bell in Philadelphia you probably saw the words inscribed on the bell. *"Proclaim Liberty Throughout all the Land unto all the Inhabitants Thereof"*. The words are taken from Leviticus 25:10.

Many people who resolve to read the Bible through get stuck in Leviticus. A certain lady on being asked if she had ever read the Bible through replied: *"I have never read it through, though I have read much of it consecutively. Three times I have started to read it through, but each time I have broken down in Leviticus. I have enjoyed Genesis and Exodus but Leviticus seemed such dull reading that I became discouraged and gave up."*

Is that how you feel when you approach Leviticus? Do you find it boring? Maybe we find it so difficult because it so <u>unfamiliar.</u> It is from a different culture as well as having a different content. We are moving away from our present situation by 3,000 years and 2,000 miles. It is a totally different world and that is why we may find it so strange. We do not arrive at church today with a lamb or pigeon and then give it to the leader who then slits its throat in front of the whole congregation. *We don't do that, do we?*

Then again this book seems so <u>irrelevant</u>. I mean, what has

Leviticus got to say to me today? What truth from Leviticus can I rest on as I go into work with an ungodly crowd on Monday morning? Well, let us try to bring Leviticus to life shall we? Think about the:

1. The Period of the Book.

The laws of Leviticus were given in the wilderness. The book covers a period in Israel's history of less than two months at the beginning of the second year after the exodus from Egypt, from the first day of the first month to the twentieth day of the second month. (Exodus 40:17 and Numbers 10:11 - 1443 B.C.)

2. The Place of the Book.

Do you see how Leviticus opens? It opens with the word *"And"*. Thus, Leviticus is a continuing story of Exodus. Exodus ended with the design of the tabernacle, Leviticus begins with the declaration from the tabernacle. The tabernacle was designed as a place for the people to meet with God, and in Leviticus God meets with His people.

Dr. G. Scroggie says:

"Mark the connection between Exodus and Leviticus. In the one the people are brought nigh to God, and in other they are kept nigh. In Exodus we read of God's approach to us, but in Leviticus of our approach to God. In the one book Christ is the Saviour, and in the other He is the Sanctifier. Exodus reveals God as Love. Leviticus reveals God as Light. In the one we are brought into union with Him, and in the other we are brought into communion. Exodus offers us pardon, but Leviticus calls us to purity."

Now it is interesting that Genesis is the book of beginnings. It tells you how everything began from the creation of the universe to Israel becoming God's people. The book of Exodus is all about Israel coming out of Egypt by the blood of the lamb. Leviticus gets its name from the tribe of the Levites. Levi was the name of Jacob's third son and Leviticus means *"pertaining to the Levites"* and the Levites were the persons responsible for the service of the tabernacle. (See Numbers 3:1-13) *Now,* as David Pawson reminds us, *there is a pattern emerging here if you see it?* Genesis is a *universal* book. It is about everybody, the human race and the whole universe. Exodus is a *national* book. Its focus is on one people, the nation of Israel. But in Leviticus the focus is even more narrow - only on one tribe out of the whole nation. So we could say that Genesis is *universal,* and Exodus is *national,* but Leviticus is *tribal.* Is that why so many get stuck in Leviticus? We are interested in universal things, even national things, but we are less concerned when the focus is just on one tribe, especially if that tribe is not ours. So here we are in Leviticus focusing on one tribe (Levi), zooming in on one place Mount Sinai (Leviticus 27:34), taking into account regulations that were given over a period of just over one month. So what is:

3. The Purpose of the Book.

The purpose is to provide guidelines to the priests and people for the appropriate worship of God. In Exodus, God had prepared a place for worship, the tabernacle. In Leviticus, God reveals a pattern for worship. The Israelites are to understand that they are separated by God, to God and for God. So Leviticus was written to show Israel how to live as a holy nation in fellowship with God. Now note:

4. The Parts of the Book.

Henrietta Mears divides Leviticus into 2 main themes. The offerings, in the first part of the book, remind us to *"Get Right"*. The feasts, in the latter part of the book, remind us to *"Stay Right"*. The first part covers Chapters 1 to 17 and the second part covers chapters 18 to 27. Now what is it that so clearly breaks the book into these two parts? Well, the first part has to do with worship; the second part has to do with practice. In the first part, everything relates to the tabernacle; in the second part, everything relates to conduct. Part one shows the way to God by sacrifice;

part two shows the walk with God by sanctification. In the first part, purification is provided; in the second part, punishment is to be inflicted. The first part has to do with the people's cleansing; the second part has to do with the people's clean living.

Do you see how the book opens in Leviticus 1 verse 1? *"And the Lord called unto Moses, and spake unto him out of the tabernacle of the congregation, saying".* The contents of Leviticus are God's Word communicated to and through His servant Moses.

Andrew Bonar says:

"There is no book in the whole of Scripture that contains more of the very words of God than Leviticus. It is God that is the direct speaker in almost every page."

The Lord Jesus Himself believed that Moses was the human author of this book as He quoted from it in the New Testament. (See Matthew 8 verse 4 and Leviticus 14 verses 2 to 10) As has been said, the book divides into 2 parts:

(1) THE WAY TO GOD BY SACRIFICE (Chapters 1 to 17)

This speaks to us of <u>the Work of the Son for us.</u> Leviticus is a book of sacrifice and blood, themes that are repulsive to modern minds. Mankind wants a *"bloodless religion"*. They want morality without sacrifice, and yet this is impossible. Every Israelite was aware of the fact that, since the beginning, God had insisted on sacrifice as the ground upon which He was to be approached. However, now the time had come for the sacrifices to be made a vital part of their daily lives. So right here we are introduced to:

(a) THE OFFERINGS.

These were the offerings of the tabernacle. There were five main offerings and each kind is described by a separate chapter in Leviticus 1-5.

1. The Burnt Offering (Chapter 1)

2. The Meal Offering (Chapter 2)

3. The Peace Offering (Chapter 3)

4. The Sin Offering (Chapter 4)

5. The Trespass Offering (Chapter 5)

Now these five offerings can be divided into three and two. The first three are *"sweet savour"* offerings. (See Leviticus 1:9; 2:2; 3:5 & 16) The remaining two are non-sweet savour offerings. Each one shows us a different aspect of the person and work of the Lord Jesus. The two sin offerings, that is the sin offering and the trespass offering, depict what Calvary means to us, the three sweet savour offerings depict what Calvary means to God.

John Phillips says:

"The sin offerings reveal how the holiness of God is satisfied by the work of the Cross, the sweet savour offerings tell us how the heart of God is satisfied by the work of Christ. The sin offerings set before us the reasons for the cross, the sweet savour offerings set before us the results of the cross. In the sin offerings God deals with our wickedness, in the sweet savour offerings God deals with our worship. In the sin offerings God deals with us as sinners, in the sweet savour offerings God deals with us as saints."

1. Look at the Sin Offerings

There were two kinds of sin offerings. Both were designed to bring before us the enormity of our guilt before God. We tend to take a complacent view of our sin, but the Lord does nothing of the kind. Our sin kindles His wrath on the one side and His compassion on the other. Now:

1. The Sin Offering:

This reminds us that Christ was *"made sin for us"* (2 Corinthians 5:21).

2. The Trespass Offering:

This underscores the individual acts of sin. (See Leviticus 5:1-3)

In both offerings, sin was looked upon as a debt to be paid and, of course, that debt was fully and finally paid by Christ. But:

2. Look at the Sweet Savour Offerings

1. The Burnt Offering: Christ's Devotion was Full

It was complete. You see, the burnt offering was all for God. There was no sharing here. All for God, for God must come first. What a picture of our Lord's dedication of Himself to God. *"Lo, I come: in the volume of the book it is written of Me, I delight to do Thy will, O My God: yea, Thy law is within My heart."* (Psalm 40:7-8) Is your devotion to the Lord full? Have you presented your body as *"a living sacrifice, holy, acceptable to God"?*

2. The Meal Offering: Christ's Devotion was Flawless

The word *"meat"* means *"meal"* for there is no blood involved in this offering. It could be fine flour, flour baked into cakes, or even dried ears of corn. But everything about the meal offering was designed to set before us the marvellous sinless humanity of our Lord Jesus. The flour, for instance, was to be fine flour, flour ground and ground until it was completely smooth and free from all unevenness. There was no roughness, no unevenness in the Lord Jesus. He was perfectly balanced: *"holy, harmless, undefiled, separate from sinners"* (Hebrews 7:26). May the Spirit of God so work in us that we become like Him, balanced, even, fragrant and pure.

3. The Peace Offering: Christ's Devotion was Fruitful

The idea of this offering was that of communion, for the offerer and the priest sat down together in the presence of God and feasted upon the sacrifice together. (See Leviticus 7:28-34) It was kind of a *"Lord's Supper"* in Old Testament times.

Fellowship with God means fellowship also with God's people. Now are you beginning to see this elaborate sacrificial system? *It formed the very core of Israel's public worship.* God is holy and He will not permit sin in His presence. In order to establish a relationship between God and sinners a sacrifice has to be made, substituting a pure life for a sinful one. Atonement – *"at-one-ment"* - means the reconciling through substitution of those who have been estranged. So the life of the animal is accepted in the place of the life of the sinner. (See Hebrews 9:22) But all was pointing to Christ. Leviticus often uses the word *"atonement"* meaning "to cover". You see, the blood shed on the altar in this book could only *"cover"* for sin until Christ shed His blood on the Cross, paying the real price that God demanded for sin's cleansing.

> *Not all the blood of beasts,*
> *On Jewish altars slain,*
> *Could give the guilty conscience peace,*
> *Or take away the stain.*
>
> *But Christ the heavenly Lamb,*
> *Took all our sins away,*
> *A sacrifice of nobler worth,*
> *And richer blood than they.*

Of course, if fellowship with God is to be maintained, there must not only be a sacrifice (Chapters 1 to 7) but a priest. So:

(b) THE PRIESTHOOD.

The priesthood is introduced to us in Chapters 8 to 10. Now, what was a priest? Well, the term *"priest"* means *"one who officiates"*. A prophet was someone who represented God to the people, a priest was someone who represented the people to God. Now, of course, "Leviticus" means *"pertaining to the Levites the priests"*. You see, if you were going to function in the priestly office you had to be a Levite. (Exodus 28:1 and Numbers 3:7) Aaron, Israel's first high priest, is a remarkable type of Christ our great high priest, and Aaron's sons foreshadow the believers as priests. In Chapter 8, we have the consecration of the priests.

1. They were Purified

There was a _Judicial Cleansing:_ a bullock was the sin offering that had to be slain to atone for Aaron and his sons. (Leviticus 8:14) There was also a _Moral Cleansing:_ for Moses "_washed them with water_" (Leviticus 8:6). Do we not need to be cleansed continually from the daily defilement of sin? The Psalmist says: "_Wherewithall shall a young man cleanse his way? by taking heed thereto according to Thy word_" (Psalm 119:9).

2. They were Sanctified

Look at Leviticus 8 verses 22 to 24. Do you see what happened? Moses put the blood of the sacrifice on Aaron's right ear, on the thumb of his right hand, and on the great toe of his right foot. Then he did the same for Aaron's sons. The lesson is plain. The consecrated ear is open to hear the Word of God; the consecrated hand is ready to serve the Lord, and the consecrated foot is guided by the Lord. Our Lord's ear was always open to hear and obey His Father's voice; His hands were busy ministering to those in need, and His feet were always walking in the paths of righteousness. _Tell me, are you set apart like that?_ It is evident that Nadab and Abihu were not, for they served the Lord presumptuously and God cut them off. (See Leviticus 10:2)

3. They were Qualified

Aaron and his sons were anointed with oil, a symbol of the Holy Spirit. Do you recall that it was said of the Lord Jesus: "_Behold My servant ... I will put My Spirit upon Him._" (Matthew 12:18) As Christ stepped out of Jordan after His baptism, the Spirit came upon Him like a dove. (See Matthew 3:16 and Luke 4:18) Do you realize that you cannot function without unction? That we need that conscious, constant dependence on the Holy Spirit otherwise our ministries will be wanting? Of course, today we do not "_have_" a priesthood - we "_are_" a priesthood. Peter says we are a holy priesthood, a royal priesthood (1 Peter 2:5-9). Tell me, are we fulfilling our priestly duties? Do you know what _dumb_ priests are? Brethren who never lift their hearts to God in prayer and praise? (Hebrews 13:15) Do you know what *disobedient* priests are? Believers who have never taken seriously their responsibility to give to the work of the Lord. (Philippians 4:18) Do you know what *dull* priests are? Christians who have lost their vitality to do anything worthwhile for the Lord.

If any Biblical confirmation is needed for the old proverb *"cleanliness is next to godliness"*, chapters 11 to 16 would do. For here there is brought before us:

(c) THE PEOPLE.

God's people must be a clean people. Is it not interesting here that holiness in God's people concerns the body as well as the soul? This section insists on:

1. Clean foods: Chapter 11

2. Clean bodies: Chapter 12 to 13:46

3. Clean clothes: Chapter 13:47-59

4. Clean houses: Chapter 14:33-57

5. Clean contacts: Chapter 15

6. A Clean nation: Chapter 16

In Chapter 16, there is brought us *"The Day of Atonement"* - Yom Kippur - which was the high point of all sacrifices. Here was provision for any and every sin not covered by the specific offerings mentioned in the first seven chapters.

This first section of the book ends with:

(d) THE ALTAR

Look at Leviticus 17 verses 3 to 9 and Exodus 27 verse 1. Time and again, it is the door of the tabernacle. It is the brazen altar. There is only one place where God has chosen to meet with penitent sinners and that is the Cross of which the altar at the door of the tabernacle was a type. There is no other sacrifice, no other priest, no other altar. *"None other name under heaven given among men, whereby we must be saved"* (Acts 4:12). Indeed, in this very chapter, we read: *"For the life of the flesh is in the blood … it is the blood that maketh an atonement for the soul"* (Leviticus 17:11). It is through the shed blood of Calvary's Lamb - nothing more, nothing less, nothing else - that we have our salvation.

> *The life is in the blood,*
> *And must for sin atone,*
> *One sacrifice and once for all,*
> *The blood of Christ alone.*

(2) THE WALK WITH GOD BY SANCTIFICATION (Chapters 18 to 27)

If the way to God underscores the *work of the Son for us*, then the walk with God underscores the *work of the Spirit in us*. I wonder, as you have read the Old Testament, have you ever put yourself in Jewish shoes? *You see,* as David Pawson points out, *for a Jew the reason for reading Leviticus is clear, it is literally a matter of life and death.* To the Jews, there is only one God and that God is the God of Israel. Since there was only one God and they were His people on earth, there was a special relationship between them. On God's side, He promised to do many things for them. To be their government - to be their minister of defence and protect them; to be their minister of finance and meet all their needs; to be their minister of health so that none of the diseases of Egypt would touch them. God would be everything they needed. In other words, He would be their all in all.

But, in return, the Lord expected them to live right and do right things. They were to be righteous and holy before the Lord. Indeed the key text of the book is right here in Leviticus 19 verse 2: *"Ye shall be holy: for I the Lord your God am holy"*. This is the key that unlocks the book. God tells them they must not do something just because the nations around them are doing it. They are to be different, to be distinct, to be separate from all the other nations. They were to be holy because He is holy. You see, when the Lord saves you, He expects you to be like Him, He expects you to live His way, to be holy as He is holy. That is why in these closing chapters we read about:

(a) HOLY PEOPLE   (Chapters 18 to 20)

Here were a people who were to separate themselves from the practices of the surrounding nations. Look at Chapter 18 verses 3 and 4: *"After the doings of the land of Egypt … shall ye not do: and after the doings of the land of Canaan … shall ye not do"*. You see, the Israelites were to maintain a distinctive lifestyle. This was to be achieved by obedience to the laws that God gave through His servant Moses. Rules forbidding sexual misconduct (Leviticus 18:20) are found alongside compassionate provisions for the needy (Leviticus 19:9, 13, 14 & 33). Do you see the value that God puts on pure sexual relationships? (Leviticus 18:20-22) Incest, adultery, homosexuality, bestiality - for all these perversions there was judgment (Leviticus 18:29).

What the Lord is really saying here is that the way to be really happy is to be really holy. You see, happiness and holiness belong together and the lack of holiness brings unhappiness. Do you realise that most of us get it the wrong way round? God's will for us is that we be holy in this world and happy in the next, but many of us want to be happy now and holy later. And then:

(b) HOLY PRIESTS (Chapters 21 and 22)

If the people as a whole were to be holy unto the Lord, how much more the priests? These chapters tell us what the priest *must not do* (Leviticus 21:1-15); *must not be* (Leviticus 21:16 to 22:16), and *must not offer* (Leviticus 22:17-33). It is interesting to notice that the tabernacle was a three-fold structure: the Outer Court, and the Holy Place and the Holy of Holies. This seemed to correspond to the three-fold way in which the nation was arranged, the congregation, the priesthood, the High Priest. You see, just as the parts of the tabernacle became successively holier, so it was to be with the nation. Israel's sanctification was to reach its climax in the High Priest who wore the golden crown inscribed with the words *"Holiness to the Lord"* (Exodus 28:36). In leadership, are we an example to the flock in holy living? And then:

(c) HOLY PERIODS (Chapter 23)

You see, Israel had not only 5 offerings - it had 7 feasts. They had a calendar of worship to observe. Now there is no corresponding Christian calendar in the New Testament. We have no instructions about observing Christmas or Easter, but for the Jewish people a calendar was a vital part of their walk with God. Seven feasts are mentioned here in Chapter 23 and all had to be kept. Seven feasts that portrayed the basic facts of redemption, even though this was something that the nation of Israel could not discern at this time. Certainly these seven feasts were memorials of past events but they were more than that. *They were foreshadowings of future events.* Now these seven annual feasts were:

1. Passover: speaks of the death of Christ (1 Corinthians 5:7).

2. Unleavened Bread: speaks of a separated walk.

3. The First Fruits: typical of the resurrection (1 Corinthians 15:23).

4. Pentecost: which looked forward to that day in history when the Holy Spirit came down (Acts 2:1).

An interval of four months then elapsed between the Feast of Pentecost and the Feast of Trumpets. (Leviticus 23:24)

5. The Feast of Trumpets: speaks of Israel's regathering (Isaiah 27:12-13; Joel 2:15 and Matthew 24:31). But, it also applies to us for we are waiting for the sound of the trumpet.

6. The Day of Atonement: illustrates to us the day of Israel's cleansing.

7. The Feast of Tabernacles: pictures that future kingdom where

Jesus *"shall reign where'er the sun"*.

The feasts are seven in number and this being the number of completion, the picture is complete in every detail. Here we have God's prophetic calendar, a perfect outline of God's dealing with the Jew and the Gentile from first to last. Now I want you to notice that these feasts are divided into sections of four and three.

(1) The First Four Feasts were Literally Fulfilled by Christ at His First Coming:

The Passover, Unleavened Bread, First Fruits, and Pentecost followed each other closely. Indeed all these took place in the first three months in Israel's calendar.

Then came that interval of four months during which there was no feast of Jehovah. Rather, there was a long pause between the Feast of Pentecost and the Feast of Trumpets. Now that is significant. Indeed, it seems to be that the truths foreshadowed in the first four feasts are related to the church, while the last three feasts are related to the nation.

(2) The Last Three Feasts will be Literally Fulfilled by Christ at His Second Coming:

The interval between the feasts in Israel's religious calendar illustrates the time gap between the first and second advents of the Lord. As there were no feasts as far as Leviticus Chapter 23 is concerned between Pentecost and Trumpets, so there are no feasts during this present age.

The church, of course, has one feast, that is the Lord's Supper. This feast embraces all the truths found in these feasts. Passover reminds us of the bread and wine, symbols of His death; Unleavened Bread, speaks of holiness of life that is so necessary for a true remembrance of Christ; First-fruits bring to mind the fact that He is risen; Pentecost, an unbroken loaf, suggests the oneness of the body of Christ. In the Feast of Trumpets, we show forth the Lord's death till He come.

Now do you know where we are living right now? We are living between the Feast of Pentecost and the Feast of Trumpets, and during that time Israel was busy in wheat harvest. Are you involved in the harvest? Sure, you have come to God through the Lamb, you have experienced resurrection life through Christ, you are putting sin out of your life, but are you involved in the harvest? When the Saviour comes again, will He find you faithful? Will He find you involved in this great spiritual harvest? Will He see you:

> *Gathering in the lost ones for whom our Lord did die,*
> *For the crowning day is coming by and by.*

(d) HOLY PRINCIPLES

The seventh day of each week was to be kept as a *"Sabbath"* of solemn rest (Leviticus 23:3 and Exodus 20:8-11) This Sabbath principle was also to be applied to the land once the Israelites were settled. (See Leviticus 25:2-7) Indeed these closing chapters deal with Israel's occupation of Canaan. Time and again in this closing portion of the book we read about *"the land"*. The words *"If ye .... then I will"* are key terms here. (See Leviticus 26:3 & 4) Likewise, *"But if ye will not hearken .... then I will punish you"* (Leviticus 26:14-18). These were not empty promises and threats. There are rewards for trusting and obeying God, but there are also punishments for those who distrust and disobey Him.

> *"Trust and obey, for there's no other way,*
> *To be happy in Jesus, but to trust and obey."*

So The Way to God is Through Sacrifice!

Our Walk with God is Through Sanctification!

Being conformed to the holiness of God! There is no book in the Bible that is stronger on the holiness of God than Leviticus. We learn about God's holiness from this book. Do you recall what the Hebrew letter says? *"Let us .... serve God acceptably with reverence and godly fear: For our God is a consuming fire"* (Hebrews 12:28-29). Do you know where the writer got that? He got it straight out of

Leviticus and it is vital for us who have lost sight of the holiness of God. Do you know what God's Word is to you? *"Ye shall be holy: for I the Lord your God am holy"* (Leviticus 19:2). Leviticus tells us to be holy in every part of our lives - even down to our toilet arrangements! You see, a godly life is godly through and through or it is not godly at all. Have you a desire to be holy?

A lot of believers are interested in Heaven, but they are not interested in holiness. They are interested in health, but not holiness. They want happiness, but not holiness. But what God wants for us more than anything else is to be holy. How are you getting on? Are you a holy person? Holy at all times, in all places, with all people.

"Ye shall be holy: for I the Lord your God am holy" (Leviticus 19:2).

CHAPTER 5
Numbers

One day towards the close of the 18th Century, a gentlemen and lady sat side by side in a stagecoach as it rumbled its way through the English countryside. The lady appeared to be occupied with the contents of the book in her hand, at times reading from its open pages, at times meditating on what she had just read. She was obviously enjoying her meditation, the words of a lovely hymn:

> *"Come Thou fount of every blessing,*
> *Tune my heart to sing Thy praise,*
> *Streams of mercy never ceasing,*
> *Call for songs of loudest praise."*

She turned to the gentleman, to her a stranger, and sought to interest him in what was thrilling her soul. Holding before him the open page, she asked if he knew the hymn. At first he appeared embarrassed and a little annoyed, then he tried to avoid her question but she persisted telling him of the blessing the words had brought to her heart. After a period of silence he burst into tears: *"Madam"*, he said, *"I am the poor unhappy man who composed that hymn many years ago and I would give a thousand worlds if I had them to enjoy the feelings I had then"*.

The man on the stagecoach was Robert Robinson (1735-1790) and the hymn was the product of his pen some thirty years previously. Robert Robinson was *"Prone to wander"*. He was *"prone to leave"*. But the record tells us that in life's eventide, he experienced the restoring grace of God. Are we not all prone to wander and prone to leave the God we love? The bent of the human heart is ever to stray from the pathway of fellowship with God, but over against every human departure and every human wandering there is restoring grace.

The book of Numbers is all about *"wandering"*. It has special significance for us today. Again and again this book is referred to in the New Testament. Indeed the Holy Spirit has called special attention to it in that classic statement concerning Israel's early history. The apostle says:

"Moreover, brethren, I would not that ye should be ignorant, how that all our fathers were under the cloud, and all passed through the sea; And were all baptized unto Moses in the cloud and in the sea; And did all eat the same spiritual meat; And did all drink the same spiritual drink: for they drank of that spiritual Rock that followed them: and that Rock was Christ. But with many of them God was not well pleased: for they were overthrown in the wilderness. Now these things were our examples, to the intent we should not lust after evil things, as they also lusted." (1 Corinthians 10:1-6)

The word *"examples"* is "types" (*tupoi*). In other words, the things recorded in the book of Numbers are, as Sidlow Baxter puts it: *"made immortal by their having been Divinely resolved into types for our learning"*.

When we think of Canaan, which was Israel's destination, we are not to think of Heaven. Rather, **Canaan represents God's full purpose for His people.**

At Kadesh-Barnea, Israel failed to enter into their inheritance. Instead of claiming Canaan by faith, they wandered in the wilderness in unbelief. How like us! Sure, we have been delivered from Egypt by the blood of the Lamb, but we have not yet entered into our inheritance in Christ. Yes, we are saved, but we have not fulfilled God's purpose for our lives. We have not trusted God to overcome the giants, knock down the walls, and give us the inheritance that He has promised. We are just wandering aimlessly in the wilderness. Wasted years. Is this your life? You see:

1. Numbers is a very Sad Book

One commentator has said: *"It should have taken them 11 days to travel from Egypt to the Promised Land, but it actually took them 13,780 days"*. Do you recall that only two of them who set out reached their home. Caleb and Joshua. The rest were stuck in aimless living, *"killing time"* until the judgment of the Lord was complete. Over time they all died in the wilderness and a new generation took up the journey.

2. Number is a very Statistical Book

It is full of numbers. Take the title. In the Hebrew the title is always taken from the first words of the scroll. *"And the Lord spake unto Moses ...."* (Numbers 1:1). When the Hebrew Scriptures were translated into Greek, the translators gave it a new title, *Arithmoi* from which we get the word "arithmetic". Latin translators gave the book the title *Numeri*. In English, we know it as Numbers. You see, the book begins and ends with censuses. The first was taken when Israel left Sinai one month after the tabernacle had been erected. (See Exodus 40:17 and Numbers 1:1) The second was taken when they arrived at Moab prior to entering the land of Canaan almost 40 years later. These were male censuses used for military conscription. So the book of Numbers tells us that there is nothing wrong with counting. David was punished by the Lord for counting his men, but this was because he was motivated by pride. Other parts of the Bible include examples of counting and taking stock. We are told, for example, of the 3,000 that were saved on the Day of Pentecost. Christ encouraged His disciples to count the cost of following Him. Now, note:

3. The Time Line of the Book

This is important.

(a) The Passover occurred on the fourteenth day of the first month of the year and the nation departed from Egypt on the fifteenth day of the first month. (See Numbers 33:3 and Exodus 12:2 & 6)

(b) The tabernacle was erected at Mount Sinai exactly one year after the exodus, on the first day of the first month of the second year. (See Exodus 40:2 & 17)

(c) One month later, the nation prepared to leave Sinai for the Promised Land, on the first day of the second month of the second year. (See Numbers 1:1)

(d) On the twentieth day of the second month of the second year *"the cloud was taken up from off the tabernacle of the testimony. And the children of Israel took their journeys out of the wilderness of Sinai"* (See Numbers 10:11&12).

(e) The book of Deuteronomy opens with a reference to the first day of the eleventh month of the fortieth year. This is 38 years, eight months and ten days after the nation departed from Sinai (Deuteronomy 1:3 and Numbers 10:11-12) This means that Numbers covers a period of time known as 'the wilderness wanderings' which lasted 38 years, nine months and ten days.

Now that is a lot for us all to take in. Maybe we could simplify all this by saying that perhaps the book would be better known by its Hebrew name *("bemidhbar")* which means *"in the wilderness"*, for this is the setting from *"the wilderness of Sinai"* (Numbers 1:1) to *"the wilderness of Paran"* (Numbers 10:12) - this is where Kadesh Barnea was - and finally on to *"the plains of Moab"* (Numbers 22:1). This means we can divide the book geographically:

(1) FROM SINAI TO KADESH BARNEA (Chapters 1 to 12)

The key word here is **WALKING.** You see, Numbers commences where the book of Exodus concludes. And just as Exodus is connected with Genesis and Leviticus with Exodus so Numbers is connected with Leviticus. Do you see how the book opens? *"And the Lord spake"* (Numbers 1:1). Now, in Leviticus the subject is the believer's worship, but in Numbers, it is the believer's walk. Leviticus speaks of purity, but Numbers speak of pilgrimage. Leviticus speaks of our spiritual position, but Numbers speaks of our spiritual progress. In the one the Sanctuary is prominent, and in the other the Wilderness is prominent. Indeed this is exactly where the book opens: *"in the wilderness of Sinai"* (Numbers 1:1). And here we see:

(a) THE NATION COUNTED (Chapters 1 to 4)

Look at verses 2 and 3 of Chapter 1. The wording here makes it clear that the primary purpose of the numbering was a military one. It gives us the man-power of the newly formed nation. The total being 603,550 and it is on the basis of this adult male census that the sum of the whole nation is reckoned at 2.5 million people.

How do you organize that kind of number? Well, our God is a God of semblance and order. He does nothing haphazardly, or half-heartedly. With meticulous detail, He positions each tribe while they are in the camp and when they are on the move. Always the tabernacle had to be central. Encamped, three tribes are located on each of the four sides of the tabernacle. On the move six tribes, those to the east and south, move out first. The tabernacle follows. The six remaining tribes, those dwelling to the west and north, bring up the rear.

What a spectacle this must have been! When the camp set out on a journey, everyone moved according to a fascinating pattern. Moreover, the Levites were given to assist Aaron and the priests in the duties of the tabernacle. (Numbers 3:5-13) We might ask: *Why is God so fussy about all these details?* I think the Lord was saying: *"Be careful, for I am in your midst"*. What a timely word for us in our day and generation. For if ever *"carelessness"* pertained to the things of God, it is today. I suppose a modern word for this would be *"casualness"*, the *"any old thing will do for God"* attitude. Has that attitude permeated your life? Have you been casual in relation to prayer, the Word, worship, evangelism?

Now, as well as being carefully arranged, the camp had to be spotlessly clean for these were *"God's people"* and so we see:

(b) THE NATION COUNSELLED (Chapters 5 to 10)

If the first chapters give us the outward formation of the camp, the next six deal with the inward condition. The key verse is Numbers 5 verse 3 where God says: *"That they defile not their camps, in the midst whereof I dwell"*. The Holy One Himself being in the midst of that camp, the camp must be holy. So:

Chapter 5 commands that lepers be quarantined outside the camp.
Chapter 6 gives us the regulations concerning the Nazarite vow, a voluntary vow of dedication to God.
Chapter 7 brings before us the freewill offerings of the princes.
Chapter 8 describes the consecration of the priests.
Chapter 9 shows us the people keeping the Passover.
Chapter 10 brings before us the trumpets of silver, for as the pillar give guidance for the eye, the trumpets give guidance for the ear.

What can we learn from all this? That we need to be: *"Vessels unto honour, sanctified, and meet for the master's use"* (2 Timothy 2:21). One thing that has struck me time and again going through the opening books of the Bible is that *"cleanliness is next to godliness"*. Do you not think that has some support from this book of Numbers? A dirty, uncared-for home is an insult to God. A dirty, uncared-for Christian is an insult to God. Yes, God wants us clean spiritually, but He wants us clean physically too. (See Chapter 19) It is a testimony to His presence in our midst. So the nation was counted, then counselled and then we see:

(c) THE NATION CHASTISED (Chapters 11 and 12)

Do you see how Chapter 11 opens? Think of it, after only three days' journey the people are complaining. Do you know what Paul said about these years? He said this: *"about the time of forty years suffered He their manners in the wilderness"* (Acts 13:18). What ill-mannered children they were! Someone has suggested that a better title for Numbers would be: *"The Book of Murmurings"*. Do you know what their biggest problem was? The same problem as ours. It is called murmuring. I mean the Israelites were constantly moaning. We have seven distinct episodes of grumbling and moaning from Chapter 11 to Chapter 21. You see, the children of Israel complained about:

1. **The Journey (Numbers 11:1-3)**
2. **The Food (Numbers 11:4-6)**
3. **The Giants (Numbers 13:33 to 14:3)**
4. **The Leaders (Numbers 16:3)**
5. **The Divine Judgment (Numbers 16:41)**
6. **The Desert (Numbers 20:2-5)**
7. **The Manna (Numbers 11:6 and Numbers 21:5)**

No doubt they were stimulated by *"the mixt multitude"* who came out of Egypt with them. (See Numbers 11:4 and Exodus 12:38) These were people who had witnessed the power of God displayed on Israel's behalf, but they had never been *"under the blood"* themselves and they were a constant irritant in the camp. Do you know folk like that? Let us nail this for what it is. *Murmuring is a serious sin.* So serious that God came down in judgment in the midst of His camp. Sidlow Baxter says: "Those who murmur without cause are soon given cause to murmur".

Paul says: *"Do all things without murmurings and disputings"* (Philippians 2:14). Let me give you a word about murmuring. Don't do it! Paul says: *"Neither murmur ye, as some of them also murmured, and were destroyed of the destroyer"* (1 Corinthians 10:10). You see, you need no talent to grumble; you need no brains to grumble; you need no character to grumble; you need no self-denial to set up the grumbling business. Have you discovered that it is one of the easiest things in the world to do? These people thought that because God was in the tabernacle, He did not know what they said when they went to their own tents. What a big mistake! Is that what you are thinking? When I go outside into the car-park, and groan to my cronies about the leaders, God does not hear? Does He not? Grumbling probably does more damage to the people of God and the work of God than any other sin.

(2) FROM KADESH BARNEA TO KADESH BARNEA (Chapters 13 to 19)

Not only did Israel move from Sinai to Kadesh Barnea, they moved from Kadesh Barnea to Kadesh Barnea! In other words, they were going round in circles. The key word here is **WANDERING.** Now look at Numbers 12 verse 16. This is where Kadesh Barnea was. (See Chapter 13:26) Sidlow Baxter says: *"It only took forty hours to get Israel out of Egypt, but it took 40 years to get Egypt out of Israel".* Within two years, the people of Israel were at Kadesh Barnea, the gate of Canaan. Thirty eight years later they were at it again, at the very same spot. Why? Well, they trusted the Lord to bring them out of Egypt, but failed to trust Him to bring them into Canaan. You see, Kadesh became a watershed in every sense of the term. It is a name written in flaming letters, for Kadesh proved a turning point in the entire enterprise so far as that whole generation was concerned. Before Kadesh, the children of Israel were pilgrims advancing with purpose at the commandment of the Lord. After Kadesh, they were simply wanderers going around in circles. They were like the proverbial door on its hinges, all the time moving backwards and forwards, but never getting anywhere. *It was only when they had come full circle and were brought back again to Kadesh, that the Lord moved to bring the new or second generation of the people into the land of Canaan by the hand of Joshua.* (See Numbers 20:1) Israel's downfall at Kadesh is a solemn reminder to us today that it is a dangerous thing to trifle with the will of God. You may end up spending your life wandering around just waiting to die. You see, sooner or later, each of us will face our own Kadesh Barnea crisis, when we will have to make a choice. Will we press on to the Canaan life of victory, or will we return to the purposeless and unsatisfying life of the desert?

Now Canaan is often referred to as representing Heaven. But this can be only so in the rather limited sense that Canaan came at the end of the journey. Its real significance is much more immediate. Canaan represents God's full purpose for His people. He would not only bring Israel out of Egypt, and through the desert. He would also bring them into Canaan.

In the same way, the Lord has much more in mind for us than that our salvation should simply be an escape from Hell. Bless God, it is that, but it is much more. His purpose in saving me, said Paul, was *"to reveal His Son in me"* (Galatians 1:16). The same apostle declared in another place: *"whom He did foreknow, He also did predestinate to be conformed to the image of His Son, that He might be the firstborn among many brethren"* (Romans 8:29). This means that there can be no finality to Christian experience in this life. On the contrary, there is a constant pressing on towards the mark. (See Philippians 3:14) There can never be the eradication of the sinful nature in your life.

The spiritual equivalent to that generation missing the land is not that present day believers may miss Heaven at the last. *Rather, it is the very real possibility of missing the full purpose of our calling in the present, of failing to realise in the here and now, that good and acceptable and perfect will of God.* Have you come a certain distance in spiritual things, only to vegetate in a kind of spiritual vacuum? Have you become like a stagnant pool, rather than like a watered garden? Kadesh Barnea carries a solemn warning for us all. Are we going backward or forward? Is it to be the old life of failure or the new life of fruitfulness?

Let us have a look at Israel on the borders of Canaan at Kadesh Barnea and notice:

(a) THE REQUEST BY THE PEOPLE

Where did the idea of sending forth the spies come from? Deuteronomy 1 verses 19 to 23 indicate that sending the spies was an idea that appears to have originated with the people. The Lord seemingly condescended to their request and Moses too went along with the idea. But why should twelve men be sent into Canaan to spy out the land? The Israelites already knew what kind of land it was for God had already more than once described it as: *"a land flowing with milk and honey"* (Exodus 3:8). To Moses the prophet the Lord said: *"And I am come down to deliver them out of the hand of the Egyptians, and to bring them up out of that land unto a good land and a large, unto a land flowing with milk and honey"* (Exodus 3:8).

Was God's promise concerning this land not sufficient? Was His description of this land not enough? Apparently not so! Israel come with this proposal: *"We will send men before us, and they shall search us out the land"* (Deuteronomy 1:22).

Sometimes, the Lord allows us to carry out our own unbelieving plans to our own confusion. If we will *"lean on our own understanding"* (Proverbs 3:5), the Lord sometimes lets us take our own way until we discover what utter folly our fancied wisdom is. You see, this request originated in the will of man.

(b) THE REPORT TO THE PEOPLE

The exploring team was split. There was the Timorous Ten, and the Triumphant Two. Do you recall what the ten said? *"The people be strong." "The cities are walled." "We be not able to go up against the people." "And there we saw the giants."* The Bible says: *"And they brought up an evil report of the land."* (Numbers 13:32) Evil, not because it was untrue, but because it left God out of the picture.

What a contrast they were to Caleb and Joshua. Look at Numbers 13 verse 30: *"Let us go up at once, and possess it; for we are well able to overcome it"*. Now, Caleb and Joshua had seen all that the ten saw. They neither underestimated their foes, nor minimised the magnitude of the task. The difference was just this. The ten matched the strength of the giants with their own strength; the two matched the strength of the giants with the omnipotence of God. The ten gazed at the giants, the two gazed at God. The ten saw the foes, the two saw the fruit. The ten saw the problems, the two saw the promises of God.

> *Ten men who failed to see God,*
> *Saw cities impregnably high,*
> *Two men, looking off unto God,*
> *Saw doom for those cities draw nigh.*
> *Ten men who failed to see God,*
> *Discouraged their fellow-men,*
> *Two men perceived God everywhere,*
> *Are you one of the two .... or the ten?*

How did it all end? Well look at:

(c) THE REACTION OF THE PEOPLE

What a picture we have in Numbers 14. The people are weeping, murmuring, rebelling: "*Let us make a captain, and let us return into Egypt*" (verse 4). The Lord responds by saying: "*How long will it be ere they believe Me?*" (verse 11). God's judgment was threefold:

(1) The nation would wander for 40 years, one for each day the spies had explored the land.

(2) During that time the older generation, twenty years and upward, would die and not enter the land, except for Caleb and Joshua.

(3) The ten unbelieving spies died because of the evil report they delivered. (See Numbers 14:37)

The Jews had lamented that they wanted to die in the wilderness (Numbers 14:2) and they had complained that their children would die in Canaan (verse 3), but God had declared that their children would live in Canaan and the adults would die in the wilderness. Out of their own mouths God passed judgment.

Be careful what you say to the Lord when you complain. He may take you up on it. Do you know something? *Moses led the world's longest funeral march, and Caleb and Joshua watched their generation die.*

Dr. Leon Wood makes the following observation:

"Figuring 1,200,000 as having to die in 38 and a half years, gives 85 per day. Figuring 12 hours per day maximum for funerals gives an average of seven funerals per hour for all 38 and a half years - a continuous foreboding of God's punishment on them."

Does God deal with His people in chastisement when they sin? Yes. Only two out of the original multitude that left Egypt came into the Promised Land. Did Israel learn from it? Not a bit! for when we come into Chapter 16, we see:

(d) THE REBELLION FROM THE PEOPLE

There was rebellion from Korah and 250 of the princes of Israel. Korah was a cousin of Moses (Numbers 16:1), a Levite who was not content to assist in the tabernacle. He wanted to serve as priest as well. (See Numbers 16:10) It appears that Korah and his followers defied Aaron, while Dathan and Abiram questioned the authority of Moses. However, they were united in their plot. These men wanted to *"lift themselves up"* before the congregation. Certainly the whole nation was holy to God, but He had placed some people in positions of leadership as He willed. The same is true of the church today. All saints are beloved of God, but some have been given spiritual gifts and spiritual offices for the work of the ministry (See Ephesians 4:11-12 and 1 Corinthians 12:14-18).

Yet somehow rebellion, against God's Word, God's house, and God's men, is more prevalent today than any other time in history. People do not want to recognize, regard, or respect spiritual, moral, or pastoral authority, even when that authority has the best interests of the people at heart. Yet God says: *"Obey them that have the rule over you, and submit yourselves: for they watch for your souls, as they that must give account"* (Hebrews 13:17).

When we come to Chapter 20, we must remember that the 38 years of wandering are past and we now enter the third great movement of the book:

(3) FROM KADESH BARNEA TO MOAB (Chapters 20 to 36)

The keyword here is **WAITING**. The old generation is no more. A new generation has arisen. Aaron is gone and Eleazar is appointed high priest. Moses is soon to go and Joshua is soon to come. Israel is to move over to the plains of Moab and get ready for entry into the Promised Land. Do you see Numbers 20 verse 22? This was a mountain on the border of Edom. You see, they are on the move again. Thus, in this closing section of the book we are taken up with:

(a) THEIR JOURNEYING (Chapters 21 to 25)

The journey from Kadesh to Moab would take about four to five months. Do you see what Numbers 22 verse 1 says? Balak, the king of Moab, becomes increasingly disturbed. He does not want the Israelites as his neighbours so he sends for Balaam, a false prophet, to curse the Israelites as they draw close to his realm.

Few men in the Bible raise as many questions as Balaam. The New Testament talks about:

1.*The Way of Balaam*: *"who loved the wages of unrighteousness"* (2 Peter 2:15).

2. *The Error of Balaam*: for he concluded that God would have to curse Israel because of their many sins. (Jude 11)

3. *The Doctrine of Balaam*: *"who taught Balac to cast a stumblingblock before the children of Israel, to eat things sacrificed unto idols, and to commit fornication"* (Revelation 2:14).

Three times he tried to curse the people of God, but each time only blessings and not cursing came out. The story is told in Numbers 22 to 24. There have been many 'Balaams' who have tried to curse Israel, but remember God's promise to Abraham: blessings will be upon those who bless Israel and cursing will be upon those who curse Israel.

He then decided that if could not get to curse them, he would get God to do so. So he hatched a plot. Do you know it was? **Women!** (See Numbers 25:1-3 and 31:16) There are three things that any servant of God must avoid – gold, glory – and girls. Balaam's plan involved girls! He instructed Balak to place sensuous women before the marching Israelite army. He did and they wilted. Before they knew it, they "lay down with dogs and got up with the devil's fleas". Soon they went to "church" with these women and worshipped their idols. The result? God slew 24,000 Israelite men. (See Numbers 25:9) Do you want to know what *"the doctrine of Balaam"* is? It is worldliness! It is having one foot in the church and one foot in the world. It was Horatius Bonar who said: "I looked for the church and I found it in the world. I looked for the world and I found it in the church". Is that your thinking? Well, let me warn you. It is all right for the boat to be in the water, but it is perilous to get the water into the boat. What Balaam could not do one way, he accomplished another way.

(b) THEIR NUMBERING   (Chapters 26 to 27)

40 years after the exodus from Egypt, a new census is taken of the children of Israel and only two men of the original multitude that came out of Egypt are still alive. The Lord keeps His word, of judgment as well as of promise.

(c) THEIR OFFERING   (Chapters 28 to 30)

Typically, all the offerings speak of Christ and it is significant that God speaks of them here as *"My bread"* (Numbers 28:2). The heart of God feeds, as it were, on Christ and is perfectly satisfied.

The book ends with:

(d) THEIR DIVIDING   (Chapters 31 to 36)

The Land was divided. The territory they were to possess was given and arrangements made in faith for the division of the land. At last the people were about to enter the Promised Land. Do you notice the last phrase of the book? *"The children of Israel in the plains of Moab by Jordan near Jericho."* (Numbers 36:13) The book of Numbers ends on a note of expectation, but alas those wasted years! Have you ever noticed this? That the movements of God's people out of His will are not on His calendar? (See Numbers 16 to Numbers 20:21)

From the time that Israel despised the Promised Land (Numbers 14:31) until they returned to its borders after 38 years of wandering there is no record, save the stoning of the Sabbath breaker and the sin and doom of Korah. (See Numbers 15:32 to Numbers 16:1) During these years they were like a regiment of soldiers marking time, but no progress.

On a sundial these words are written: *"I number none but the cloudless hours"*. Beware - every hour spent out of fellowship with God or short of His purposes for your life will in the annals of eternity be unnumbered, uncounted, a blank.

It was at Kadesh Barnea they went wrong. It was 38 years later at Kadesh Barnea they got right. (See Numbers 20:14-22) Spiritually speaking, are you wandering aimlessly? Do you need to get right at the spot where you have gone wrong? Listen again to these words of Robert Robinson:

> *"Prone to wander, Lord I feel it,*
> *Prone to leave the God I love,*
> *Take my heart, O take and seal it,*
> *Seal it for Thy courts above."*

CHAPTER 6

Deuteronomy

According to Karen Bolla, a Johns Hopkins researcher in the U.S.A., these are the things people most often forget:

Names: 83%

Where something is: 60%

Telephone numbers: 57%

Words: 53%

What was said: 49%

Faces: 42%

And if you can't remember what you just did, you join 38 percent of the population!

John Newton was plagued with a terribly treacherous memory. His autobiography is filled with the sad, sad story of his forgettings: *"I forgot"; "I soon forgot"*, and *"This too I totally forgot."* These words occur repeatedly. So it came to pass that after his wild and sinful years, he was gloriously saved and then entered the Christian ministry. It was then that he printed a certain text in bold letters and fastened it right across the wall over his study mantelpiece. The words of the text were taken from the book of Deuteronomy: *"Thou shalt remember that thou wast a bondman in the land of Egypt, and the Lord thy God redeemed thee"* (Deuteronomy 15:15). This was John Newton's text and in the sight of it he prepared every sermon.

"I forgot, I soon forgot, this too I totally forgot."

"Thou shalt remember, remember, remember."

Deuteronomy is a book of remembrance. It consists of a series of addresses given by Moses, warning the Israelites, whom he was soon to leave, of the danger of forgetfulness. *"Beware, lest ye forget"*, he said again and again, and *"Thou shalt remember."* These two warnings run like a refrain from page to page in this book.

"Take heed to thyself, and keep thy soul diligently, lest thou forget the things which thine eyes have seen." (Deuteronomy 4:9)

"And thou shalt remember all the way which the Lord thy God led thee these forty years in the wilderness." (Deuteronomy 8:2)

"But thou shalt remember the Lord thy God: for it is He is that giveth thee power to get wealth." (Deuteronomy 8:18)

This word *"remember"*, occurring 14 times in the book, invites the children of Israel to look over their shoulder. They are told that they must not forget the great things that God has done for them. Christians are also to remember. With spiritual insight we can remember that once we were slaves of sin and the Lord our God brought us out *"through a mighty hand and by a stretched out arm"* (Deuteronomy 5:15). Why, the Lord's Supper is a memorial feast! It ever keeps before us the central tenet of our faith, namely the Cross of Calvary. *"This do in remembrance of Me"*, said the Saviour. So Deuteronomy is a book of remembrance.

Actually, the original Hebrew title of the book is translated *"these are the words"*. Do you see how the book opens? *"These be the words"* (Deuteronomy 1:1). What happened was this. When a scroll was opened in a Jewish synagogue, the first part would be unrolled to read the opening words. The book then became known by these opening words. So the book of Deuteronomy is simply called in Hebrew: *"The words"*. However, when the Hebrew Old Testament was translated into Greek, they had to think of a more appropriate title. Deuteronomy comes from two words in the Greek language which means *"The Second Law"*. Now this book does not contain a new Law replacing the one already given. Rather, it is a second stating of the Law.

Deuteronomy was written by Moses when he had less than one month to live. (See Deuteronomy 1:3; Chapter 31:9-10, 24-26 and Chapter 34:8 and Joshua 5:6-12). You can almost see him, like a dying father *"on this side Jordan, in the land of Moab"* (Deuteronomy 1:5). He is appealing to them in a series of addresses. There are several reasons why Moses restated the Law on the border of Canaan. For one thing there was:

1. A New Generation

The old generation had perished in the wilderness, except for Caleb and Joshua, and the new generation needed to hear the Law again. We have short memories and these people were 20 years of age and under when the nation failed at Kadesh Barnea. It was vital that they knew God's Word afresh.

2. A New Challenge

Up to now their life had been unsettled. They had been pilgrims, but now they were to enter their Promised Land and become a settled nation. There would be battles to fight and they needed to be prepared. The best way to prepare for the future is to understand the past. *"Those who cannot remember the past are condemned to repeat it"*, said a famous philosopher. Moses wanted the nation to remember what the Lord had done.

3. A New Leader

Moses was on the way out and Joshua was on the way in.

Moses knew that the success of the nation depended on the people obeying God, no matter who their human leader might be. If they were grounded in the Word of God and loved the God of the Word, they would follow Joshua and win the victory.

4. A New Trial

You see, a settled people in the land would face different problems from a pilgrim people in the wilderness. Moses wanted them to possess the land and keep that possession, so he warns them of the dangers and points the way of success.

In a spiritual sense, many of us believers stand with Israel in the opening verses of this book. Sure, we are redeemed from Egypt, but we have not yet entered into our spiritual inheritance. We stand *"on this side Jordan"* (Deuteronomy 1:5) instead of in the Promised Land of blessing. We need to hear God's Word again and step out by faith and claim our inheritance in Christ. Canaan represents God's full purpose for His people. Do you recall how the hymn writer puts it?

> *"More and more, More and more,*
> *Still there's more to follow,*
> *Have you on the Lord believed?*
> *Still there's more to follow."*

Now there are four looks in this book: The backward look, the inward look, the forward look and the upward look.

(1) THE BACKWARD LOOK

As Moses begins this series of addresses to the new generation in Israel, he reviews the past history of the nation. Now it is a sin to live in the past, but we can never understand the present or prepare for the future if we are ignorant of the past. Warren Wiersbe declares: "We cannot live in the past, but we can learn from the past". As Deuteronomy opens, the children of Israel are on the border of the land of Canaan. Now this first section of the book surveys God's dealings with His people from their stay at Horeb, Mount Sinai (Deuteronomy 1:6) to Beth Peor, located east of the Jordan River, probably opposite Jericho. Moses is reminding them that although it only takes 11 days to walk from Sinai to the Promised Land, their parents took 13,780 days. (Deuteronomy 1:2 & 3) Kadesh Barnea proved a turning point in the entire enterprise so far as that previous generation were concerned. Only two - Caleb and Joshua - urged the people to trust God and go on. You see, as Moses looks backward:

(a) TRAGIC FAILURES ARE RECOUNTED

In his first message, Moses gives the people *a history lesson of their failures.* He recounts what has brought them to this place they have occupied for 40 long, wandering years. Do you see what he says in Deuteronomy 1 verses 32 to 35? *"Yet in this thing ye did not believe the Lord your God ..."* Then look at Deuteronomy 1 verses 44 to 46. You see, this new generation would not know why the nation was organized as it was, and why the nation had not entered its inheritance sooner.

So Moses points out that their sin at Kadesh Barnea was rebellion based on unbelief. (See Deuteronomy 1:26) The people are reminded that their plight was not due to a divine blunder, but rather because of their own human behaviour. They had brought this upon themselves, and had no one to blame but themselves. They chose not to turn to God and trust in God. They chose not to look to God or lean on God.

They had enough faith for God to get them out of Egypt, but not enough faith for God to get them into Canaan, so for the past 40 years they wandered.

Is this where you are in your Christian experience? Are you like a stagnant pool or a watered garden? Are you going backward or forward? Are you in the old life of failure or are you in the new life of fruitfulness?

Tragic failures are recounted - for look at Deuteronomy 3:23-26. Moses requested that he be permitted to enter the land. The response from God was: "No!" Why was this simple request denied? Do you recall that it was God's judgment on Moses for striking the rock? (Numbers 20:7-12) The constant bickering of the Hebrews had worn him down and he allowed his anger to rise to the surface. *Think of it, one moment of anger, one moment of disobedience, one moment of mistrust, one moment of frustration and the price to pay and the blessing he missed was great.* Do you know something? We need the Lord in our fortieth year of ministry just as much as in our first. We need the Lord at the end of our service just as much as at the beginning. We need the Lord more on the final lap of the journey than we ever did on the first lap of the journey. Sadly, many fail when it comes to the end of their ministry.

(b) TRIUMPHANT VICTORIES ARE RECALLED

In spite of all their tragic failures, God had been faithful, and triumphant victories had been achieved throughout their nation's history. There were:

1. The Nations they Avoided

Edom, the descendants of Esau, Jacob's brother (Deuteronomy 2:4) and Moab and Ammon, the descendants of Lot, Abraham's nephew. Since these nations were blood relations of Israel, God did not permit the Jews to fight them.

2. The Nations they Defeated

En route to Canaan, the Lord gave them victory over the attacking forces of King Sihon (Deuteronomy 2:24) and King Og (Deuteronomy 3:1) and the Lord foiled the plans of Balak, king of the Amorites (Deuteronomy 3:8). You see, what was happening was this: *the land east of the Jordan was being secured so that the Israelites could cross the river and take Canaan.* Moses reminds them of God's faithfulness, and urges them to be grateful and obedient. Look at Deuteronomy 4 verses 7 to 9 and then verse 31. In spite of their failures, God had been faithful. They had His presence, His promise, His provision, His protection and His providence all in the midst of their camp. No matter what had been the obstacle, when they whined, God heard them; when they worshipped, God honoured them, and when they wandered, God helped them.

Is this not one of the central themes of the book of Deuteronomy?

God is faithful. Think of all the times *we* have forsaken Him, failed Him, forgotten Him, and fled Him, yet, there has never been a time where He has forsaken us, failed us, forgotten us, or fled us. He has heard us when we prayed; He has helped us when we were down, and He has healed us when we were sick. God is faithful. What a source of comfort that is to us in days like our own, when things sometimes seem to have run out of control.

> *"God is still on the throne,*
> *And He will take care of His own,*
> *His promise is true,*
> *He will see us right through,*
> *God is still on the throne."*

(2) THE INWARD LOOK

The source of all national greatness lies in a right relationship with God. This is so with all peoples, but especially with the nation of Israel, since God's purpose in granting them nationhood was that they might be a witness for Him to all mankind. Moses, therefore, warned Israel against forgetting the Law of the Lord.

Now in this section from Chapter 5 to Chapter 26 there are set before us:

(a) THE SINAI LAWS

Moses begins by expounding the Decalogue, the Ten Commandments, given by the Lord on Mount Sinai. He then reminds the congregation of their obligation to worship and serve the true God and instructs the Israelites to communicate these laws to future generations. Now, as we have noted, the word "Deuteronomy" means *"second law"*, for here there is a second stating of the Law to a new generation. In this section there are three passages that deserve our attention:

1. The First One has to do with God's Word

Look at Deuteronomy 6 verses 4 to 9. That word *"hear"* means in

Hebrew "*Shema*", to hearken or publish. The *Shema*: "*Hear, O Israel: The Lord our God is one Lord*" (Deuteronomy 6:4) is considered by Jews to be the most important passage in Deuteronomy. Orthodox Jews still repeat the *Shema* twice a day. This part of the Law was to be taught by the parents to their children. It was to be discussed, described, declared, and detailed at home. Every Jewish parent was to teach their children to:

Love God *Sincerely*: "*with all thine heart*".

Love God *Sacrificially*: "*with all thy soul*".

Love God *Supremely*: "*with all thy might*".

God's Word was to be central in the home. Look at Deuteronomy 6 verses 8 and 9. The Jews took this so literally that they made little boxes called phylacteries or frontlets. They put the *Shema*, or Law, in these boxes and tied them around their heads with a piece of leather to go "*between thine eyes*". If you have visited Israel and stayed in a Jewish hotel, there would have been a rectangular metal box on the doorpost of your room. It is called a *mezuzah*. The Word of God was to be central in their homes.

Is the Word of God central in our homes? Are we teaching it to our children? We might not be Old Testament Jews, but it would be a glad day in our nation, a glad day in our churches, and a glad day in our homes were we to give God's Word pre-eminence.

Did you know that this section of the Old Testament may have been "*a special favourite of the Lord Jesus*"? You see, the Saviour only quoted from this book when He faced temptation, by the devil, in the wilderness. The Lord Jesus was:

Tempted Physically

"*If Thou be the Son of God, command that these stones be made bread*" (Matthew 4:3). "*But He answered and said, It is written, Man shall not live by bread alone, but by every word that proceedeth out of the mouth of God*" (A quotation from Deuteronomy 8:3).

Tempted Spiritually

"If Thou be the Son of God, cast Thyself down ...." (Matthew 4:6). *"Jesus said unto him, It is written again, Thou shalt not tempt the Lord thy God"* (A quotation from Deuteronomy 6:16).

Tempted Materially

"All these things will I give Thee, if Thou wilt fall down and worship me" (Matthew 4:9). *"Then saith Jesus unto him, Get thee hence, Satan: for it is written, Thou shalt worship the Lord thy God, and Him only shalt thou serve"* (A quotation from Deuteronomy 6:13).

The Hebrew letter says Christ *"was in all points tempted like as we are"* – physically, spiritually, materially – *"yet without sin"*. If this book of Deuteronomy was good enough for Christ, is it good enough for you? Steve Wagers says: *"They may take the Word of God out of the schoolhouse, courthouse, and White House; but they can't take it out of your house and my house"*.

"Upon thine hand" - the Word must control all we **do.**

"Between thine eyes" - the Word must control all we **see.**

"Upon the posts of thy house" - the Word must control all we **are.**

Many measure the success of their home by their brains, beauty, brawn, and bigness. God wants us to measure the success of our home by the Bible.

2. The Second One has to do with God's Will

Look at Deuteronomy 6 verse 23. I love that phrase: *"He brought us out ... that He might bring us in"*. We have thought, thankfully, on that negative *"out"*. Have we given as much attention to the positive *"in"*? God brought them out of Egypt that He might bring them into Canaan. He brought them out of bondage that He might bring them into blessing. Christian songs may portray Canaan as Heaven, but this can only be in a limited sense that Canaan came at the end of the journey. **Canaan represents God's full purpose for His people.** Therefore, when God brought Israel out of Egypt, it was for the purpose of bringing them into Canaan, the land of security, sufficiency, and stability. It was that which God had promised to His people and prepared for His people. In the same way, when God saved us, He *"brought us out"* of this old, sinful world. But He *"brought us out"* that He might *"bring us in"* to a land where we would not have to be blinded with sin, burdened by sin or bound to sin. He *"brought us out"* that He might *"bring us in"* to a land where we do not have to be overcome, but where we can be overcomers.

3. The Third One has to do with God's Way

Look at Deuteronomy 10 verse 12. Do you see those two little words? *"And now!"* They are gathering up the significance of the book. As Sidlow Baxter says: *"This is distinguishingly the 'and now' book"*. The people have reviewed the faithfulness of God. They have seen His power (Deuteronomy 4:20); His patience (Deuteronomy 1:25 & 26); His presence (Deuteronomy 2:7); His provision (Deuteronomy 2:7) and His preservation (Deuteronomy 3:2-3). *"And now"* - what about it? What is it that is required of them as they enter the Promised Land? Simply this: *"To fear the Lord thy God"* (Deuteronomy 10:12). If we could summarize it in one word, do you know what that word is? <u>Obedience.</u> It has been pointed out that the word *"do"* occurs 50 times in Deuteronomy.

If this was expected of Israel, is anything less expected from us with all our exalted privileges in Christ? Do you recall what the Saviour says: *"He that hath My commandments, and keepeth them, he it is that loveth Me". "If a man love Me, he will keep My words."* (John 14:21 & 23) Does the Saviour have to put a question mark over your love for Him?

(b) THE SACRED LAWS

These were laws that have direct relevance to living in a settled community in Canaan. For example:

1. There is to be one place of worship. (Deuteronomy 12:11)

2. Idolaters are to be stoned on the word of two or three witnesses. (Deuteronomy 13:6-10)

And so on. These were laws for living in Canaan.

(c) THE SECULAR LAWS

Orderly government had to be established and so there had to be laws for kings, judges, law courts, the administration of punishment, and so on.

(d) THE SOCIAL LAWS

There were laws concerning marriage, adultery, divorce, homosexuality, health, welfare and warfare.

What are we to make of all this? Just this. God is interested in the whole of our lives. We are great people for dividing life into sacred and secular but all of life is for God. Living right is not just what you do in church on Sunday. It concerns the whole of life. Do you realise that God wants you to be right in every area of your life?

(3) THE FORWARD LOOK

This section looks forward to:

(a) ISRAEL ENTERING THE LAND

When they moved into the land of promise, they were to pronounce the blessings from Mount Gerizim and the curses from Mount Ebal. (Deuteronomy 11:29) In other words, God was saying to this covenant nation: *"If you obey Me, I will bless you; if you disobey Me, I will curse you"*. Throughout Deuteronomy, we see divine sympathy constantly interwoven with divine severity. John Phillips writes: *"Law and love, goodness and grace, wooings and warnings go hand in hand in the economy of God."* And then:

(b) ISRAEL ENJOYING THE LAND

"Obedience brings blessing." That is the message of the first section of Deuteronomy 28. Look at verses 1 and 2. God promises Israel material blessings in all areas, city, farm, fruit, cattle, coming in and going out. He promises to defeat their enemies and establish them in the land as a holy people. Do you see that in verse 10 the nation was to be a world-wide witness of God's grace? Do you see from verse 46 they have become a world-wide witness of God's judgment? Now keep in mind that Israel <u>owned</u> the land because of God's covenant with Abraham, but she <u>possessed</u> and <u>enjoyed</u> the land only if she obeyed God's covenant as a holy nation. In just the same way, we have all the blessings we need in Christ. Paul says we are *"blessed with all spiritual blessings in heavenly places in Christ"* (Ephesians 1:3), but we only enjoy those blessings as we trust the Lord and obey His voice. Someone has said that when we read this chapter it is like reading the whole history of Israel for the last 4,000 years for we see also:

(c) ISRAEL EXITING THE LAND

Deuteronomy 28 is one of the most amazing pieces of prophecy every recorded. It predicts the entire history of the Jewish people, from Egypt to the Millennial Reign of Christ.

Warren Wiersbe says:

"To spiritualize these covenant blessings and curses and apply them to the church is to twist the Scriptures and to fail to 'rightly divide the Word of truth.' These are literal curses and they fell upon Israel because she broke her covenant with God by worshipping idols and disobeying His law."

Look for example at verse 45. The word *"destroyed"* here does not mean completely wiped out for God could not violate His covenant and destroy the nation of Israel. It means *"<u>to be crushed</u>"*, referring to the terrible trials that would fall on Israel because of her disobedience. The nation would be "a sign and a wonder" to the world even as it today. Israel would be scattered among the nations. Look at verses 63 to 66. They would be scattered among the nations. They would experience sorrow and fear. What a picture of Jewish history, full of persecution. Some believe this could refer to Hitler's Holocaust, where over 6 million Jews were savagely slaughtered.

But do not stop there, for here we also see:

(d) ISRAEL ENTERING THE LAND AGAIN

Deuteronomy 30 promises that God will turn the captivity of Israel and restore her to her land (verse 3). Of course, they have returned to the land today. They have done so in unbelief, but God is blessing that land. Today Israel has a population of six million and they are still coming.

In a coming day, Antichrist will appear. A temple will be built and, since the Jews believe that only Messiah can rebuild the temple, they will believe that Antichrist is the Messiah and they will worship him. God will then refine them through the Tribulation. Then the Lord will return in power and great glory and when the nation sees their pierced Messiah, they will be saved. There is a future, in the purpose of God, for Israel. The church has not replaced this nation.

It is interesting that in these closing chapters of the book, a future state is moving in and a faithful servant is moving out. So we have in closing:

(4) THE UPWARD LOOK

Moses, the leader of Israel for the past 40 years, is now 120 years of age. He is about to pass from the scene, and the moving out of this faithful servant is described in 4 stages. Notice:

(a) MOSES THE SPEAKER

What a portraiture of God Moses gives in these closing chapters!

1. A God who goes Before us

"And the Lord, He it is that doth go before thee" (Deuteronomy 31:8).

2. A God who walks Beside us

"He will be with thee" (Deuteronomy 31:8). Are you living in the shadow of some great disappointment? Some physical handicap, some personal dilemma. The Lord is with you.

3. A God who is Beneath us

Moses in this farewell says: *"The eternal God is thy refuge, and underneath are the everlasting arms"* (Deuteronomy 33:27).

Do you see that God *surrounds* us on all sides? Where is God? He is *Above us*, for *"there is none like unto the God of Jeshurun, who rideth upon the heaven in thy help"* (Deuteronomy 33:26). Where is God? He is *Around us*, for *"the eternal God is thy refuge"* (verse 27). Where is God? He is *Before us*, for *"He shall thrust out the enemy from before thee"* (verse 27). Where is God? He is *Beneath us*: *"And underneath are the everlasting arms"* (verse 27). *"This God is our God for ever and ever: He will be our guide even unto death"* (Psalm 48:14).

(b) MOSES THE SINGER

Look at Deuteronomy 31 verse 30: *"Moses spake in the ears of all the congregation of Israel the words of this song, until they were ended"*. He wrote 3 historic songs. He wrote a song that became the first song service in the Bible in Exodus 15 after deliverance from Egypt. He wrote this song in Chapter 32 and his final song is heard in Psalm 90.

(c) MOSES THE SEER

Here he asks God's blessing on the various tribes. Did you ever notice the spiritual position of God's people here? We are *in God's hand* (Deuteronomy 33:3); we are *at God's feet* (verse 3); we are *between God's shoulders* (verse 12), and we are *upheld by God's arms* (verse 27).

We can say: *"Who is like unto thee, O people saved by the Lord"* (Deuteronomy 33:29). What a privilege it is to be a child of God!

(d) MOSES THE SOLITARY

Look at Deuteronomy 34 verses 1 and 4. One thing to be learned from the life of Moses – especially to be learned by those who are leaders – is that God views seriously sin in the life of a leader. Because of his own disobedience (told in Numbers 20), he was not able to occupy the land; but God allowed him a sneak preview of coming attractions. God held His own private funeral procession and ceremony with Moses. With eyes that were not dim, and strength that had not been diminished, Moses stretched out on the ground and died, and God laid him to rest. *God buried Moses in a place that, to this day, is undiscovered, undisclosed, and undetected.* The exact site is only known to God Himself. I have often wondered what kind of eulogy or obituary God offered for Moses in this private ceremony. We do not know all of it, but we are given part of it in Deuteronomy 34 verses 10 to 12.

In the movie *"Gladiator"*, Caesar was about to turn his kingdom over to a man named Maximus. In that powerful moment, the Emperor looked into the eyes of Maximus and said: *"I am dying, Maximus. When a man sees his end, he wants to know there was a purpose to his life."* Then, he asked a most penetrating question: *"How will the world speak of my name in years to come?"* We know what God had to say about Moses, but, I wonder, what would God have to say about you, or about me?

Robert Baker, in an article called *"Country Road 13"* in *Christianity Today,* made an outstanding statement:

"As I grow older, I care less about what people think about me and more about what God thinks about me; because, I expect to be with God much longer in my existence."

What kind of eulogy will the Lord give about you?

CHAPTER 7

Joshua

A school teacher asked a classroom of children: *"Who knocked down the walls of Jericho?"* There was a long silence before a small boy said: *"Please, Sir, I didn't"*. Later that day in the staff room, the teacher recounted the incident to the headmaster. *"Do you know what happened in my classroom today? I asked who knocked down the walls of Jericho and that boy Smith said: 'Please, Sir, I didn't'".* The headmaster replied: *"Well, I have known Smith some years. They are a good family. If he says he didn't do it, I am sure he didn't."* The headmaster reported the boy's answer to a visiting school inspector, whose response was: *"It's probably too late to find out who did it. Get them repaired and send the bill to us."*

The joke, of course, is that everybody should know who knocked down the walls of Jericho. It is one of the better known stories of the Bible. If they do not know the story from the Bible, then they have heard the Negro spiritual song *"Joshua fought the battle of Jericho".* But, sad to say, this may be the only part of the book that people do know.

When we come to the book of Joshua, we are coming to the first of twelve historical books which start at Joshua and finish at Esther. Now in our English Bible it is the book after Deuteronomy. There seems to be a logical flow from the death of Moses at the end of Deuteronomy to the commission of Joshua at the start of this book. To the Jews, however, the position of the book is quite different. You see, the end of Deuteronomy marks the end of the Torah, the law of Moses. These five books are read annually in the synagogue with Genesis 1:1 starting the New Year and Deuteronomy 34:12 being read at the end of the year. Each of the five books is named after its first words seen at the start of the scroll when the books came to be selected for reading. Joshua is the first book to be known by the name of its author. This book records the continual story of the children of Israel, their arrival at the river Jordan and their entry into and conquest of the land of Canaan. *Joshua completes what Moses commenced.*

The great event in Moses' life was the passage through the Red Sea; the great event in Joshua's life was the passage through the Jordan. The one tells of deliverance from bondage; the other of entrance into blessing. Joshua bears the same relationship to the five books of Moses as the book of Acts bears to the four Gospels. Now let me point out some things by way of introduction:

(1) THE PENMAN OF THE BOOK

In the last chapter of this book we read: "*And Joshua wrote these words in the book of the law of God*" (Joshua 24:26). He obviously did not write the entire book as his own death is also recorded in the last chapter. Joshua was originally named Oshea or Hoshea which means "*salvation*", but Moses changed it to Jehoshua (Joshua) which means "*Jehovah saves*". It is the word from which the New Testament name "*Jesus*" is derived.

(2) THE PERIOD OF THE BOOK

If the conquest of Canaan was completed around 1400 B.C., then this book was written shortly after this date. The book of Joshua covers a period of around 25 years. The conquest itself was completed in around 7 years according to Caleb. (See Joshua 14 verse 10 and Deuteronomy 2 verse 14)

What about:

(3) THE POINT OF THE BOOK

What is the aim of this book? To show us the victory of faith. In the book of Numbers, we see the failure of unbelief. But the book of Joshua shows *the victory of faith.* Spiritually interpreted, the exploits of Israel under Joshua proclaim that great New Testament truth: *"This is the victory that overcometh the world, even our faith"* (1 John 5:4). Joshua has been called "the Ephesians of the Old Testament" because most scholars see Canaan as a type of the believer's inheritance in Christ. Canaan represents God's full purpose for His people. Let me illustrate it like this: **Egypt** is a picture of the world, the bondage to sin. The **Wilderness** is a picture of the defeated, despondent Christian life. **Canaan** is a picture of victory, claiming our inheritance. Canaan illustrates the words of Christ: *"I am come that they might have life, and that they might have it more abundantly"* (John 10:10).

Now, some Bible readers cringe at the mention of the book of Joshua because of its military violence. There is thus:

(4) THE PROBLEM OF THE BOOK

Joshua is probably the bloodiest book in the Bible. That is because a wicked civilization, known for its idolatry, religious prostitution, sorcery and even child sacrifice at times, was now coming under divine judgment. The discovery of the Ugarit tablets, in the early part of the 20th Century, gives us an idea of the extent to which the religious system in the land of Canaan had corrupted itself. Do you recall that centuries earlier, in the time of Abraham, God was not yet ready to do anything about this wicked civilization: *"The iniquity of the Amorites is not yet full"* (Genesis 15:16). But now, a longsuffering God was finally ready to deal in judgment with sin. God was offended to the point of commanding the total extermination of the inhabitants of Canaan.

Should any remain, they would corrupt the faith. The Lord said: *"But thou shalt utterly destroy them .... that they teach you not to do after all their abominations, which they have done unto their gods; so should ye sin against the Lord your God"* (Deuteronomy 20:16-18). Right from the start, the Lord warned His people to be holy, to remain separate and distinct. They were not to intermarry or make other alliances. God was saying, in effect, to His chosen nation: *"If you are careless, you will not change them. Instead they will change you. Your worship of the one true God will get diluted, and then polluted."*

Is it not sad when some Christians think they know better than God? They want to live as close to the world as they possibly can, yet God's unchanging standard is: *"Come out from among them, and be ye separate, saith the Lord, and touch not the unclean thing"* (2 Corinthians 6:17).

Now let us look at:

5. THE PARTS OF THE BOOK

Joshua is a book of graphic movement, for, as Sidlow Baxter put it, we see Israel going up, winning through and settling in. Notice then, Israel:

(1) ENTERING THE LAND (Chapter 1:1 to Chapter 5:12)

"Joshua the son of Nun" (Joshua 1:1) walked onto the pages of history at a crucial time in the life of Israel. He was born in Egyptian slavery round about 1500 B.C. If Josephus the historian is accurate, Joshua had lived for some 40 or 45 years in bondage to Egypt. Then he had spent 40 years in the wilderness under the leadership of Moses and, finally, as the leader of those who conquered Canaan for about 25 years. *"Moses my servant is dead; now therefore arise"* (Joshua 1:2). What a shattering statement! Yet as Matthew Henry says: *"God buries His workman, but carries on His work"*.

Israel was encamped on the eastern side of Jordan. Canaan with its giants and walled cities lay before them. The tribes of Israel were unseasoned in war, but here God speaks to Joshua and encouraged him. He fixed his attention on the written Word, the fact of the divine Presence and the certainty of the divine Promise. So Joshua is assured of:

1. The Divine Presence: *"As I was with Moses, so I will be with thee"(verse 5).*
2. The Divine Promise: *"I will not fail thee"(verse 5).*
3. The Divine Plan: *"Unto this people shalt thou divide"* (verse 6).
4. The Divine Power: *"Be thou strong and very courageous"* (verse 7).

So the Lord speaks to Joshua, Joshua speaks to the people and the people speak to Joshua. You see, here in this opening chapters we have:

(a) THE PREPARATION OF THE PEOPLE

Notice that for Joshua and the people there was:

1. Inward Preparation: The Law

When Joshua was about to lead the people into the Promised Land, the only words of God he had were Genesis, Exodus, Leviticus, Numbers and Deuteronomy, the first five books of the Old Testament. God said to Joshua: *"This is your military manual. This will be your map. This is how you will accomplish the job I have given you."* Did you notice what God told him to do with *"the law"*? Look at verse 8. He was to read the book, meditate on it day and night, and obey its commands. John Bunyan wrote on the flyleaf of his Bible, this phrase: *"This book will keep you from sin; sin will keep you from this book"*. Can you not testify to that fact? When you get away from the Lord, the last thing you want to do is read the Word. But it is impossible to have victory in the Christian life apart from the Word of God. Is the Word central in your life? Do you follow it exclusively? *"Turn not from it to the right hand or to the left"* (verse 7) Do not go this way. Do not go that way. Whatever it says - you do it.

2. Outward Preparation: The Spies

Joshua sends out two spies for a new look at the land they are about to possess. Do you recall that 40 years previously twelve spies had been sent out? The negative report from ten of them had contributed to Israel's refusal to enter the land. This time just two are asked to go in, reflecting the number who had brought back a good report on that first occasion.

Is it not interesting what Rahab said? Look at verses 9 to 11 of Chapter 2. Rahab declares: *"I know that the Lord hath given you the land"*. She confesses: *"The Lord your God, He is God in heaven above, and in the earth beneath"*. There were no Bibles in Jericho, no prophets in Jericho. Jericho was a city under the curse, yet here is one soul who has faith in the living God. Do you know something? We can never limit the grace of God. Is this not a tremendous encouragement to us? You see, there are no human situations, however unpromising, however unlikely, in which the grace of God cannot operate. Did you know that Rahab became the wife of Salmon and the mother of Boaz? (Matthew 1:5) Did you know that Boaz was the great grandfather of King David and from his line came our wonderful Saviour? *Think of this - from the Land of Canaan to the Line of Christ.* Such is the grace of God!

3. Onward Preparation: The Ark

Look at Chapter 3 verses 3 and 11. Now a literal rendering of verse 11 would be: *"Behold the ark of the covenant. The Lord of all the earth is about to proceed before you into Jordan"*. You see, the ark represented the presence of God. Joshua was saying: *"You want to know if the living God is among you? Here's how you will know. The ark of the covenant is in your midst."* They had the presence of God in the here and now. Is this not one of the most important things when facing the challenge of the future? When facing the unknown? To know that the Lord is with us. You see, they were guided by the Word of God, guarded by the Power of God and graced by the Presence of God.

(b) THE PASSAGE OF THE PEOPLE

Would you look at Chapter 3 verses 15 to 17? The Jordan parted and the people went over on dry land. Harry Ironside said: *"The Jordan River was parted so many times that the fish didn't know which way to swim!"* Now the Jordan River speaks of death. This river which rises high in the mountains north of Canaan plunges downwards and is called "The Descender". It buries itself at last in the waters of the Dead Sea from which there is no outlet. **As the Red Sea was a judgment on Sin, so the Jordan River is a judgment on Self.** In the language of the New Testament, the Jordan is entering into the truth that: *"I am crucified with Christ: nevertheless I live; yet not I, but Christ liveth in me: and the life which I now live in the flesh I live by the faith of the Son of God, who loved me,* and gave Himself for me" (Galatians 2:20).

Now it is interesting that the Psalmist speaking of these two waters says this: "The sea saw it, and fled: Jordan was driven back" (Psalm 114:3). Do you see the difference? The Red Sea fled before Israel, but the Jordan had to be driven or turned back. In one sense, it was easier for God to get His people out of Egypt than to get them into Canaan. In just the same way, it is easier to get a sinner out of Egypt than to get a Christian into Canaan. In a sense evangelism is easier than edification, salvation simpler than sanctification. It is one thing to bring a child into the world, but quite another to bring that child up in the world. Just the same way, getting into Canaan is far more difficult than getting out of Egypt. Not that it has to be that way, but we die hard. We want a Canaan with no Jordan. You see:

The Memorial in Jordan speaks of Death (Joshua 4:9)

The Memorial over Jordan speaks of Resurrection: (Joshua 4:20)

To a person who asked him the secret of his service, George Müller said: "There was a day when I died, utterly died" and as he spoke, he bent lower and lower until he almost touched the floor. He continued: "Died to George Müller, his opinions, preferences, tastes and will .... died to the world, its approval or censure .... died to the approval or blame even of my brethren and friends .... and since then I have studied only to show myself approved unto God."

Do you realise that there can no victory without death to self?

(c) THE PURIFICATION OF THE PEOPLE

It was here at Gilgal the men submitted to painful surgery. (See Joshua 5:8 & 9) Now remember to be a Hebrew male meant being circumcised. (Genesis 17:9-14) Through this ritual, the Jews became a "marked people", because they belonged to the true and living God. That covenant relationship had been suspended. During the wilderness wanderings, God did not require the mark of circumcision, but now that the old generation had died and the new generation were in their inheritance, it was vital that they renew their covenant relationships with the Lord.

Israel's sin at Kadesh Barnea was a reproach to them, but that was all in the past for now each bore in his body the mark that reminded him that he belonged to God.

Now do you recall the two memorials?

<u>The Memorial in Jordan that speaks of Death</u>
<u>The Memorial over Jordan that speaks of Resurrection</u>

When Paul speaks of our death with Christ, he speaks of something else. Paul says: *"For ye are dead .... Mortify (put to death) therefore your members which are upon the earth; fornication, uncleanness, inordinate affection, evil concupiscence, and covetousness, which is idolatry"* (Colossians 3:3-5). Paul is speaking of sexual vice, impurity, sensual appetites, unholy desires and all greed and covetousness. How are you getting on in the realm of mortification? *"You have died in Christ."* Are you therefore putting to death your earthward inclinations by the power of the Holy Spirit?

(2) CONQUERING THE LAND (Chapter 5:13 to Chapter 12:24)

This is what the book of Joshua is all about. It is a record of the conquest of Canaan. It is interesting to notice the strategy that Joshua adopted for the invasion of the land. It was God-inspired and God-led. His strategy was simply to enter Canaan via Jericho, thus driving a wedge through central Canaan, separating the territory to the north from that to the south. He then moves in on the nearest enemies to the south. Having conquered them he turns his attention to those in the north. So you see, you can look at this:

(a) FROM THE GEOGRAPHICAL PERSPECTIVE

Joshua drove a wedge straight through the middle of Canaan, and then having divided the enemy into two halves, he conquered the south then the north. This strategy prevented the forces in Canaan from uniting, dealing with each area in turn. It is a striking tribute to Joshua's God-guided military genius that by adopting exactly the same strategy General Allenby was successful in occupying Palestine in World War 1. There was:

1. The Central Campaign

This took in two cities which were deemed the most significant, namely Jericho and Ai. Jericho soon fell as Israel obeyed God, but Ai's conquest was hindered by sin in the camp. After subduing Ai, Joshua made a serious mistake. He made a league with the Gibeonites, forgetting the injunction of Chapter 1 verse 8 and the warning of the book of Deuteronomy in verses 1 and 2 of Chapter 7.

2. The Southern Campaign

This took place when a powerful southern coalition, headed by Adoni-zedek, king of Jerusalem (Joshua 10:1), attacked Israel's new allies, the Gibeonites. A forced march from Gilgal brought Joshua and his army to the scene where victory was secured. The final campaign was:

3. The Northern Campaign

This centred around the waters of Merom. (See Joshua 11:5) The strength of this new alliance in the north struck fear into Joshua's heart and so *the Lord said unto Joshua, Be not afraid because of them: for tomorrow about this time will I deliver them up all slain before Israel"* (Chapter 11:6). Then Chapter 12 completes the account by giving us a summary of the kings and major cities which fell before the sword of Israel.

So you can look at this from the geographical perspective, but what about:

(b) THE SPIRITUAL PERSPECTIVE

1. Israel were Helped by the Lord

Look at Chapter 5 verses 13 to 15. Joshua saw *'the captain of the host of the Lord'*. Now who was this? Bible scholars call this *"a theophany"*, that is a manifestation of God. I believe that this was one of the pre-incarnate appearances of the Lord Jesus recorded in the Old Testament – and so it would more correctly be called *"a Christophany"*. Here was Joshua taking a look at the city of Jericho and assessing its fortifications for the possibilities of its being overthrown. Suddenly *"he lifted up his eyes"* and saw this Stranger. Why had the Lord Jesus come? To assure Joshua that he was not alone - the Lord was with him. Joshua had read in the Book of the Law what Moses had said to the Lord after Israel had made the idolatrous golden calf: *"If Thy presence go not with me, carry us not up hence"* (Exodus 33:15). This was in response to the promise of God: *"My presence shall go with thee, and I will give thee rest"*. Joshua was not alone. God was with him. Oh, you say: *"He had several million Jews working with him"*. No, I am not referring to that. **Have you ever considered the loneliness of leadership?**

When I was a young believer, I came to Lurgan Baptist Church Bible Class and I was greatly helped through the ministry of Pastor Mullan. I also went to conferences all over. I am sure I did in those days what you are doing now. It is easy to look into the pulpit and say: *"These people have no problems. They have it made."* Now I am beginning to understand the loneliness of leadership. You see, a leader has to make decisions that have far-reaching consequences. However, Joshua was not alone - God was with him. In Joshua 1 verse 5, he had the promise of God. In verse 17, the people of God assured him of this. Even the enemy knew that God was with Joshua. (See Joshua 2:11). But now Joshua experiences this in a very personal way. It is one thing to read in the Bible that God is with me. It is something else to experience this. Oh you say: *"I don't think that this God is with me the way He was with Joshua."* I think He is. The Lord has promised to be with ALL His people – the preacher in the pulpit and the people in the pew. We read in Hebrews 13 verse 5: *"For He hath said, I will never leave thee, nor forsake thee"*. The Gospel of Matthew begins by calling His name, Emmanuel, God with us. That is the way it begins. Do you recall how it ends? *"Lo, I am with you alway, even unto the end of the world"* (Matthew 28:20).

We have the assurance that in every circumstance of life the Lord is with us. Here is Joshua about to begin this campaign in Canaan and the Lord is assuring him that He is with him. Some day when you are discouraged and think you are all alone, read the story of this man, Joshua, who conquered cities. Joshua came and declared _war_.

In the New Testament, Paul came and declared _peace_. He would show up at a city and declare peace: "_Be ye reconciled to God_" (2 Corinthians 5:20). Paul got to Corinth and was so discouraged that the Lord appeared one night and said: Paul, "_Be not afraid … I am with thee_" (Acts 18:9-10).

Paul went to Jerusalem. They arrested him. He is in jail and that night the Lord said: "_You've witnessed in Jerusalem. Now you must testify in Rome_" (See Acts 23:11).

They are on board ship. A storm comes. The Lord has a message for him: "_Paul, don't be afraid. I'm going to give you everyone on board this ship_" (See Acts 27:24).

So Paul gets to Rome and writes to Timothy: "_At my first answer no man stood with me_" (2 Timothy 4:16). Fancy that! But Paul said: "_The Lord stood with me, and strengthened me_" (2 Timothy 4:17).

Do you realize that as you battle with the giants, possess the inheritance, and proclaim the Gospel, the Lord is with you? Have you not discovered that? That He is your Helper. But:

2. Israel were Harassed by the Foe

1. Look at the First Foe: Jericho

In order for Canaan to be claimed, Jericho had to be conquered. Easier said than done! Jericho was a fortified city. It was surrounded by massive walls. They tell us that its walls were 30 feet high with a 6 foot thick outer wall and a 12 to 15 foot gap between that and a 12 foot thick inner wall. _Now what do you think the real battle was at Jericho? Was it with the Canaanites? The enemy?_

The more I read this chapter the more I am convinced that the real battle was not with the Canaanites at all. The real battle was with God's own people. You see, all this blowing of trumpets, all of this numerical listings of seven, all this walking around the walls. *Was this necessary to knock down a city wall?* God could have just spoken and Jericho would have disappeared. I think the real battle of Jericho was with the human heart, not with the city wall. God was seeking to overcome the Israelites rather than simply seeking to overcome the Canaanites. When victory came, it would convince God's people that the overthrow of Jericho was a victory of faith. Indeed, the Hebrew letter reminds us: *"By faith the walls of Jericho fell down"* (Hebrews 11:30). *How do we overcome Jericho, the world?* That invisible, spiritual system of evil. Well, John says: *"This is the victory that overcometh the world, even our faith"* (1 John 5:4). John says: *"You Christians do not have to walk around defeated because Jesus Christ has made you victors. He has roundly trounced every enemy and you share in His victory."* (See Romans 8:37: "We are more than conquerors!") Now, by faith claim His victory.

2. Look at the Second Foe: Ai

If Jericho reminds us of the *world,* Ai reminds us of the *flesh,* that part of man's nature wherein his natural desires have free rein. Look at Joshua 7 verse 4. Three thousand fled before the men of Ai. Do you know why? There was sin in the camp. Achan stole that which had been devoted to God. Do you see that word *"accursed"* or *"devoted"* in verse 11? The Hebrew term refers to the irrevocable giving over of things or persons to the Lord, often by totally destroying them. (See Chapter 6:21) The Lord said to Joshua: *"Israel hath sinned"*. One man sins - and the whole Israelite army are defeated. One Christian in the assembly of saints is not walking with God – and the whole of the Gospel Meeting is affected. Achan took of the accursed thing, but God said: *"Israel hath sinned"*. The ramifications of sin! Do you see what Achan did? He robbed God. He appropriated what was God's. Are you putting your hand on something that belongs to God? Are you caught up in the web of materialism? You see, while it is not wrong for us to own things, the problem comes when things own us. Is that where you are? Are you controlled by things? Money, business, materialism? How do we overcome Ai, the flesh? God says: *"Neither will I be with you any more, except ye destroy the accursed from among you"* (Joshua 7:12). In New Testament language, self must be crucified. (See Colossians 3:5) Is this God's Word to you? Are you living a life of defeat instead of victory? Are you no longer conscious of God's presence with you? Is it because of unconfessed sin in your life?

3. Look at the third Foe: Gibeon

If Jericho reminds us of the world and Ai reminds us of the flesh, then Gibeon reminds us of the **devil**. Alan Redpath offers wise counsel: *"Every victory that the Christian wins is an invitation for a full-scale attack by the enemy of his soul. Every time a child of God steps into an experience of blessing, he is on the verge of another attack. Our blessings and battles go side by side."*

Joshua makes one of the few mistakes of his otherwise impeccable career by making a treaty, a league, with the Gibeonites. The Gibeonites deceived Joshua into thinking that they had come to help him, when their ultimate goal was to hinder him. The Gibeonites deceived Joshua about their _Country; Contents; Clothes; Consecration to God_ and _Commitment to Joshua_ (Joshua 9:6-13).

Joshua failed to heed God's Word: *"Thou shalt make no covenant with them, nor shew mercy unto them"* (Deuteronomy 7:2). Look at Joshua 9 verse 14. Israel failed to seek the Lord. *"Oh, what peace we often forfeit!"* Do not be friendly with the enemy. Do not be fooled by the enemy. Do not be fellowshipping with the enemy. Never, never trust your own judgment in anything. *"Trust in the Lord with all thine heart; and lean not unto thine own understanding. In all thy ways acknowledge Him, and He shall direct thy paths"* (Proverbs 3:5-6).

(3) POSSESSING THE LAND (Chapters 13 to 24)

The word *"possess"* appears nearly twenty times. These closing chapters are all about:

(a) THE DIVISION OF THE LAND

Canaan is divided among the 12 tribes. Individual tribes had to be assigned their various territories and each tribe had to clean out pockets of resistance that still existed in the land even though it was basically in Israel's control. The work of a nation was over. The work of each tribe had now to begin. Then:

(b) THE DEATH OF THE LEADER

Chapters 23 and 24 contain Joshua's farewell speeches. He first speaks to the leaders in Shiloh (See Chapter 18:1) and then he addresses all the people in Shechem. Here is an old soldier on the journey home. He is on his way. He is getting ready to die. Do you see what it says in Chapter 24 verses 29 to 31? *"Israel served the Lord all the days of Joshua, and all the days of the elders that outlived Joshua".* *Oh, what an influence he had. Joshua kept Israel in the place of God's blessing. You see, one man committed unreservedly to the Lord and His Word can make an enormous impact.*

J. Wilbur Chapman was preaching in England, and went to see General Booth. During the course of the conversation, J. Wilbur Chapman asked General Booth: *"General, tell me what has been the secret of your success all these many years?"* General William Booth slowly bowed his head and replied: *"I will tell you the secret. God has had all there was of William Booth".*

Henrietta Mears sums it up: *"The greatness of your service will be the greatness of your surrender".* It is not a matter of us getting more of God. It is simply a matter of God getting more of us.

Can I ask: *"Do you have the Lord?"* My next question is: *"Does the Lord have you?"* Totally? Completely? Fully? Your answer will determine whether or not you will, if ever, move into the Canaan land of victorious Christian living.

CHAPTER 8

Judges

In 1745, Charles Edward Stuart suddenly appeared at Glenfinnan in the Scottish Highlands. He was a tall, good-looking young man and an exciting, dynamic leader. The heir of the Scottish kings and queens, Stuart had returned to Scotland to recapture the throne. George II, the British king, was an arrogant, cruel man who spoke only German, and the Scots hated him. The Highlanders loved their Prince Charles and committed themselves to follow him and dethrone the foreigner. At first they were successful in battle. But suddenly, *at the Battle of Culloden,* their dreams came to an abrupt end. The Scots were crushed by the English army, and although Charles escaped, his troops were slaughtered.

The Prince found his way to France to plan and dream about the day he would return to take his ancestral throne. But he never did. In fact, to meet Charles twenty years later was to confront a tragedy. *He had become a hopeless alcoholic, his body and health broken.* His life had become a record of disgrace and shame, a long trail of broken marriages, discarded mistresses and public scandals. His former friends wanted nothing to do with him. The Scots may still sing about their *"Bonnie Prince Charlie,"* but there was little that was *"bonnie"* about Charles at the end of his life. The life of Charles Stuart is the story of a great beginning followed by a tragic downward spiral into the slavery of sin. His life seemed to be one cycle of sin after another, taking him lower and lower and lower. You see, sin unchecked in our lives has a way of doing that to us. It is possible to *begin brilliantly and end ignominiously.* Some believers are like the Russian satellite that went up on the back of a rocket, but came down like a rock and required a team of searchers in Northern Canada to find the fragments. A good start does not guarantee a successful conclusion.

119

This downward spiral of sin does not only operate in the lives of individuals. *It also operates in groups and nations, and it is vividly illustrated for us in the nation of Israel during the period of the judges.* Here were a people who had experienced a great beginning as God worked mightily in their midst, but as time went on, they moved further and further away from the Lord into the quicksand of sin. Eventually, they bore almost no resemblance to the people God had liberated from Egypt, kept in the desert and taken into Canaan in victory.

All the history in the book of Judges is accurate history, but the arrangement is not based on chronology. Instead, it is presented in a repeated cycle of sin, oppression and delivery. In Judges, we go round in circles or cycles, but it is all in a downward spiral.

If ever a verse has the ring of the 21st century about it, it is the one that is hanging at the back door of the book of Judges: *"In those days there was no king in Israel: every man did that which was right in his own eyes"* (Judges 21:25). It does not say that *"every man did wrong"*, but *"every man did that which was right in his own eyes"*. Do not miss this. Their own evaluation and estimation of their deeds was not that it was wrong, but right. However, it was right in their own eyes, not in the eyes of God. Is this not why things are the way they are in our nation, our homes, our churches, and our lives? It is right, but in our own eyes. *You see, our estimation of right compared to God's estimation of right makes our right become wrong.* For what is right in our eyes is not always what is right in God's eyes. Read the verse again: *"In those days there was no king in Israel: every man did that which was right in his own eyes"*. The result was an age of Hebrew history blacker with moral pollution and darker with religious apostasy than almost any other age.

Judges has been called one of the saddest books of the Bible. It records the story of a nation that had once known the wonderful works of God, a nation with a glorious history, but a nation that turned away from its grand heritage to reap a grim harvest.

There are several things that I want you to notice by way of introduction to this book:

(1) The HISTORY of the Book

The second main group of books in our English Old Testament is called the historical books. Judges is the second of the twelve historical books, and it was written around 1000 B.C. It was obviously written after Israel began to be ruled by a king for that key phrase of the book says: *"In those days there was no king in Israel",* implying that there was a king when the history was published. In addressing people in the synagogue in Antioch in Pisidia, Paul summarized this period: *"And after that He gave unto them judges about the space of four hundred and fifty years, until Samuel the prophet"* (Acts 13:20). So the book of Judges takes us from Joshua's conquest in 1400 B.C. until Eli and Samuel judged prior to the establishment of the monarchy. Jewish tradition ascribes the authorship to Samuel.

(2) The SUMMARY of the Book

The summary is given in Judges 2 verses 11 to 23. Do you recall when you were a child? Your parents would have taken you to the park and put you on a merry-go-round. That is the best way to describe the book of Judges. For in this book we go round in circles. It is the same cycle that is repeated over and over and over again. Look at these verses in Chapter 2. There is *SIN; SUFFERING; SUPPLICATION and SALVATION.* Look at the same cycle in Chapter 3 verses 7 to 10: *SIN; SUFFERING; SUPPLICATION and SALVATION.* Now that cycle is repeated at least 6 times in the book of Judges.

Does it not reflect the lives of many people who do not know the Lord? They get up, go to work, come home, watch the television, and go to bed again, ready to repeat the same cycle the next day. It is life on a large roundabout. You get nowhere and achieve nothing. What about:

(3) The RELEVANCY of the Book

"Family feud leaves 69 brothers dead. Powerful Government leader caught in love nest. Gang rape leads to victim's death and dismemberment. Girls

at party kidnapped and forced to marry strangers. Woman judge says travellers no longer safe on roads." Sensational headlines like that are usually found on the front pages of tabloids, but those headlines describe some of the events that occur in the book of Judges. Have we got murder today? They had it in the period of the Judges. Have we got rape today? It happened in the Judges. What about homosexuality? Well, it was there also.

This was a society without standards and a time without truth. *Well, how do you live in a society without fixed standards?* When everyone is doing that which is right in their own eyes, how do we believers keep on track? Doing that which is right in the eyes of the Lord! You see, this book is so relevant because it provides us with living examples of people who faithfully served God in dark and ugly times. Did you know that when the writer of Hebrews listed Old Testament characters who walked by faith in their generation he mentioned the major judges: Gideon, Barak, Samson, Jephthah. Now these men were not perfect. Some of them committed grave sins, yet they were used by God and they challenge us with our limitations and failures to have an impact for righteousness in our society.

Now there are three pictures in this book that I want you to see:

(1) A PICTURE OF TRIBAL APATHY

The tribes are brought before us in the opening chapter. Nine and a half tribes settled in Canaan and did not destroy or even drive out the Canaanite nations as God had commanded. There was failure through compromise and every page of the book of Judges drives home this central truth. All of Israel's failure was due to compromise.

As Sidlow Baxter says:

"Incomplete mastery of an evil at the outset always means constant trouble from it afterwards, and often defeat by it in the end."

So it was for Israel. So it is with us. There is no use taking hold of a nettle with a tender hand. Israel failed through compromise and lived to rue it. You see, what we need to remember is that although Israel had conquered the whole land of Canaan in a general sense, there still remained pockets of enemy heathen nations here and there. When Joshua was an old man, the Lord said to him: *"There remaineth yet very much land to be possessed"* (Joshua 13:1). Joshua failed to complete 'mopping-up operations'. Pockets of paganism remained dotted here and there, holding remnants of the Canaanites. The tribes of Israel owned all the land, but they did not possess all of it. Therefore, they could not enjoy all of it. What *a picture of tribal apathy* is set before us in these opening chapters. Indeed Israel failed on three counts:

(a) They Failed to CONQUER THE LAND

While these opening verses record the early victories of Judah and Simeon, the rest of the chapter is a record of repeated defeats. Do you notice that time and again the Lord keeps pounding out the message: *"They did not drive them out."* (Chapter 1:27-33) Now, is this what God told them to do? No! (See Deuteronomy 7:1-6) Why were Israel to drive them out? *"Lest they make thee sin against Me"*, said the Lord. (Exodus 23:33). Is that not exactly what happened? The nations in the Land of Canaan became *Thorns* (Judges 2:3) that afflicted Israel and *Traps* that ensnared Israel. You see, the Jews eventually became so accustomed to the sinful ways of their pagan neighbours that those ways did not seem sinful any more. (See Judges 2:11-13) Then they became interested in how their neighbours worshipped, until finally Israel started to live like their enemies and imitate their ways. *The Thorns had become Traps.* I can just hear the Israelites rationalize their behaviour by saying: *"These people don't seem that bad. They look harmless. They appear to be fine people who have been given a bad press. We don't want to be mean, cruel, or unkind, so we'll see if we just can't all get along"*.

Do we not do the same thing? Do we not, at times, settle for less than complete victory in our lives over sins and bad habits? And while we seek to make justification, rationalization, and accommodation for these things, the *"little foxes"* come in and *"spoil the vines"* (Song of Solomon 2:15). You see, for believers today, the first step away from the Lord is *"friendship with the world"* (James 4:4) which then leads to our *"being spotted by the world"* (James 1:27). The next step is to *"love the world"* (1 John 2:15) and gradually become *"conformed to this world"* (Romans 12:2). This can lead to being *"condemned with the world"* (1 Corinthians 11:32), the kind of judgment that came to Lot, Samson and Saul.

Have the thorns become traps in your life personally? Things that you have allowed to remain in your life are now bringing you into bondage. I think of believers who have entered into marriage with unbelieving partners and today they are nowhere spiritually. If you had asked them at the time of their courtship they would have said: *"You have no cause to worry. This is purely platonic. It is harmless"*. But that little thorn grew, until it entrapped them. The thorns so easily become traps personally and corporately.

We need to beware of falling standards. Sometimes Christians say: *"I don't care what way they come to the meetings - as long as they come"*. Is that how God feels about His people? I'm not referring here to the unsaved. Get them in whatever way you can. But does God have standards for His people? Yes! What a responsibility we as parents have to bring up our children in the light of the Word of God, not in the light of the ways of the world. We would not insult the Queen if we were invited to the Palace by wearing 'any old thing'.

(b) They Failed to CONSIDER THE LAW

This was the reason for their failure and defeat. God promised Joshua constant victory and success if he honoured the book - see Joshua 1 verses 7 and 8 - and Joshua repeated this promise to the nation before he took his leave of them. He said:

"Be ye therefore very courageous to keep and to do all that is written in the book of the law of Moses, that ye turn not aside therefrom to the right hand or to the left; That ye come not among these nations, these that remain among you" (Joshua 23:6-7).

But do you see what happened in Judges? Look at Judges 2 verse 2. The people had not obeyed God's voice. *What was Central in Joshua became Peripheral in Judges.* Is God's Word central in your life? Someone has said: *"The Bible that is falling apart usually belongs to someone who is not!"*

Do you notice one of the tragic results of neglecting God's Word in Judges 2 verse 10? A generation grew up who did not know the Lord. They had not even won their own children to the Lord. They had failed to teach them the Word of God as God had instructed them. (See Deuteronomy 6:7)

How often that happens in nations, in families, in churches! The first generation may be dedicated, devoted. Then the second generation comes along and they are not just as committed and consecrated. Then, when it comes to the third generation, they forget what the first generation was like. It is possible to hear great spiritual truths and to be blessed with sound ministry – and then get to the stage of 'yawning in the face of God'. We could write over verse 10: 'Second Generation Syndrome'. The Word of God must be central in our churches, in our homes, in our lives.

Yes, they failed in these respects and then:

(c) They Failed to CLEAVE TO THE LORD

Look Judges 2 verse 11: *"The children of Israel did evil in the sight of the Lord"*. The Hebrew text is far more strongly worded. *"The children of Israel did **the evil.**"* They threw themselves into the supreme sin, the sin of all sin. Look at verse 13: "They served Baal and Ashtaroth". Baal and Ashtaroth were false deities in the Canaanite pantheon of gods. Baal was the god of the storm and rain who rode on the clouds and was responsible for the crop-watering rains. Ashtaroth, Baal's consort, was the goddess of war and fertility. In Canaanite religion, the fertility of the land depended on the sexual relationship between Baal and his partner. In other words, the sexual union of these gods in the heavens was expected to result in an abundant harvest. But, you see, the Canaanite faithful did not sit back and say: *"Let Baal do it"*.

No! Instead their watchword was: *"Serve Baal with gladness"*. They practised sacred prostitution as part of their worship. A Canaanite man would go to a Baal shrine and have sexual intercourse with one of the sacred prostitutes serving there. The man would fulfil Baal's role, the woman would fulfil Ashtaroth's. The idea was to encourage Mr. and Mrs. Baal to follow their example! Thus the rain, grain and wine would flow again. Can you see why the Israelites were drawn, time and time again, toward Baal worship?

Do you see why God wanted His people to drive them out? (See Deuteronomy 20:16) That they might be separate and distinct and thus protected from contamination. (See Deuteronomy 18:9-12) But *"they did not utterly drive them out"* (Judges 1:28). The result? They were overcome by them. Why? There was no distinctive separation. Do you know something? God's call to separation is for our preservation. *"Come out from among them, and be ye separate, saith the Lord"* (2 Corinthians 6:17). Do you think that you can form deep relationships with the ungodly and not be affected spiritually? Do you believe that you can frequent places where God is not welcome and it will not harm you? Do you think that you can watch questionable films and it will not affect your daily walk with God? Paul says: *"Be not conformed to this world"* (Romans 12:2). *"Do not let the world around you squeeze you into its mould."* The amazing thing is this: God loved Israel in spite of the nation's sin. That is why He raised up judges to deliver His sinful people and to call the nation back to Himself. So we have here also:

(2) A PICTURE OF SUPERNATURAL ACTIVITY

Judges is the name given to these leaders God raised up to rule during these dark days. Look at Chapter 2 verses 16 to 19. You can see that:

1. God raised them up: they were divinely appointed;

2. God was with them: they were divinely empowered;

3. God worked through them: they were divinely used.

These judges had a specific role to perform. They were God's men for dark days.

(a) THEY ARE DESIGNATED

They are appointed for a specific task. Consider:

1. Their Role

The Hebrew word translated *"judge"* means to *"to save, to rescue, to defend and to deliver"*. Now, when we think of judges, we think of the courthouse, dignified officials wearing stately robes, but these folk were not like that. Do you recall the old Westerns? Wyatt Earp and Matt Dillon? Well, the judges were probably more like them. They were like those Sheriffs in the Wild West with forceful personalities. They are called *"deliverers"* and that was often their function.

2. Their Area

These judges were not national but *local* leaders. When we read about Gideon and Samson we tend to think that they were delivering the whole nation, but Israel was now divided into groups of tribes, spread over an area roughly the size of Wales. So when we read that a judge ruled for 40 years it may only apply to tribes in the north. Samson, for example, delivered the southern tribes and Gideon the northern tribes.

3. Their Number

There is a division of opinion over that. Some say eight, some say twelve, and others say fourteen. I think what we can say is this: there are six major judges. These six judges are identified with the six major apostasies of Israel. The six major apostasies are identified by these words: *"And the children of Israel did evil in the sight of the Lord"* (See Chapter 2:11). Thus the six major judges are: Othniel, Ehud, Deborah, Gideon, Jephthah and Samson. The six minor judges are: Shamgar, Tola, Jair, Ibzan, Elon, and Abdon.

(b) THEY ARE DIFFERENT

If you were trying to find in the book of Judges a stereotype of the kind of person the Lord uses, you would be confused.

With tears streaming down her face, she looked at the pastor and said: *"I want more than anything else to make my life count for the Lord Jesus. When you were talking about what He has done for us and our position in Him, that really got through to me. But how can He use somebody like me?"* Then she talked about Christians she respected and their qualities which she admired and envied. They inspired her, but they also discouraged her because she lacked their personalities or gifts or talents. So how could the Lord have anything significant for her to do? Have you ever thought like that? *"How can God use someone like me?"* Well, our God is the God of infinite variety who uses people of all kinds, shapes and colours and He has a wonderful, unique purpose for each of us. Nowhere is this seen more clearly than in the judges God used. Look at these six major judges:

1. Othniel was the Judge with a Glorious Heritage

Othniel had the privilege of belonging to a family that was led by an outstanding believer. Caleb was one of the two greatest men of his generation. It was God Himself who said: *"Caleb hath followed Me fully"* (Numbers 14:24). Othniel's name means *"the lion of God"* and it was he who captured Kirjath-sepher (Judges 1:12-13) which means *"The city of the Book"*. As John Phillips reminds us, we need Othniels today. Men who are living in victory, men who will lead the church then the nation back to the Book and to God's great lion, Jesus Christ. We believers have a glorious heritage. Young person, do you appreciate your heritage?

2. Ehud was the Judge with a Physical Limitation

Look at Judges 3 verse 15. Ehud – a man left-handed. A *"man handicapped in the right hand"*. It is ironic that Ehud was from *"Benjamin"*, a name meaning *"Son of my right hand"*, yet he was able to use only his left hand. A lefty from Benjamin! What an encouragement this is to people with physical disabilities who have the wrong idea that God cannot use them in His service. Do you know the life-story of Joni Eareckson? As a young woman she became a quadriplegic in a diving accident. For years, Joni struggled with the terrifying fact that she would never again be able to walk or use her arms. Then, as God worked in her heart, she began to develop her skill. The Lord began to use her in a wonderful way to share His truth. When she accepted what she was, the Lord began to use her as she was. Have you an obvious handicap? A defect? Accept your so-called limitations and the Lord will open new areas of ministry for you for His glory.

3. Deborah was the Judge with Unusual Talents

While not a "Woman's Libber", Deborah was a liberating woman. Her name means *"bee"* and this accurately describes a busy, efficient, productive woman. Indeed, just as a bee is capable of stinging its enemy, so Deborah was God's instrument who through Barak delivered a fatal sting to the enemies of Israel.

Some have found the raising up of Deborah strange. Some have said: *"I can't believe God raised up a woman to be a leader in Israel at this time"*. Do you know why God did it? *There was no man willing to lead.* Now, we are living in a day when some women are wanting the place that Scripture has given to men. So today we have women ministers and women bishops. But do you ever think about the men who remain silent and act like women? How many brethren in the church there are whose voices are never raised in prayer, in worship and in ministry?

4. Gideon was the Judge with a Transformed Personality

Notice the first words on Gideon's lips: *"Oh, if, why, where, now."* (Judges 6:13)

A little girl was listening to her mother tell some great stories about people like Moses, Joshua, Samson and Daniel. Finally, she turned to her mother and said: *"Mummy, you know, God was much more exciting back then!"* I think Gideon felt like that. He loved to hear what God had done for Israel in the past, but where were the miracles now? Where was God now? You see, Gideon is a man with an exercise, with a concern, with a heart for the people of God. Sure, he is frightened, but he becomes fearless as the Lord says: *"Go in this thy might, and thou shalt save Israel from the hand of the Midianites: have not I sent thee?"* (Judges 6:14) It is as though God has taken His might and put it inside Gideon so that Gideon is now full of the might of the Lord. God wore Gideon like a suit of clothes. I wonder, are you like Gideon? Fearful, hesitant, feeling inferior? Well, one of the great truths of Scripture is that when God looks at us, He does not see us for what we are but for what we can become as He works in our lives, as we are moulded, mastered and motivated by Him.

5. Jephthah was the Judge with a Needless Vow

Do you recall Harry Ironside's prayer? *"O God, keep me from becoming a foolish old man."* It is good to start well, better to go on well, best to finish well. Now, in many ways, Jephthah was a man with many admirable qualities, but he made a vow that was needless. Look at Judges 11 verses 30 and 31. He vowed to offer to the Lord *"whatsoever cometh forth of the doors of my house to meet me"*. Was Jephthah vowing to make a human sacrifice? If he was, then he was doing something contrary to Scripture. Some think that his vow meant that his daughter had to spend the rest of her life in virginity, unmarried.

Do you recall Moses' instruction about vows? *"When thou shalt vow a vow unto the Lord thy God, thou shalt not slack to pay it: for the Lord thy God will surely require it of thee; and it would be sin in thee"* (Deuteronomy 23:21; See also Ecclesiastes 5:4-5). It was easy for Jephthah to make such a vow, but he never thought that his only child would run out to meet him. How often do you make vows that you do not honour? Have you ever been on a sick bed and you have said: "Lord, if You raise me up, I will do something more for You!"? Have you been moved under the ministry of the Word and said to the Lord: *"I want to do this or that for Your glory"*. Has it ended there? Have you been honest with God in this matter? Have you said: *"I have opened my mouth unto the Lord and I cannot go back"*?

6. Samson was the Judge with a She Weakness

According to Hebrews 11 verse 32, Samson was a man of faith, but he certainly was not a faithful man. He was not faithful to his parents' teaching, to his Nazarite vow or to the laws of his God. He was a man of great potential and even greater tragedy because his life was a story of waste.

Everything about Samson was exceptional. He was exceptional in his birth, in his upbringing, in his unusual ministry of the Spirit, in his strength, in his victories, even in his defeat and downfall and in his final triumph. *But, alas for Samson, the man who could conquer his enemies could not conquer his lust.* You see, when it came to women, Samson melted before his passions. He had three sad love affairs - his bride (Judges 14:1, 7 & 20); a prostitute (Judges 16:1) and Delilah (Judges 16:4). He was indeed the *"He man with a she weakness"*.

In the story of Samson, we read: *"He went down"*. Stephen Olford declared: "It is both ominous and dangerous when a Christian starts going down".

Let me leave you with one principle from Samson's life - Don't toy with temptation! When we toy with temptation, it traps us. Do you recall Paul's words to young Timothy? *"Flee also youthful lusts"* (2 Timothy 2:22). Samson chose not to flee and he lost his character, but Joseph not to stay and he maintained his testimony. Everytime you are faced with lust: Flee, abandon ship. Ralph Emerson says: *"Call on God, but row away from the rocks"*. Is that what you need to do? Are there things in your life now that you need to deal with in a drastic way? Are there areas in your life that need to be changed if you are going to preserve your character? Don't toy with temptation! Don't trifle with sin! Don't play with fire!

> *"Fight manfully onward, dark passions subdue,*
> *Look ever to Jesus, He will carry you through."*

(c) THEY ARE DEFIANT

The judges were different in so many ways, but they had one thing in common - they dared to step out in faith for God. As Hudson Taylor looked over 30 years during which he had seen 600 missionaries respond to his vision to reach China, he said: *"God does not do His work by large committees. He trains someone to be quiet enough, little enough, and then He uses him."* By that standard, which is God's standard, all of us qualify. The issue is not whether He can or will use us. The great question is this - Will you trust Him to do so?

(d) THEY ARE DEPENDENT

Even Othniel with all his abilities and talents was successful only because of what the Holy Spirit did through him. (See Judges 3:10) Do you recall Isaiah's words? *"They that wait upon the Lord shall renew their strength"* (Isaiah 40:31). God exchanges our weakness for His strength.

Then we have:

(3) A PICTURE OF NATIONAL ANARCHY

It is interesting that the book of Judges starts with compromise and ends with corruption. At the beginning, Israel are fighting the enemy, but by the end they are fighting each other. Initially they are under the rule of God - *(Theocracy)* - but by the end they are under the rule of nobody - *(Anarchy)* (See Judges 17:6). This situation leads later to them wanting to be under the rule of a king - *(Monarchy)*. In these closing chapters, the emphasis changes from the enemy without to the cancer within. There is utter disregard of God's will, their own walk and other people's welfare. There is:

(a) SPIRITUAL DISORDER

Chapters 17 and 18 are disgusting reading, bringing before us spiritual order concerning a corrupt man, a corrupt mother, corrupt money, corrupt ministry and corrupt might.

(b) MORAL DISORDER

In Chapter 19, there is brought before us an awful story of lust, homosexuality and violence. The body of a concubine is cut in pieces and sent to all the tribes of Israel.

(c) POLITICAL DISORDER

Inter-tribal warfare breaks out. So, the book of Judges ends with those words: *"In those days there was no king in Israel: every man did that which was right in his own eyes"* (Judges 21:25; See also Judges 17:6; Judges 18:1 and Judges 19:1). Today, there is no king in Israel. That is why evil and lawlessness are rampant in this world. The King has not come yet, but the fact that all is going so wrong down here (see 2 Timothy 3:1) is a sure sign of the nearness of His coming. You see, the only true remedy for the period of the Judges was the coming of the King, David, who is mentioned in the next book of Ruth. As it was then, so it is now. We are on the threshold of the glorious reign of the King, whose right it is to reign! (See Jeremiah 23:6) In the Corinthian epistle, it says of the Lord Jesus: *"He must reign"* (1 Corinthians 15:25). He must reign – and He will reign. The King is Coming. *"For now is our salvation nearer than when we believed."* (Romans 13:11)

> *"Where is the promise?, the signs all say*
> *His Coming is not far away*
> *Rejoice ye saints, He may come today*
> *He's bound to come."*

"Maranatha"- the Lord is coming. (1 Corinthians 16:22)

Are you ready? Can you say: **"Even so, come, Lord Jesus"** (Revelation 22:20)

CHAPTER 9
Ruth

The story is told of Dr. Samuel Johnson, the great literary giant of the 18th Century, reading a work to a largely agnostic London literary club as though it were a production he had recently written. The club thinking that it was a modern composition was vocal and unanimous in its praise of the manuscript. *But then Dr. Johnston informed the group the story was in fact from a book they all rejected, the Bible.* And the story? Why, it was the book of Ruth! Though only four chapters in length the book of Ruth has long been recognized, even by those who do not believe the Bible, as a literary masterpiece. But for all its literary beauty and excellence, it is so much more than that.

Ruth and Esther are the only Old Testament books named after women. Esther was a Jew who married a Gentile. Ruth was a Gentile who married a Jew. God used both of them to save the nation.

Dr. Graham Scroggie says:

"Ruth is like a lovely lily in a stagnant pool. Here instead of unfaithfulness is loyalty, and instead of immorality is purity. Here instead of battlefields are harvest fields and instead of the warriors' shout is the harvesters' song."

Remarkable for its brevity, its eighty-five verses are easily read in twenty minutes. Precious for its deep unfolding of the person of God, the truth of redemption, the workings of providence, this charming and beautifully written story is both simple and sublime, a gem of literature and a wonder of language.

There are several things that I want to mention by way of introduction to this book:

1. The STUDY of this Book

We can study this little book from many angles. Ruth may be looked at:

Historically: This includes the history of Elimelech and his family, the departure of Ruth from Moab to the country of Bethlehem, and her marriage to Boaz.

Devotionally: When life's great choice came to Ruth, she decided aright, and from that day onward her steadfast path of faith and trust is an outstanding pattern for believers today.

Prophetically: Here we see the Jew set aside temporarily that the Gentiles might receive salvation. (See Acts 15:14) Naomi's blessing came after Ruth's wedding, just as Israel will be restored and blessed after Christ and His church are united.

Typically: Much truth centres on the seven personalities in the Book. Elimelech, Mahlon and Chilion are types of backsliders from God, whose restoration to the Lord is not revealed. Naomi is a backslidden saint who is happily restored to the Lord. Ruth is a picture of a sinner who through links with believers trusted the Lord. Orpah is a sad type of those who show some interest in spiritual things, but turn back and perish. (See Hebrews 6:4-6) Of course, Boaz is a beautiful type of the Lord Jesus as the Redeemer and strength of His people. (See Jeremiah 50:34)

2. The SETTING of this Book

The story of Ruth occurred in the days *"when the judges ruled"* Israel. (1370 to 1041 B.C.) Thus, this book bridges the time from the Judges to Israel's monarchy. Look at Ruth 1 verse 1. This was a time of _Apathy:_ for the tribes of Israel failed to go up and take the land and to claim it for their inheritance. (See Joshua 13:1 and Judges 2:10-11) It was a time of _Apostasy:_ in which they departed from the worship of the true God and served Baal and Ashtaroth. (See Judges 2:11-13) It was a time of _Anarchy:_ for *"in those days there was no king in Israel: every man did that which was right in his own eyes"* (Judges 21:25). What a period this was! A day of darkness and disobedience and disgrace and yet amid the darkness there shines this sweet story of Ruth. You see, God never leaves Himself without a witness. The darker the times, the more definite the testimony.

3. The SCENES in this Book

The scenes are beautiful. For there are four outstanding scenes in the book of Ruth:

Scene No 1: Moab (Chapter 1:1-18) Period about 10 years.

Scene No 2: The field of Boaz (Chapter 1:19 to Chapter 2:23) Period of several months - possibly mid-April to mid-June.

Scene No 3: One day in Bethlehem and one night at the threshing floor. (Chapter 3)

Scene No 4: Bethlehem, the city. (Chapter 4) Period about 1 year. So, the book of Ruth in total covers about eleven to twelve years.

4. The SIGNIFICANCE of this Book

Never judge a book of the Bible by its bulk. Some of the most potent books of the Bible are the shortest. Ruth has only four brief chapters, but *it is a mighty midget with a marvellous message.* In fact it has several messages. It gives us a genealogy that leads to the Lord Jesus and it explains His coming from the line of David. (See Ruth 4:18-22) But surely the primary purpose of the book is to bring before us the wonderful truth of redemption. Redemption is only possible through a Kinsman-Redeemer. God could not redeem apart from a Mediator, and since only God could redeem it was necessary for Him to become that person, of whom Boaz is a beautiful picture.

5. The STRUCTURE of this Book

The structure is simple. The book of Ruth contains 4 chapters - and Warren Wiersbe summarises the book like this:

Chapter 1: Weeping, for throughout this chapter we see nothing but trouble and weeping.

Chapter 2: Working, for here we see Ruth serving in the harvest field as a gleaner coming into contact with Boaz her husband-to-be.

Chapter 3: Waiting, for after presenting herself to Boaz and asking him to fulfil his role as near kinsman (Ruth 3:9), Ruth hears wise counsel from her mother-in-law: *"Sit still, my daughter, until thou know how the matter will fall"* (Ruth 3:18).

Chapter 4: ends with the Wedding.

So we go from Chapter 1 which is filled with <u>Sorrow</u> to Chapter 2 which is all about <u>Service</u> to Chapter 3 which is a beautiful picture of <u>Submission</u> to Chapter 4 which is all about <u>Satisfaction</u>.

Or, to change it slightly, in the opening chapter we are taken:

(1) FROM THE FORBIDDEN LAND

This chapter is all about **Weeping.** J. Vernon McGee writes: *"The presence of a famine is the tell-tale mark of flagrant sin and the displeasure of the Lord".* How strange that there should be a famine in Bethlehem which means *"house of bread".* God had set two pathways before His people. The pathway of obedience and blessing or the pathway of disobedience and cursing. The Lord had promised His people that if they would obey Him, there would be plentiful rain. (See Leviticus 26:3-4) But, if they disobeyed Him: *"The Lord shall make the rain of thy land powder and dust"* (See Deuteronomy 28:24). Now, it was this famine that precipitated:

(a) A WRONG DECISION

Elimelech and Naomi and their two boys travelled east across the hills on the far side of the Dead Sea to Moab. As time passed, each of their two sons married a Moabite woman. *Things then went from bad to worse.* Naomi's husband had died and then the two sons died also. Now remember there were other men in Bethlehem Judah who had faced the same famine as Elimelech. For example, Boaz passed through the testing time of famine. Trusting the Lord, he proved the Lord, but Elimelech failed the test and went to live in Moab. This became for him the end of testimony, a place of death.

Why do I call this 'the forbidden land'? Because in its origin, Moab was *impure* (Genesis 19:35-38); in its history, Moab was *antagonistic* - when Israel travelled to Canaan, Moab refused to let Israel through their land. They would not help Israel, they hired the prophet Balaam to curse Israel and then some Moabite women seduced the Israelite men not only to corrupt their morals but to corrupt their worship. The result - 24,000 dead Israelites, because of the judgment of God. Then again, these Moabites were *idolaters.* (See Numbers 25:3) This move by this family was not only dangerous physically but spiritually. God's Word said they were not to mix with the Moabites - see Deuteronomy 23 verse 3 - yet, we read *"they came into the country of Moab, and continued there"* (Ruth 1:2).

Think of it! Ten years out of the will of God, and what a price they had to pay for their disobedience. Do you know what 'Elimelech' means? *"My God is King."* A king who is to be honoured and trusted and obeyed - but as soon as difficult circumstances arrive, Elimelech leads his family astray. A father who was backslidden took his children into Moab.

Oh, his intentions were good, for, as the opening verse suggests, *"he went to sojourn",* to live for a while, but in verse 2 we read: he *"continued there".* He settled down in disobedience.

Are you, like Elimelech, living for self rather than living for God? For time rather than for eternity? For the temporal rather than for the eternal? Have you embarked on the pathway of disobedience? Have you taken the first step downward, backward? Many a professing Christian never had any intention of staying in the world of idolatry and immorality and iniquity, but they *"continued there"*. Years lost, out of the will of God. Do you recall what they said: *"What's the harm in the first drink? What's wrong with the disco? What's the problem with flirting about with the opposite sex?"* Do you know something? They are still in Moab today!

Notice that this wrong decision:

1. Affected the Father

Look at verse 3. The father died. Naomi later testifies: *"I went out full, and the Lord hath brought me home again empty"* (Ruth 1:21). Do you know what "Naomi" means? *"My pleasant one."* But here pleasantness becomes bitterness.

Sometimes God has to take drastic measures to bring us back to where we belong. It never pays to rebel against God. Naomi discovered that. Jonah discovered that. Are you discovering that?

2. Affected the Family

Look at verse 4. One sin leads to another. Elimelech left Israel to move the 50 miles to Moab and this eventually led to these forbidden marriages. Are you forming a relationship which is outside the will of God? Scripture is very clear about whom we should date and whom we should marry. Do you recall Paul's words? *"Be ye not unequally yoked together with unbelievers."* (2 Corinthians 6:14). Christians should marry *"only in the Lord"* (1 Corinthians 7:39). Elimelech died and in due course Mahlon and Chilion died also - and the land of Naomi's dreams became the land of their despair.

(b) A WRONG DIRECTION

Backslidden Naomi desires to return home, but she is not wise enough to invite her daughters-in-law to accompany her. Do you know something? *You need to beware of the advice of a carnal Christian.* You never find a professing Christian getting into the wrong place without doing great damage to the Lord's name and work. Imagine Naomi sending these women back to their heathen idols! She thought that their only interests were fleshly, but Ruth had higher desires than mere bread and home. Orpah returned to the old life *"but Ruth clave unto her"* (Ruth 1:14).

Ruth's statement in verses 16 and 17 is one of the literary gems of all time. What a wonderful acclamation of faith! Is this not absolutely amazing? Ruth was a Moabite, a descendant of Lot, a pagan, a worshipper of many false gods, yet we see her turning her back on the gods of her people and putting her trust in the God of Israel.

Ruth chose five things for her life:

1. A New Path: *"Whither thou goest, I will go"*

2. A New Place: *"Where thou lodgest, I will lodge"*

3. A New People: *"Thy people shall be my people"*

4. A New Person: *"Thy God shall be my God"*

5. A New Purpose: *"Where thou diest, will I die"*

What she was simply saying was: *"If you die, I've no intention of returning to Moab and idolatry"*. She was making a decision that would never be reversed or altered. She would follow to the end. Do you know what that is? Commitment.

Is this not what we need in marriage? Commitment. Too many are marrying for better or for worse - but not for long.

Is that not what we need in service? Commitment. You see, things get tough and we want to quit.

Is that not what we need in relationships? Commitment.

"I will go" (verse 16) was her steadfast decision - in spite of Naomi's unscriptural direction.

Then there was:

(c) A WRONG DISPOSITION

Can you see that day when Naomi and her daughter-in-law came home? Two widows, one a backslider and the other a new convert. Do you see verse 19? *"And they said."* "They" is feminine. The town gossips said: *"Is this Naomi?"* You see, she was pleasant when she left, but when a believer gets away from the Lord, you can see it etched in their face.

Listen to Naomi: *"Call me not Naomi, call me Mara".* *"Mara"* means *"bitter"*. At the beginning of Chapter 1, Naomi made a wrong decision; in the middle of the chapter, she gives a wrong direction and by the end of the chapter, she has a wrong disposition. She is blaming God: *"The Almighty hath dealt very bitterly with me".* *"The hand of the Lord is gone out against me".* No! God's hand was working for her. *"I went out full, and the Lord hath brought me home again empty."* No! That was not true. Sin sent out her full and sin brought her home again empty.

Do you know what bitterness is? It is having wrong thoughts about God. Someone says: *"You don't understand. God has been cruel to me".* No, He has not. You are judging His hand apart from His heart. *God is too kind to do anything cruel, too wise to make a mistake and too deep to explain Himself.*

(2) INTO THE HARVEST FIELD

This chapter is all about **Working**. There is a commercial with an old gentleman advertising for a certain company and he says: *"We earn money the old fashioned way - we work for it".* Incidentally, is this not God's way? Even the apostle Paul worked so that he would not be a burden to the believers at Thessalonica (1Thessalonians 2:9). There is nothing wrong with a pastor or a Bible teacher or an evangelist or a missionary working if the means are not there to sustain them.

Can you see Ruth? One day, she said to Naomi: *"Mother, I'm going to have to get a job. We can't live much longer this way".* Naomi said: *"Daughter-in-law, you don't understand. We have social security in this country".* It was a very unusual form of social security. In the book of Leviticus, we see God's way of caring for the poor. (See Leviticus 19:9-10 – and Deuteronomy 24:19-22) If the reaper in the field missed some of the grain along the way, they could not go back and pick it up. Anything left over in the fields must be left for the poor. This was God's way of caring for the poor. Naomi says: *"Ruth, you can go if you desire, but it is hard work".* I can imagine Ruth said: *"I'll do it, mother".*

So:

(a) RUTH IS GLEANING

Sometimes, we hear folk talking of Ruth reaping, but Ruth was not a reaper. She was a gleaner. Look at Ruth 2 verses 2, 3, 7, 8 and 23. There is a difference. The reapers were gathering in the harvest, the gleaners were gathering in the ears of corn left by the reapers. The reapers were not gathering for themselves, but for their Master. Ruth, however, was gathering grain for herself and for the sustenance of Naomi.

Now, if the reapers represent the servants of God who minister the Word and seek to bring souls to Christ, then Ruth pictures the new convert who needs to gather for herself before she can gather for her Master. Sometimes young Christians want to go out witnessing right away when they themselves have never ever gleaned yet. They want to feed others when they themselves are terribly underfed.

Gleaning was not a dignified employment, but Ruth did it thoroughly and wholeheartedly. Now let me ask you, how serious are you in your study of the Word? Let me tell you, if you intend to glean from the Word of God, it will require diligence, determination, time and perseverance. Someone said to Dr. Barnhouse one day: *"Sir, I would give the world to know the Word of God like you".* Barnhouse said: *"That's how much it will cost - the world".*

(b) GOD IS GUIDING

While Ruth was gleaning, God was guiding. Do you notice that little phrase in verse 3 of Chapter 2: *"She went, and came, and gleaned in the field after the reapers: and her hap was to light on a part of the field belonging unto Boaz"*. *"Her hap"* or literally *"her lot"*. From a human point of view, it is just a 'happenstance', a pure coincidence, but then God's children have no accidents. They have only appointments. Can you imagine the Lord poking one of the angels in glory and saying: *"Now watch this"*?

There were no fences dividing the fields, only boundary markers. There was no sign that proclaimed: *"Boaz Incorporated, Visitors Welcome"*. Can you see Ruth? She is going down to the fields. She looks to the left, then to the right. She says: *"I think I'll go to the right"*. Guess what? She steps right into the fields of Boaz. About that time, the Lord knocks an angel off a heavenly couch and says: *"What did I tell you, there she is. She is in the fields of Boaz."*

Ruth's heart was right with God. She was marked by sweet submission. She was fulfilling her daily obligations when *"her hap"* occurred.

F. B. Meyer was crossing from Dublin to Holyhead one dark night. He asked the Captain of the ship: *"How do you find Holyhead harbour on such a dark, starless night as this?"* The Captain replied: *"Do you see those three lights just ahead? These must be lined up behind the other in one straight line of vision, and I follow them, keeping the ship in line with the three, until I safely enter the harbour."* Dr. Meyer, using the illustration, compared the three lights to the light of God's Word, the inward conviction of the Holy Spirit, and the divine arrangement of circumstances in the Christian's life. The Lord is constantly working *with us* (Mark 16:20) and *in us* (Philippians 2:13) and *for us* (Romans 8:28) and accomplishing His gracious purposes.

Do we not have a wonderful God? A God who guides, overrules and whose providence reaches every area of our lives.

(c) *BOAZ IS GOVERNING*

Do you know what Boaz means? *"In him is strength."* How good it is to know that God has good people living in bad times. You see, here was a man who was concerned about his workers and wanted them to enjoy the blessing of the Lord. He governed <u>Graciously.</u> When he entered the field, he said: *"The Lord be with you"* (Chapter 2:4). He governed <u>Conscientiously.</u> Immediately he saw Ruth he said: *"Whose damsel is this?"* (verse 5). J. Vernon McGee translates it: *"Well, where in the world has she been that I have not met her before."* Is that not how you felt when you met your wife? This was love at first sight.

Boaz took an interest in Ruth the stranger. Do you? Do you take an interest in the strangers that come into the meeting? Do you know God's Word: *"Be not forgetful to entertain strangers: for thereby some have entertained angels unawares"* (Hebrews 13:2)? Do you know what the complaint of 21st century worshippers is? It is this - they come and go without a welcome. We are all so busy with our little cliques that the stranger comes and goes unnoticed and unwelcome. Will you have a word for the stranger? *"A word spoken in due season, how good it is!"* (Proverbs 15:23).

In Scene One, Ruth is coming from the forbidden land; in Scene Two, Ruth is in the harvest field, then, in Scene Three, Ruth goes:

(3) ONTO THE THRESHING FLOOR

This chapter is all about **Waiting.** In those days, the threshing floor was a very important place. They would take the grain that had been harvested to the threshing floor. The grain would be threshed and then winnowed. Men would sleep at the threshing floor to protect the harvest. Away back in Moab, Naomi told Ruth to find *"rest"*, a husband among her own people, but now she realises that there is rest with the people of God and in the will of God. This brings into play the Hebrew practice of appointing a Go'el, that is a kinsman redeemer. This law states that a brother or male relative is obliged to make every provision possible for the family of his deceased kinsman, either by redeeming the widow's property or marrying her. (See Leviticus 25:25) The kinsman, of course, had to be able and willing to redeem. So the time has come for Ruth to present her claims to Boaz and give him the opportunity to be her kinsman redeemer. Here we see:

(a) PREPARATION FOR THE REDEEMER

Do you notice that there were three things that were needed before Ruth could take her place at the feet of Boaz - and these things have a clear application for believers today. We must be:

1. Washed in order to Worship

Look at Ruth 3 verse 3: *"Wash thyself"*. This was not ceremonial. Naomi just wanted to make sure Ruth was clean. If we want to enter into a deeper fellowship with the Lord, we must *"cleanse ourselves from all filthiness of the flesh and spirit, perfecting holiness in the fear of God"* (2 Corinthians 7:1). We tend to be hard on those who talk of sinless perfection, but we are inclined to go the other way and even make excuses for our sin. There is positional holiness. There will be perfect holiness when we get to Heaven. However, there is such a thing down here as practical holiness. The Word of God does say: *"Follow peace with all men, and holiness, without which no man shall see the Lord"* (Hebrews 12:14). Have your feet become soiled? Has your mind become polluted? Has your spirit become arrogant?

2. Anointed in order to Witness

Naomi says to Ruth: *"Wash thyself therefore, and anoint thee"*. *"Get that little bottle of perfume out. You know, that one that's called 'Midnight in Moab', and use it generously."* The gracious Holy Spirit is the anointing today. Christ's opening words as He began His public ministry were these: *"The Spirit of the Lord is upon Me, because He hath anointed Me to preach the gospel to the poor"* (Luke 4:18). If the spotless Son of God needed the Spirit's power, how much more do we?

3. Clothed in order to Walk

Naomi continues: *"And put thy raiment upon thee"*. *"Ruth, put off your widow's garments, and put on that special garment reserved for festive occasions."* Peter says: *"Be clothed with humility"* (1 Peter 5:5). Paul says: *"Walk worthy .... with all lowliness and meekness, with longsuffering, forbearing one another in love"* (Ephesians 4:1-2). *"Ruth, dress for the occasion."*

Our dress and appearance are very important subjects and no more so than in this present age. Many believers *"dress down"* for church and *"dress up"* for work. Are there principles to govern our dress? Paul says: *"In like manner also, that women adorn themselves in modest apparel"* (1 Timothy 2:9). The word *"apparel"* conveys the idea of a garment that does not accentuate the precise figure of a woman's body. Does your dress complement your Christian profession? Are you promoting sin by the way you dress? Does your appearance glorify the Lord?

(b) PRESENTATION TO THE REDEEMER

Ruth says to Boaz: *"Spread therefore thy skirt over thine handmaid: for thou art a near kinsman"* (Ruth 3:9). This is not an invitation to immorality, but a *'formal proposal of marriage couched in the picturesque language of the time.'*

I heard about a timid young man who wanted to ask his very eager girlfriend to marry him. He finally got up enough courage to call her on the phone: *"Will you marry me?"* he said. She replied: *"Sure, what's your name?"*

Don't be that way! Wait on the Lord.

Notice what Boaz promises: *"I will do to thee all that thou requirest"* (verse 11). He promises to fulfil her wishes when he has satisfied himself that a closer relative will renounce his right and duty. Boaz <u>Accepted Her</u>: *"Blessed be thou of the Lord"*. Boaz <u>Assured her</u>: *"My daughter, fear not"*. Boaz <u>Assisted her</u>: *"Don't go back to Naomi empty handed"*.

(c) PROCLAMATION ABOUT THE REDEEMER

1. Do you see the Proclamation of Ruth?

"And she told her all that the man had done to her" (Ruth 3:16). Is that what you are doing? Telling others of all that the Lord Jesus has done for you?

2. Do you see the Proclamation of Naomi?

"The man will not be in rest, until he have finished the thing this day" (Ruth 3:18).

What was said of Boaz could well have been said about Christ. I see Him as they drive nails into His hands. The crowd spits on Him and rails on Him. *"The man will not be in rest, until He have finished the thing this day."*

They lift the Cross between Heaven and earth. The religious leaders scorn and mock Him. *"The man will not be in rest, until He have finished the thing this day."*

Nature revolts. The birds leave the air. The sun refuses to shine. There is darkness over the face of the earth. *"The man will not be in rest, until He have finished the thing this day."*

Out of the darkness and degradation of Calvary, Christ cries: *"It is finished"* (John 19:30). He rests in His finished work of redemption.

This chapter begins by Naomi saying to Ruth: *"Shall I not seek rest for thee?"* (verse 1). It ends by saying: *"The man will not be in rest, until he have finished the thing this day"*.

That brings us to this final scene of this lovely story:

(4) AT THE CITY GATE

This chapter is all about a **Wedding.** Do you see here:

(a) THE BASIS FOR THIS UNION

You see, it all centred in the kinsman redeemer. Beyond Boaz, we see here our Kinsman Redeemer, the One in whom we have redemption. The word *"redeem"* means *"to set free by paying a price"*. To be a kinsman redeemer, you had to have:

1. The Right to Redeem

You had to be a near kinsman. We read in Leviticus 25 verse 25: *"If thy brother be waxen poor, and hath sold away some of his possession, and if any of his kin come to redeem it, then shall he redeem that which his brother sold."* Look at Ruth 2 verses 1, 3 and 20 and Chapter 3 verses 12 and 13. So, the redeemer had to be a member of the family.

Did the Lord meet this qualification with regard to us? Well, John tells us: *"And the Word was made flesh, and dwelt among us, (and we beheld His glory, the glory as of the only-begotten of the Father,) full of grace and truth"* (John 1:14). The Lord Jesus became man. He became one of us, sin apart.

2. The Power to Redeem

Ruth and Naomi were too poor to redeem themselves, but Boaz had all the resources to set them free. He was *"a mighty man of wealth"* (Ruth 2:1). Did the Lord Jesus Christ meet this qualification? Was He able to redeem? Well, the Bible says *"He was rich"* (2 Corinthians 8:9) and *"He is able"*.

3. The Will to Redeem

This other kinsman was willing to redeem the land, but Ruth 4 verse 6 tells us that he was unwilling to redeem the lady, lest he mar his own inheritance. He said: *"I must preserve my own name"*. But Boaz was not concerned about preserving his name. His only concern was doing the will of God in rescuing Ruth. How like our adorable Lord. Willing to make Himself of no reputation, willing to take upon Himself the form of a servant, willing to humble Himself, willing to die to secure our redemption.

Do you notice that interesting statement in Ruth 4 verse 9: *"I have bought"*? It does not tell how much Boaz paid for the land and the bride. But we know the price that our Saviour paid for our redemption. Peter speaks of *"the precious blood of Christ"* (1 Peter 1:19). What a price He paid! What a debt we owe!

(b) THE BLESSING OF THIS UNION

1. For Ruth there was the Blessing of Fruitfulness

Ruth gave birth to a son. In the East, the biggest disgrace that a woman could experience was to be barren.

2. For Boaz there was the Blessing of Fame

Do you see Ruth 4 verse 11? The people said to Boaz: *"Do thou worthily in Ephratah, and be famous in Bethlehem"*. The word *"famous"* means to obtain a name. Do you recall the nearer kinsman? He was trying to protect a name. Do you know who he was? No, and neither does anyone else. But Boaz's name has lived throughout history because of his redemptive work. Mark it down. God honours those who honour Him.

3. For Naomi there was the Blessing of Fellowship

That baby boy in Bethlehem changed her sorrow into joy, her bitterness into blessing, her emptiness into fulness. Backslidden believer – that is what the Lord will do for you if you return to Him.

(c) THE BENEFITS FROM THIS UNION

The result of the union between Boaz and Ruth leads to the record of the royal line of Judah, through which David would come, and through David would come the Messiah. God's hand is in control. His hand is guiding, shaping and directing. Is God's providence not amazing? God's name occurs 23 times in this book for He is control.

So that little baby Obed blessed a marriage, a mother, a mother-in-law, and continues to bless us even to this day, because through that line of Boaz and Obed and Jesse and David came our precious Saviour.

Realise afresh that **history is His story. "The most High ruleth"** (Daniel 4:17). God is still on the throne. Let me personalize it:

> *"God is still on the throne,*
> *And He will take care of His own,*
> *His promise is true,*
> *He will see us right through,*
> *God is still on the throne."*

Trust Him.

CHAPTER 10

1 Samuel

In the original Hebrew Bible, 1 and 2 Samuel formed one book, as also did 1 and 2 Kings and 1 and 2 Chronicles. These three books were first divided by scholars working on the Septuagint, when they translated the Old Testament into the Greek language. The reason for the division in each case seems to have been that written Greek requires at least one third more space than Hebrew. *So the translators were forced to divide each of Samuel, Kings and Chronicles into two, either because there was a limit to the length of scroll available, or in order to make the scrolls easier to handle.*

In our English Bible, 1 and 2 Samuel appear among the historical books. In the Hebrew Bible, however, they are considered as one book among the former prophets. Now how should we approach this book of 1 Samuel? Well, we could we approach it:

1. Geographically

We need to keep in mind that the majority of action in both books of Samuel took place in and around the central highlands in the land of Israel. The nation of Israel was largely concentrated in an area that ran about 90 miles from the hill country of Ephraim in the north (1 Samuel 1:1 and Chapter 9:4) to the hill country of Judah in the south (Joshua 20:7 and Chapter 21:11) and between 15 to 35 miles east to west. The major cities of 1 and 2 Samuel are to be found in these central highlands; Shiloh, the residence of Eli and the tabernacle; Ramah, the hometown of Samuel; Gibeah, the headquarters of Saul; Bethlehem the birthplace of David; Hebron, David's capital when he ruled over Judah, and Jerusalem the ultimate *"city of David"*.

2. Historically

Abraham, the father of the Jews, lived around 2000 B.C. King David came to the throne around 1000 B.C. So this first book of Samuel covers the history of Israel from the time of the Judge, Eli the priest (1060 B.C.), to the death of Saul (1010 B.C.). David Pawson suggests that the Old Testament can be divided into four equal parts of roughly 500 years each:

1. From 2000 to 1500 B.C. Israel was led by *Patriarchs*, Abraham, Isaac, Jacob and Joseph, though they were not a nation at time.

2. From 1500 to 1000 B.C. they were led by *Prophets* from Moses to Samuel.

3. From 1000 B.C. to 500 B.C. they were led by *Princes* or kings from Saul and onwards.

4. From 500 B.C. and leading up to the time of Christ they were led by **Priests** from Joshua a priest who returned to Judah from exile under Zerubbabel's rule to Caiaphas in the time of Christ.

None of these leader types was ideal and each person brought his own flaws to the task. *You see, the nation needed a leader who was prophet, priest and king - and they found Him in the Lord Jesus.* Each stage, therefore, was a foreshadowing of the ideal leader who was to come. You see, like the book of Acts in the New Testament, the First book of Samuel is a book of transition, a book of change. The long period of the judges with its unsettled government, religious apostasy and social problems was about to end. The theocracy was about to be replaced by the monarchy. So 1 Samuel is a book of transition.

3. Spiritually

The First book of Samuel is the book of transition from the Theocracy to the Monarchy. It was always God's intention to give Israel a king. As far back as Genesis 49, Jacob had prophesied: *"The sceptre shall not depart from Judah, nor a lawgiver from between his feet, until Shiloh come; and unto Him shall the gathering of the people be"* (verse 10). In the law of Moses, instructions were given as to who could or could not be king, and restrictions were placed upon such a king.

The great sin of Israel in this book was anticipating the purpose of God and insisting on the king of their choice instead of waiting for the king of God's choice. Do you see their request in 1 Samuel 8 verses 4 to 9? *"Give us a king to judge us."* You see, they wanted to become *"like all the nations"* (Chapter 8:5). There are believers who have become spoiled because they wanted to become like the people of the world around them. But, do you notice the deeper meaning here? Look at 1 Samuel 8 verse 7: *"They have not rejected thee, but they have rejected Me, that I should not reign over them".* <u>Is this not the central spiritual message of this book?</u> The Lord had called Israel into a unique relationship with Himself and God Himself was Israel's invisible king. Through disobedience, the people had brought chastisement upon themselves from time to time, but they attributed this to the fact that they had no human and visible king, such as the surrounding nations had. Now, as Samuel ages and his sons prove corrupt, the people take the opportunity to press for a human king. You see, they wanted the seen not the unseen; the visible not the invisible; the human not the divine; the second best, not God's best.

> *"God has His best things for the few,*
> *Who dare to stand the test,*
> *God has His second choice for those,*
> *Who will not take His best."*

Incidentally, God's ideal form of government is not a democracy or a republic. It is not government of the people, by the people, for the people. That is man's ideal form of government, the very best that man can produce. God likens that to a mixture of iron and clay. But God's kind of government, the government yet to be imposed on this planet during the Millennium will be theocratic or Christocratic, that is government by Jesus Christ.

4. Biographically

First Samuel is the story of four men: Eli, Samuel, Saul and David. Their stories are so interwoven that the story of Eli overlaps that of Samuel, the story of Samuel overlaps that of Saul, and the story of Saul overlaps that of David.

I wonder, have you noticed the contrasts or comparisons in this book? Eli and Samuel, David and Saul, and Jonathan and Absalom.

(1) ELI & SAMUEL - Chapters 1-8

This first section of the book has what Raymond Brown calls "*a true to life*" mixture of joy and tragedy. The story of Samuel's birth and Hannah's delight dominates Chapters 1 to 3, while the tragedy of Ichabod's birth and Eli's grief makes sad reading in Chapter 4. You see, the events in these opening chapters centre around:

(a) HANNAH: A GODLY MOTHER

She put the Lord first in her life; she believed in prayer; she kept her vows, and she gave God all the glory. Hannah was the wife of Elkanah. Her name means "*gracious*" and she was one of the most gracious women in all the Bible. Driven to desperation because she was unfruitful, she besieged the throne of God promising that if God would give her a son she would give him right back to God. So she did. When her little boy was born, she called him "Samuel" – "*asked of God*" – as though to constantly remind herself of her promise. You see, she did not want to fall into the sin of Eli and put her son before the Lord. So she gave him to Eli and said: "*You train him to be a man of God*" (1 Samuel 1:28). How she must have upheld that little boy in prayer day and night! She had prayed for the **gift** of that son, but now she was praying for the **growth** of that son. Over her whole life can be written just that one sentence that she uttered to Eli when she brought the boy to him: "*For this child I prayed*" (1 Samuel 1:27).

A little girl was spending the night far away from home. At bedtime she knelt with her hostess to pray, expecting the usual prompting. Finding her hostess unable to help her, she prayed:

"Please, Lord, excuse me. I can't remember my prayers, and I'm staying with a mother who doesn't know how to pray".

Are you a mother who knows how to pray? For good or bad, for Heaven or Hell, a mother's influence is very great. It is not surprising to learn that Lord Byron, the prominent poet, lived a reckless and vicious life, for his mother was rash and violent. Nero was fourteen years Emperor of Rome. He was one of the most evil of all men, and his mother was a murderess. On the other hand, the mothers of Sir Walter Scott, Wesley and Augustine were remarkable for their graciousness, godliness and intelligence. Like mother, like child. That is what led one great man to say: *"Give me a generation of Christian mothers, and I will undertake to change the face of society in twelve months".*

Is it not interesting that Hannah's trial drove her to the place of worship? Do you notice 1 Samuel 1 verse 19? Is that not a challenge? You see, it seems to be the pattern that when believers face difficulties, afflictions and disappointments, they do not pray and they do not worship. They stay at home or take a weekend break from their church in order to cheer themselves up. The solution to your problem is never found in absence from the assembly of God's people. (See Hebrews 10:24-25) Hannah was a woman of prayer, and so it is no surprise that Samuel was a man of prayer.

(b) ELI: A CARELESS FATHER

Who was Eli? Well, _religiously_ he was the high priest (1 Samuel 1:9); _nationally_ he was a judge, for Eli *"judged Israel forty years"* (Chapter 4:18); but _domestically_ he was a father who had lost control. How tragic when a servant of the Lord and a high priest at that fails to win his own sons to the Lord. Do you see what Chapter 2 verse 12 says? *"The sons of Eli were sons of Belial; they knew not the Lord."* Now, grace does not run in our blood-stream. It is not always the man's fault if his children are unsaved. There are unbelieving parents who have children who become Christians, and there are Christians who have unbelieving children. There are many godly parents with ungodly children. Do not let the devil distress you about this matter. Leave the children with the Lord and continue to pray for their salvation. Sometimes God waits that He might keep your heart tender towards those in your family. <u>*But believing parents ought to do their best to lead their children to the Lord.*</u>

Because Eli was a priest, his sons became priests. To them it was not a calling, but a career; not a passion, but a position.

The story is told of the preacher who was asked: **"Was you sent, or did you just went?"** These sons *"just went"*.

Eli's sons were not interested in the Lord, only lust, for the Bible says they seduced the women who assisted in the temple. They were not concerned about the Master, only money, for the Bible says they stole from the people they were to serve. They did not care about the Scriptures, only about self-indulgence, for the Bible says *"they knew not the Lord"*.

The fact that Eli's children were unregenerate is noted among his other faults. Eli *rebuked* them, but he did not *restrain* them (1 Samuel 2:23) and therefore he came under the judgment of God. (See Chapter 2:29).

Some time ago a columnist in one of Chicago's daily newspapers received a letter from a distraught mother. She said: *"My son is seventeen years of age. He will not listen to a thing I say. He's in with the wrong crowd. He's in trouble with the police. What can I do?"* The columnist's answer was brutally frank: *"Shrink him down to seventeen months and start all over again."* How many wish they could! But what we cannot do, God can. The Gospel is not a reduction in age – it is a new birth altogether.

Eli failed with his sons, but he did not fail with Samuel.

(c) SAMUEL: A DEVOTED SON

The Jews regarded Samuel as a national leader second only to Moses. (See Jeremiah 15:1) Samuel was to lead the people out of the times of the judges into those of the kings *"and lay the foundation for a prosperous development of the monarchy."* He bridged the gap between the priests and the kings and founded the prophetic order in Israel. He was the last of the judges and the first of the prophets. (See 1 Samuel 3:20 and 7:15) He became Israel's man of destiny; an educator, who founded the *"school of prophets"*, a kind of theological seminary where young men could be trained in the Scriptures (see 1 Samuel 10:5; Chapter 19:20 and 2 Kings 2:3-7 and Chapter 6:1); a prophet, who put the Word above the world; a man who offered priestly sacrifices (see 1 Samuel 16:2 & 5); a judge, who put integrity above indulgence; a king-maker, who put greatness above glory. Moses was the deliverer who created a nation, but the nation sinned and went down deep in defeat and despair. Just when Israel's national situation and spiritual condition appeared hopeless, Samuel restored them and recreated them, and he led them on from victory to victory.

During those days, messages from the Lord were rare. One night, however, while Samuel was sleeping in the temple, the Lord called him. Eventually he said: *"Speak; for Thy servant heareth"* (1 Samuel 3:10). Later on, the Lord would say to Samuel: *"Speak servant, for thy Lord heareth".* Samuel became a man of prayer. Are you living where the Lord can speak to you? Are you living where the Lord can use you?

1. Samuel ministered at a time of Animosity

We read: *"And the hand of the Lord was against the Philistines all the days of Samuel"* (1 Samuel 7:13). Samuel was there, standing for the truth right in the forefront of the battle.

2. Samuel ministered at a time of Apostasy

The emergence of a prophet in Israel always signals a time of backsliding. The priesthood had failed, so God raised up a prophet to preach the Word of God and to exhort the people to return to God.

3. Samuel ministered at a time of Activity

When Israel demanded a king, we read: *"But the thing displeased Samuel .... and Samuel prayed unto the Lord"* (1 Samuel 8:6). You see, up till now God had not spoken to the people in widespread visions (Chapter 3:1), but now everyone knew that Samuel was God's prophet and that the Word of the Lord was with him. Do you know what his first task was? To declare Eli's doom. (See Chapter 3:18) This was the start of Samuel's prophetic ministry and it was not the last time that the word he gave would be hard to receive.

(d) ISRAEL: A SUPERSTITIOUS NATION

The *Ark* is the main theme in these chapters. We see:

1. The Ark's *Capture:* by the Philistines (Chapter 4)

2. The Ark's *Victory:* (Chapter 5)

3. The Ark's *Return:* (Chapter 6)

4. The Ark's *Rest:* (Chapter 7)

The Philistines were still occupying parts of Israel on the west coast, thus posing a real threat to the nation. Israel lost 4,000 men in the preliminary battle, and this should have told them that the Lord was displeased. *Did they repent? Did they turn to the Lord in confession and prayer?* No! Instead, they resorted to superstition and they took the Ark to the battlefield. Because Israel put their trust in the Ark of God rather than the God of the Ark, God allowed the Philistines to defeat them. The Ark was taken, Hophni and Phinehas, the sons of Eli, were slain and Eli, hearing the news, died. (See 1 Samuel 4:18) You see, instead of revering the Ark as the symbol of God's presence, they turned it into a religious relic. (See Numbers 10:35) Can the same mistake not be made with regard to Christian symbols? Consider 1 Corinthians 11 verses 29 and 30. When we rely on the outward form without the internal reality, we just become like the Pharisees of Matthew 23 verses 25 to 28.

Do you see what is happening here? After Eli's grim death, responsibility as a judge in Israel falls to Samuel – and so we move to the second section of the book:

(2) SAMUEL & SAUL - Chapters 9-15

Samuel formed the living link between the theocracy and the monarchy. It had always been God's intention eventually to give Israel a king, in His own time and in His own way. Israel's impatience forced the issue and so the Lord gave them the kind of king they demanded - Saul. Later, in His purpose, the Lord gave them the King He had intended to give them all along, David.

John Hunt was a missionary in the 19th Century to the cannibals of Fiji. Writing to a missionary colleague on one occasion about holiness, he urged his friend to join him in the prayer that they would escape: *"The curse of a useless life"*. The curse of a useless life! God had rich purposes for Saul's life, but it ended in tragedy. But it was not always so, for look at:

(a) SAUL'S INITIAL DEVOTION

In his old age (see 1 Samuel 8 verse 1), Samuel anoints Saul as King. Indeed:

1. Saul was *Anointed* at Ramah: (Chapter 9:17 - 10:1)

2. Saul was *Appointed* at Mizpah: (Chapter 10:17-27)

3. Saul was *Acclaimed* at Gilgal: (Chapter 11:15)

It all began so well. Saul was attractive, considerate, meek, controlled, just and courageous. He stood head and shoulders above his countrymen. He was handsome and humble, strong and tall, and every inch a king. When the Israelis saw him they shouted: *"God save the king"* (Chapter 10:24). God tried to save Saul, but Saul interfered!

He started well. There was initial devotion. Can you recall your initial devotion to the Lord? Do you remember the freshness of your first love? Do you remember when it was springtime in your soul? How you yearned to learn more of the Word? When your heart was filled with love for Christ? When you loved your fellow believers? There was no bitterness. There were no grudges. When you had a passion for souls? That was then, what about now? For Saul, it was from devotion to decline, for notice:

(b) SAUL'S GRADUAL DECLINE

Someone has said that power corrupts - and with power, Saul changes. George Sweeting says this: *"Collapse in the Christian life is rarely a blow-out. It is usually a slow leak"*. Spiritual decline can be so gradual that before we know it we have fallen. Saul began that downward spiral that ultimately led to his defeat, then to his disgrace and finally to his death. The Lord says in Chapter 15 verse 11: *"He is turned back from following Me"*. What brought about this decline? Well:

1. Saul was Impatient

Samuel was supposed to come to Gilgal in seven days to make a sacrifice (Chapter 10:8), but when he was late, Saul takes matters into his own hands, *"and he offered the burnt offering"* (Chapter 13:9). As king, Saul has no right to make a priestly sacrifice, but in the stress of the moment, his fault line of impatience cracks, and he rushes ahead of the Lord. The result? He lost his crown. Are you like that?

It is interesting to notice that the early Church did not start with *Activity* but with *Passivity*. It begins with a story about people who obeyed the Lord by waiting. Consider Luke 24 verse 49 and Acts 1 verse 4. Is *"steady patience"* what you need? (See Hebrews 10:36) Patience to face the problems of family life, to confront the discouragements of church life, to meet the frustrations of secular life?

2. Saul was Irreverent

Do you recall God's Word concerning Amalek? Look at Chapter 15 verse 3. *"Go and smite Amalek, and utterly destroy all that they have."* The word *"destroy"* refers to the giving of things and persons to the Lord, often by totally destroying them. In other words this spoil was to be devoted to God but look at Chapter 15 verse 9. Saul kept the best for himself and gave the leftovers to God.

Are we guilty of that? We talk about worldliness in the church, but what about worldliness in the Christian? Do you know what a worldly believer does? *He attends first to his own needs.* Are we only giving to God that which is left over? What about your *Time?* Have you time for sport, personal interests, socialising? How much time do you give to the Lord? What about your *Energy?* *"Oh"*, you say, *"I have not much of that!"* Well, you have enough to work - have you enough to worship? You have enough for pastimes - have you enough for prayer? You have enough for family - have you enough for fellowship? What about your *Money?* Do you just give the leftovers of your money to God? Do you just tip the Lord? Is God coming in for the leftovers in your life? This is what the people in Malachi's day were doing. (See Malachi 1:13) They were offering to God sacrifices that they would not have offered to their master.

3. Saul was Insubordinate

Saul declared to Samuel: *"Blessed be thou of the Lord: I have performed the commandment of the Lord"* (1 Samuel 15:13). Samuel replied: *"To obey is better than sacrifice, and to hearken than the fat of rams"* (verse 22).

Do you know what God wants from His people in this 21st century? The same thing that He wanted from His people in the 1st century. The same thing that He wanted from His people in the days of Saul. *Obedience.*

Aretta Loving, a Wycliffe missionary, was washing her breakfast dishes when she saw Jimmy, her neighbour's five year old, headed straight toward the back porch. She had just finished painting the hand rails, and she was proud of her work. *"Come around to the front door, Jimmy"*, she shouted. *"There's wet paint on the hand rails."* *"I'll be careful"*, Jimmy replied, not turning from his path. *"No, Jimmy. Don't come up the steps"*, Aretta shouted, knowing that Jimmy had a tendency to mess things up. *"I'll be careful"*, he said again. By this time he was dangerously close to the steps. *"Jimmy, stop"*, Aretta shouted. *"I don't want carefulness. I want obedience."* As the words burst from her mouth, she suddenly remembered these words to King Saul: *"To obey is better than sacrifice"*. How would Jimmy respond, Aretta wondered. To her relief he shouted back: *"All right, Loving, I'll go around to the front door"*. As he turned around the house, Aretta thought to herself: *"How often am I like Saul or like Jimmy, wanting to go my own way? I rationalise, 'I'll be careful, Lord' as I proceed with my own plans."*

The Lord does not want carefulness. **He wants obedience.** Tell me, is your spiritual decline due to a lack of obedience? Are you keeping the commandment of the Lord in relation to the *Lord's Table?* (1 Corinthians 11:24); To *Attendance?* (Hebrews 10:25); To *Prayer?* (Luke 18:1); To *Love?* (John 13:34); To *Go?* (Matthew 28:19) Is God saying to you through His Word: *"Thou hast not kept the commandment of the Lord thy God"*? (See 1 Samuel 13:13)

The late President of The Moody Bible Institute in Chicago, William Culbertson, often prayed: *"Lord, help us to end well"*. The saintly British preacher F. B. Meyer said at the close of his life: *"I don't want my life to end in a swamp"*. Sadly, some of our great preachers have not ended well. They have been like Samson – wanting to bring down the temple on the last lap of the journey.

How did Saul end?

(c) SAUL'S EVENTUAL DEFEAT

It is interesting that Saul's career as King began at *Dawn,* as the sun was coming up (1 Samuel 9:26). His career as King ended at *Dusk,* with the sun going down. At night, Saul disguised himself and went to consult a witch (Chapter 28:8). Then he went out to the battlefield and was slain (Chapter 31:6).

God's intention for Saul's life was: *"Anoint him to be captain .... that he may save"* (Chapter 9:16), but the captain became a captive to his own selfish desires and changing moods.

Saul failed miserably. He failed God. He failed the people of God. He let himself down. He lost God's blessing; he lost his crown and he lost his life. Saul ended his life in disgrace, in defeat, in disaster. What a contrast he was with the other Saul - Saul of Tarsus. One chose the *path of rebellion* against God; the other chose the *path of submission* to God. The first Saul *died a suicide* and lost his crown; the second Saul *died a martyr* and gained a crown. The first Saul died saying: *"I have played the fool"* (Chapter 26:21). The second Saul died saying: *"I have fought a good fight"* (2 Timothy 4:7). Which one represents you? The Risen Lord says: *"Behold, I come quickly: hold that fast which thou hast, that no man take thy crown"* (Revelation 3:11). **Don't lose your crown!** Be faithful to the Lord, so that one day He can present you before God's throne and give you a crown of glory.

Notice the final part:

(3) SAUL & DAVID - Chapters 16-31

Saul was the first king, but David was Israel's finest king. All the kings of Judah are measured by David. I love what John Phillips says:

"Saul was a herder of mules, but David was a keeper of sheep. Saul was used to driving, David to leading. The first time we see Saul, he had just lost his father's mules and had not the slightest idea where to find them. The first time we see David, he was keeping his father's sheep and was willing to give his life for his flock."

So we see:

(a) DAVID THE SHEPHERD

As everyone was watching Saul's reign sink, in a secluded field in Bethlehem God was raising up a youth named David. A nobody,

nobody noticed, but someone who would change the course of Israel's history forever. *"The Lord hath sought Him a man after His own heart"* (1 Samuel 13:14). God had sought out a man. Only a man, but what a man he was! Scholars tell us that David was about 15 or 16 years of age here. Do you recall what Jesse said about him? *"He keepeth the sheep"* (Chapter 16:11). When you live in the fields tending sheep, it is solitude that nurtures you. Think of it, nature was his nurse, his companion, his teacher. David's training exposed him to the danger and threats of reality. He says: *"The Lord delivered me out of the paw of the lion, and out of the paw of the bear"* (Chapter 17:37). While David was tending sheep, God was putting steel in his bones. The Lord used **obscurity, monotony, and reality** to bring David from the place of *Humility* to the place of *Honour*. Do you recognise that faithfulness in little things is God's appointed way to bigger things? (See Matthew 25:21) Before entrusting David with the nation, what did God do? He gave him a flock of sheep to protect.

Could it be that the Lord has placed you in some sphere of service for Him which is obscure? Are you unseen, unknown, unappreciated, unapplauded, and is it monotonous? The question is - Are you faithful? For although man may forget you, God will remember and reward you.

(b) DAVID THE SERVANT

David's pre-king years are most well-known for:

1. His Fight with Goliath: (Chapter 17)

2. His Friendship with Jonathan: (Chapter 18)

3. His Fame with Israel: (Chapter 18:6)

Do you know how David refers to himself time and again? As a servant! See Chapter 17 verses 32, 34 and 36.

Sometimes we think of David fighting Goliath as one victory in one day, but it was three victories in one day! When David came into the valley of Elah, his brothers chided him. David could so easily have retaliated, but he said: *"Is there not a cause?"* (Chapter 17:29) This was victory number 1 – over the flesh. Then Saul wanted David to put on his armour. David said: *"I have not proved them"* (verse 39). This was victory number 2 – over the world. Finally, David overcame Goliath. This was victory number 3 – the devil. Yet, David regarded himself as but a servant.

After piloting their spacecraft on its 250,000 mile journey back to planet earth, James Irwin noted: *"As I was returning to earth, I realized that I was a servant not a celebrity. So I am here as God's servant on planet earth to share what I have experienced that others might know the glory of God."*

Have you that servant's heart, attitude and humility?

(c) DAVID THE STALKED

David, though anointed by God, is now separated from Saul's court and is considered an outlaw and a rebel. You say: *"What is God doing?"* He is removing the props from underneath David until David is brought to the place where he is leaning on God alone. It is all part of his preparation for the throne. He needed to learn to suffer in the wilderness, to learn not to trust men and how to trust the Lord. Do you see the activity of God in the life of David? The Lord is pulling up and out the props from underneath him. His position .... gone. His wife .... gone. His counsellor .... gone. His closest friend .... gone. His self-respect .... gone.

Are you in the same position? Are you in the process of having every crutch, every prop removed from your life? For some, it is represented by a broken romance. The person you felt was God's choice has vanished. For some, it has been the death of a dream. For some, it has been the loss of a job, the loss of friend. You say: *"What is God doing?"* He is bringing you to the place where you are leaning on Him alone. Do you know the words?

> *"We must trust Him wholly,*
> *All for us to do,*
> *They who trust Him wholly,*
> *Find Him wholly true."*

CHAPTER 11

2 Samuel

The year 1809 was a very good year. Of course, no one knew it at the time because every eye was on Napoleon, as he swept across Austria like a frenzied flame in a parched wheat field. Little else seemed to be significant. The dictator of France was the talk of all Europe. That same year, however, while war was being waged and history was being made, babies were being born in England and America. But who cared about babies and bottles and cribs and cradles when Austria was falling? Someone should have cared! For, in 1809 a great host of thinkers and statesmen drew their first breaths. William Gladstone was born in Liverpool. Alfred Tennyson began his life in Lincolnshire and in Hodgenville, Kentucky in a rugged log cabin owned by an illiterate labourer and his wife were heard the screams of their new-born son, Abraham Lincoln. All this and more happened in 1809. But nobody noticed. The destiny of the world was being shaped by Napoleon over in Austria. Or was it? The *"nobodies"* nobody noticed were in fact the genesis of a new era. It was their lives, brains, writings that would influence the destiny of the entire world.

The year 1000 B.C. was also a very good year. But not because of Saul, the Napoleon of that day. Although he was Israel's elected king, he had begun to crack under the weight of his role. Rashness, compromise and flagrant disobedience to God were the traits in Saul's life until, finally, Samuel confronted him informing him that God had rejected him as Israel's king. (See 1 Samuel 15:23 & 26) That year was special because while everyone was watching Saul's reign sink, in a secluded field in Bethlehem God was raising up a youth named David, a nobody nobody noticed, but someone who would change Israel's course forever. *"The Lord hath sought*

Him a man after His own heart" (1 Samuel 13:14). God had sought out a man, only a man, but what a man he was!

David was, after all, Israel's greatest king. More is written about David and by David than any other person, except the Lord Jesus. He appears constantly in the historical books; he wrote half the book of Psalms; he is mentioned by name in both the first and last chapters of the New Testament. Is it not fitting, therefore, that we have a whole book devoted to him? As we have noted the two books of Samuel are one book in the Hebrew Bible. The Hebrew scholars who centuries before the birth of Christ translated the old Hebrew Bible into Greek decided to divide Samuel into two books. That translation became what is known as the Septuagint version of the Bible. It was not a bad idea, for in that way we have a book entirely devoted to David – 2 Samuel.

2 Samuel begins with a poem and ends with a plague; it begins with deception and ends with devotion; it begins with war and ends with worship. David came to a kingdom divided by civil war and with its affairs in total confusion, both at home and abroad. Israel's ancient enemies triumphed all along the frontiers while tribal jealousies kept the Hebrews at loggerheads among themselves. So David subdued the foreign foes of Israel, united the tribes, cleared Jerusalem of the Jebusites and made it Israel's capital. He planned for the temple, led a great revival in religious affairs, and founded a deathless dynasty. No wonder there is so much about him in the Bible!

Now I want us to consider this book in the following way:

(1) THE FIRST YEARS OF DAVID'S REIGN - Chapters 1 to 9

The keyword is **Triumphs.** Upon the death of Saul, David is crowned King by the tribe of Judah. Saul's son, Ishbosheth, clung to the remnants of his father's tattered kingdom. Thus, for 7 years there existed a civil war between Judah and Israel, between the house of David and the house of Saul. Eventually, David was crowned king over all Israel. So, in this first section of the book, we see how, despite some initial opposition, David comes to be recognized as king by all the tribes of Israel. First of all we see David:

(a) As King Over Judah in Hebron: Chapters 1 to 4

1. David's Sorrow

How would you react if your greatest enemy was killed? A lesser saint would have rejoiced, but then David was a man after God's heart, a man who had a heart for God, someone whose heart was God's completely. David felt keenly the tragedy of Saul's sin. Of course, David's dear friend Jonathan was also dead. The sin of a disobedient father had brought judgment upon innocent people. By all natural codes of conduct, David should have flung his hat in the air there on the Judean hills, but he did not. Do you see how he speaks about Saul?

Look at 2 Samuel 1 verses 23 - 25: *"Saul and Jonathan were lovely and pleasant in their lives ... How are the mighty fallen"*. What a thing for David to say about a man who for years had used half his army to hunt him down in order to hang him up on some tree - and all without a cause. Is this not the love that covers a multitude of sins? The love that suffers long and is kind? The love that many waters cannot quench? Is this not the love of God shed abroad in the human heart? Do we know anything about such love?

Is it not interesting to notice that an Amalekite brought the news and claimed to be the one who finally took Saul's life? Had Saul obeyed the Lord in 1 Samuel 15 and slain all of the Amalekites, this would not have happened. Mark it down. *The sin we fail to slay is the one that eventually slays us.* (See Deuteronomy 25:17-19).

2. David's Song

David's lamentation, called the "Song of the Bow" (2 Samuel 1:18), is touching. The book of Proverbs says: *"Rejoice not when thine enemy falleth, and let not thine heart be glad when he stumbleth"* (Proverbs 24:17). David's lament reveals *his loyalty to his King* and *his love for his friend*. "How are the mighty fallen" is his theme. In

1 Samuel 10 verse 23, Saul "stood higher" than any other man, but now he had fallen lower than the enemy. No wonder Paul says: *"Let him that thinketh he standeth take heed lest he fall"* (1 Corinthians 10:12).

3. David's Struggles

David's march to the throne was a bloody one. (See 2 Samuel 3:1) The tribe of Judah had proclaimed David king at once, but the other tribes were not so sure. Who was this fellow David anyway? Was he not a fugitive from justice? Why should David be king? Thus the kingdom was divided between "the house of Saul" led by Ishbosheth, who was a helpless pawn in the hands of Abner, and the house of David. You see, each faction was contending for the kingdom.

There was civil war – and this conflict typifies what is going on between the *"flesh and the Spirit"* (Galatians 5:17). Indeed, Abner's actions were a revelation of life *"in the flesh"*.

He sought strength in himself: The Bible says: *"Abner made himself strong for the house of Saul"* (2 Samuel 3:6);

He fulfilled his own fleshly desires: for he had physical relationships with Saul's concubine;

He demonstrated his pride by not admitting his sin;

He displayed an uncontrolled temperament: (Chapter 3:8);

He acted out of wrong motivation: (Chapter 3:9).

Is all this not simply a picture of life lived in the flesh? Paul says: *"For the flesh lusteth against the Spirit, and the Spirit against the flesh: and these are contrary the one to the other"* (Galatians 5:17). Now, by the flesh, Paul does not mean *"the body"*. The human body is not sinful. It is neutral. If the Holy Spirit controls the body, then we walk in the Spirit, but if the flesh controls the body, then we walk in the lusts or desires of the flesh. You see, *the flesh stands for that part of man's nature, wherein his natural desires have free rein.* (See Romans 7:18) The Spirit and the flesh have different appetites and that is what creates the conflict. Do you know anything about this conflict? Every believer knows about it. At times, it is like a civil war within us. Oh, we love to hold up the tottering kingdom of self. If only we could keep this or that, or do this or that, at any cost. All the time this civil war goes on, the flesh wants the throne.

This conflict lasted for seven and a half years, but eventually Abner, now frustrated with Ishbosheth, comes to the elders of Israel and says: *"Ye sought for David in times past to be king over you: Now then do it"* (2 Samuel 3:17-18). So now we see, David:

(b) As King Over Israel in Jerusalem: Chapters 5 to 9

1. David is Crowned

Look at Chapter 5 verse 3. In Chapters 1 to 4, David is King over Judah in Hebron. Now he is crowned King over Israel in Jerusalem. All the elders came and anointed David as King.

Have you ever put the crown where it belongs? How many times have you been on the verge of making Christ King of your life? Of acknowledging His Lordship in every area of your life? But then you have put it off, saying: "I'll wait a little longer. I'll allow self on the throne just a little longer". Is the Lord saying to you this: "Now then do it"?

2. David is Conquering

"David took the strong hold of Zion: the same is the city of David" (Chapter 5:7). For hundreds of years, this had been the possession, a strong hold of the Canaanites (see Joshua 15:63 and Judges 1:8) and so confident were the present occupants, the Jebusites, that even the blind and lame could defend the city from David's little ragtag army. *"Nevertheless David took the strong hold of Zion."* There is now a new capital, Jerusalem, "the city of David".

3. David is Challenged

"But when the Philistines heard that they had anointed David king over Israel, all the Philistines came up" (Chapter 5:17). Is that not an interesting thing? An old enemy comes on the scene again. It is always that way. The moment you crown Christ Lord of every area of your life, get ready. The devil is going to make an attack. He will attack initially and he will attack continually. (See Chapter 5:18 & 22) As long as we are prepared to co-exist with sin and self, the devil is happy, but you crown Christ as Lord and spiritual warfare erupts and spiritual weapons are needed. We need to enquire of God – as David did in verse 19 - and we need to wait on God – as David did in verse 23.

4. David is Corrected

In Chapter 6, David decided to bring "The Ark of the Covenant" to Jerusalem. He was eager to make Jerusalem the religious as well as the political centre of national life. His motive was good, but his method was wrong. He was right in his intention, but wrong in his implementation. He had to learn the lesson that we must all learn - *that God's work must done by God's people in God's way.* You see the Word of God was very plain as to how the Ark was to be moved. It was to be carried by the Levites, particularly the Kohathites (see Numbers 4:15) who were the descendants of one of the three sons of Levi (Numbers 3:17). The Ark was to be covered (Numbers 4:5-6) and borne on their shoulders, by two poles inserted through four rings, one on each corner of the Ark (See Numbers 7:9). The Ark was not to be touched (Numbers 4:15). Nothing was said about placing the Ark on a new cart - that was man's way. On the shoulders of the Levites - that was God's way. Do you see what David had to learn? *That God's work must be done by God's people in God's way.* He had to learn the lesson that the Word of God must guide the work of God.

It is not sufficient to have a worthy cause and a proper spirit. *God's work must be done in God's way, that is according to God's Word.* Today we often hear the cliché: *"Well, surely the end justifies the means".* So in order to increase the crowd in the pew and the cash in the purse, many churches will do anything. There are gimmicks galore. Churches that feature weight-lifters, sword specialists, daffodil teas, sponsored this or that, anything to bring in the crowds or cash. Anything we introduce into our worship, work, or witness for which we have no Scripture, no *"Thus saith the Lord"*, must be abandoned by us. So David is corrected. Something else:

5. David is Consecrated

Can you picture the scene set out in 2 Samuel 7? The kingdom had been united. Jerusalem had been taken. The Philistines had been defeated. David sat in a beautiful new palace that was built for him by Hiram, King of Tyre (Chapter 5:11). He considered the goodness of God in giving him rest from his enemies (Chapter 7:1). He recalled the joy he and his kingdom had just enjoyed as the Ark was brought to its new home in Jerusalem (Chapter 6:17). Then the thought struck him: *"Here I sit in a luxurious home, while the Ark rests in that drab tent. God deserves better"*.

He begins to formulate a plan. David proposed to build a house for God. This was his holy resolve. You see here is a young man 30 or so years of age whose heart is full to overflowing with love to the Lord. When David thinks of all that God has done for him, he pours out his heart in adoring gratitude to the Lord. Later on in this passage, we find him sitting in the Lord's presence saying: *"Who am I, O Lord God? and what is my house, that Thou hast brought me hitherto?"* (Chapter 7:18)

Do you ever sit in the presence of the Lord and ponder His blessings to you? Can you not testify that God's love has surrounded you, God's grace has sustained you, God's hand has strengthened you? In the light of all that, are you prepared to say: *"Here am I, Lord. I gave myself unreservedly to You"*? Is it not the *"mercies of God"* that Paul uses as a basis for his appeal to the saints at Rome? He says: *"I beseech you ....by the mercies of God"* (Romans 12:1). Was it not this thought that motivated C.T. Studd to say: *"If Jesus Christ be God and died for me, then no sacrifice can be too great for me to make for Him"*? What have you rendered *"unto the Lord for all His benefits"* toward you? (Psalm 116:12)

Now, the Lord appreciated David's desire to build Him a house, but a man of war, a man with blood on his hands, could not build a house of peace. (See 1 Chronicles 28:6) Rather than David building a house for God, God said a wonderful thing to David: "I will build you a house". The Lord promised to build a house for David. **Prophetically**, this is known as the Davidic Covenant and it is important to notice that 5 promises were made to David and Israel:

(1) *A Promise of Residency*: "*May dwell in a place of their own*". (Chapter 7:10)

(2) *A Promise of Security:* "*Neither shall the children of wickedness afflict them any more*". (Chapter 7:10)

(3) *A Promise of Posterity:* "*I will set up thy seed after thee*". (Chapter 7:12)

This clearly has reference to David's physical descendants. David's line would always be the royal line.

(4) *A Promise of Authority:* "*I will stablish the throne of his kingdom for ever*". (Chapter 7:13) David's throne was to be established forever.

(5) *A Promise of Perpetuity:* "*Thine house ... shall be established for ever*". (Chapter 7:16)

The ultimate fulfilment of these promises is in Jesus Christ. (See Luke 3:31) Do you recall the message of the angel to Mary? "*And the Lord God shall give unto Him (Christ) the throne of His father David*" (Luke 1:32). It is our conviction that Christ will fulfil this Davidic Covenant when He sits on David's throne and rules during the Millennial Kingdom.

Prophetically, here is God's future programme for Israel, but **practically** *is this not what God does for us?* He does "*exceeding abundantly above all that we ask or think*" (Ephesians 3:20). Do you know something? It is impossible to out-give God.

(2) THE FURTHER YEARS OF DAVID'S REIGN - Chapters 10 to 19

The key word is **Troubles**. This marks a dreadful turning point in the life of David. His early life, chequered as it was, is characterized by triumphs, but his remaining years will be marked by troubles. Now what was it that brought about this turning point in David's life? There were:

(a) TROUBLES IN THE FAMILY

David sinned. Did you ever think about:

1. The Cause of David's Sin

2 Samuel 11 verse 1 records: *"At the time when kings go forth to battle ... David tarried still at Jerusalem"*. Note David's **idleness**! David was now about fifty years old. He had been on the throne approximately twenty years. It was the springtime of the year, March or April. Joab was on the battlefield; David was in the city. Someone has said: *"While Joab laid siege against Rabbah, Satan laid siege against David"*. Can you see him as he rises from his bed? He is proud, prosperous and the most powerful potentate in that part of the world. David can have anything he wants. Then he sees beautiful Bathsheba. The Hebrew conveys the idea that she was physically attractive beyond description – and David fell.

Now, he did not fall suddenly. Some chinks had already begun to form in his spiritual armour. Go back to 2 Samuel 5 verse 13. What do you find there? David's **indulgence**! He increased the number of his wives and concubines. This was in direct violation of God's commands. In Deuteronomy 17 and verse 17, we read that God's king was not to multiply wives to himself. As David's harem grew, so did his lust. For years, David had been feeding his fleshly appetite, thus paving the way for adultery with Bathsheba. This king who took another man's wife already had a harem full of women. Do know one of the lies of the devil? If you satisfy your physical drives, they will be abated. No. They will increase. Are you gratifying the flesh? Consider 2 Timothy 2 verse 22: *"Flee* *also youthful lusts"*. Are you playing with sin in your thought life? What about pornography on the television and the internet? Do you know the chorus: "Oh be careful little eyes what you see"?

David proceeds to break five of the Ten Commandments. He covets his neighbour's wife; he bears false witness against her husband; he steals his wife; he commits adultery with her, and finally he arranges the murder of her husband. Bathsheba becomes pregnant. David seeks to cover it. The baby dies and David takes Bathsheba into the palace as his wife. However, David has no peace of mind. He carries around unconfessed, unforgiven sin - and a year later God sends Nathan to confront David with his sin, and there is:

2. The Confession of David's Sin

Look at 2 Samuel 12. The prophet tells David the story of the traveller who comes to a rich man – and the rich man takes from a poor man his little lamb and kills it to feed the traveller. David is outraged at the story, but then Nathan applies it to the King: *"Thou art the man"*. "You are the man who stole the poor man's lamb!" In response, David confesses: *"I have sinned against the Lord"* (verse 13). Benjamin Franklin once stated: "How few there are who have courage enough to own their faults and resolution enough to mend them".

What do you do when you fail? Do you conceal your sin or do you confess your sin? David writes Psalm 32 and Psalm 51 and in that latter Psalm says: *"Against Thee, Thee only, have I sinned"* (verse 4). It is not my brother or my sister, but it is me, O Lord, standing in the need of pardon, power and purity. There is one thing that God will not accept for sin and it is an alibi. The Bible says: *"If we confess our sins, He is faithful and just to forgive us our sins, and to cleanse us from all unrighteousness"* (1 John 1:9). Have you confessed your sin as a believer? Do you keep short accounts with the Lord?

Don't miss:

3. The Consequence of David's Sin

Years ago, an old country preacher said: *"Sin will take you further than you want to go; sin will keep you longer than you want to stay, and sin will cost you more than you want to pay"*. There's a lot of wisdom in that - and I believe David would say "Amen" to that statement. Sin from start to finish is a costly business and that is especially so with sexual sin. Forgiveness is no guarantee that we shall escape the consequences of sin. Do you know what David said when he heard the story of the little lamb? *"He shall restore the lamb fourfold"* (Chapter 12:6). Do you know something? David paid fourfold for his sin:

(1) *The little baby died:* (Chapter 12:15-23)

(2) *Amnon, one of David's sons, violated or raped Tamar, one of David's daughters:* (Chapter 13:14)

(3) *Amnon was slain by Absalom:* (Chapter 13:23-29)

(4) *Absalom was slain:* (Chapter 18:9-15)

David paid fourfold for his sin. Indeed, the whole subsequent history of David is a record of the consequences resulting from his sin. You see, though God forgave him, David had trouble to the end of his life. Now this did not mean that David lived under a cloud. This did not mean that he had no more joy. He did pray: *"Restore unto me the joy of Thy salvation"* (Psalm 51:12). God answered his prayer. David wrote many songs after this incident and he went out and won many victories, but how better it would have been if he never had yielded. Oh, there is family forgiveness, for God promises to forgive our sins: *"He is faithful and just to forgive us"* (1 John 1:9). However, God is also faithful and just to reap what we sow. In His *Grace,* He can forgive our sins, but in His *Government* He permits us to suffer the consequences.

Trevor Knight puts it perfectly when he says: "When we have done with sin, sin has not done with us". But then there was:

(b) TROUBLES IN THE COUNTRY

As David continues to reap the sad harvest of his sins, there was:

1. The Rebellion of the Prince

David's life becomes chaotic. He had committed adultery with Bathsheba, now rape invades his own household. His son Amnon commits a dreadful sin against his half-sister Tamar, and David is simply "very wroth". (Chapter 13:21) Was the memory of his own sins checking him, controlling him? Absalom had a dual purpose in mind when he found out what Amnon had done. He wanted to avenge Tamar by killing Amnon, but at the same time he would be removing the obvious heir to the throne. (See Chapter 3:2) He murdered Amnon and fled from his father, his home and his country. (See Chapter 13:37)

After three years, David permitted Absalom to return from exile, but he refused to see his son for a further two years. (See Chapter 14:24, 28 & 33) Even when they were reconciled, the difficulties between father and son were far from over. Absalom caused untold distress in Israel and led a rebellion against his father.

Despite all these problems, David persisted in his love for Absalom so that when his son fell in battle, King David mourned with inconsolable grief: *"O my son Absalom, my son, my son Absalom! would God I had died for thee, O Absalom, my son, my son!"* (Chapter 18:33).

2. The Reactions of the People

Consider 2 Samuel 15 verse 13 to Chapter 16 verse 23. While David was reigning, his real enemies would not dare to oppose him, but Absalom's revolt gave them what appeared to be a wonderful opportunity to resist the king and do so successfully. It was a time of sifting the true from the false. Ittai was loyal to the king. The two priests, Zadok and Abiathar, also started to follow their king, but David sent them back to the city. Hushai was also sent back to the city to pose as an ally of Absalom. His counsel could change that of Ahithophel. Is it not a sad picture as David and his small army flee the city and cross the Kidron River? The sweet Psalmist of Israel betrayed! Ziba lied to David about Mephibosheth. Shimei openly showed his hatred for David and the "Judas" in David's situation was his former friend Ahithophel. (See Psalm 55:12-13)

What do you do when your world is falling apart? David's world was falling apart. The walls of David's life were crumbling around him, but David's eye was upon his God. He cries: *"But Thou, O Lord, art a shield for me; my glory, and the lifter up of mine head"* (Psalm 3:3). He discovered that true security and true serenity and true sufficiency are only found in God.

> *"Be not dismayed, what'er betide,*
> *God will take care of you,*
> *Beneath His wings of love abide,*
> *God will take care of you.*
>
> *No matter what may be the test,*
> *God will take care of you,*
> *Lean, weary one, upon His breast,*
> *God will take care of you."*

3. The Reckoning of the Lord

This rebellion was part of the price that David paid for his sin, but God also overruled the events so as to purge David's kingdom and separate the loyal from the disloyal. A day of reckoning finally arrived. Sometimes God's judgments fall swiftly, while at other times He waits and acts slowly. Do you see here that:

1. Ahithophel dies: (Chapter 17:23)

2. Absalom dies: (Chapter 18:1 to Chapter 19:15)

3. Shimei is pardoned: (Chapter 19:16-23, but note 1 Kings 2:36-46)

4. Ziba and Mephibosheth are reconciled: (Chapter 19:24-30)

5. Barzillai is rewarded: (Chapter 19:31-39)

This entire episode of David's rejection and return certainly illustrates the attitudes people today have toward Christ. There are the loyal few who stand by their absent King, and there are the selfish majority who prefer to rebel. But what will happen when the King comes back? What are we, His followers, doing to hasten His return? (See 2 Peter 3:12)

(3) THE FINAL YEARS OF DAVID'S REIGN - Chapters 20 to 24

The keyword is **Testimonies**. Look at:

(a) THE WITNESS OF THE KING: Chapter 22

Here David writes a song full of gratitude and hope unto the Lord. While David was not without problems in his latter days, he was not without the Lord.

(b) THE WITNESS TO THE KING: Chapter 23

Here is recorded for us the names, deeds and exploits of David's mighty men.

(c) THE WITNESS AGAINST THE KING: Chapter 24

At the end of his life, David is tempted by Satan to conduct a census of Israel's fighting men. (See 1 Chronicles 21:1) What lay behind David's desire for a national census? Probably it was pride. He had won a number of great victories (See 1 Chronicles 18 to 20) and perhaps he wanted to bask in the glory of success.

There is an interesting series of contrasts between this sin and his sin with Bathsheba:

(1) This was a sin of the spirit (pride), while the other was a sin of the flesh (adultery).

(2) Here David acted with deliberate persistence, while his sin with Bathsheba came as the result of the sudden overwhelming desires of the flesh.

(3) This sin involved the nation, and 70,000 people died, his other sin was a family matter, with 4 people dying.

(4) Yet, in both sins, God gave David time to repent.

The terrible plague that decimated the nation was halted when David took the place of mediator and stood between the avenging angel and the suffering people. This takes place at Araunah's threshing floor. David sees this threshing floor as an ideal place to build the temple of God. In an act of worship, David buys the place, and it was there that later Solomon built the temple. (See 2 Chronicles 3:1)

There is a lovely lesson here. God was able to turn the curse into a blessing. It is interesting to note that Solomon, born to Bathsheba who had been involved in David's adultery, became the next king and actually built the temple on the piece of ground associated with David's greater sin of numbering the people.

Is God's providence not amazing? Certainly we ought not to *"do evil, that good may come"* (Romans 3:8), but we can rest in the confidence that *"all things work together for good to them that love God"* (Romans 8:28). God can turn the curse into a blessing. God can forgive and bring blessing.

Let us therefore like David put ourselves *"into the hand of the Lord; for His mercies are great"* (2 Samuel 24:14).

CHAPTER 12

1 Kings

Steve Wagers tells of a popular secular magazine in the 1990s which did an article on the subject of success. The article: *"The Best of the New Generation"* dealt with successful people under the age of 40 who were being used to impact and change America. They were recognized for things like taking risks, having initiative or being creative and persistent. Nothing was mentioned about morals, integrity, Biblical values or character. It revealed that success in our society does not involve the condition of the heart.

1 and 2 Kings is a stark reminder that while it is possible to do a right thing in the wrong way, it is impossible to do a wrong thing in the right way. Right is right, wrong is wrong, because God is God. While character may not matter to society, it does matter to the supreme, sovereign Lord.

The First book of Kings may be described as: *"The rise and fall of the nation of Israel"*. The two books of Kings, like the books of Samuel, were originally one book. Together they cover a period of Israel's history from the accession of King Solomon in 970 B.C. to the final exile of the people of Judah to the land of Babylon in 586 B.C.

As we come to 1 Kings, there are a few things needed by way of introduction. Firstly there is;

1. A Difficulty we need to Identify

The difficulty stems from the arrangement of the Old Testament books. The way our Old Testament books are arranged is not chronological, and that largely accounts for the difficulty here.

If, for example, we were to read the Bible straight through, we would come to the history of Esther before that of Job - yet Job lived more than 1,000 years before Esther. We come to the end of Judah's captivity in Daniel, and yet in the next book in our Bible, Hosea, neither Israel nor Judah has been carried into captivity by anyone yet. So do you see the difficulty? If we do not understand the arrangement of the Old Testament books, we will inevitably end up with a confused and hazy view of Old Testament history. Then there is:

2. A Division we need to Specify

The book of 2 Samuel and the early part of 1 Kings describe the powerful position of Israel on the world stage, but most of the book of Kings is concerned with the nation's downfall. Under David and Solomon the nation was eventually united and the empire stretched from Egypt to the Euphrates. But, from Solomon's time onwards, they headed downhill, through civil war and a divided kingdom to exile in a foreign land. After the death of Solomon the nation was divided in two. The two parts were:

(a) The Northern Kingdom

The headquarters were first at Shechem then at Samaria. This northern kingdom was composed of 10 of the 12 tribes. These 10 tribes were eventually taken away into captivity by Assyria. They never returned.

(b) The Southern Kingdom

The headquarters were at Jerusalem and this kingdom was composed of two of the twelve tribes, namely Judah and "little Benjamin" (1 Kings 12:21). These two tribes were taken away captive by Babylon and ultimately returned to Jerusalem.

The Northern Kingdom was known by the name "Israel", the Southern Kingdom was known by the name "Judah", it being the larger tribe of the two. Then there are:

3. Details we need to Clarify

If a number of facts are kept in mind, then the accounts of the Divided Kingdom as given in Kings and Chronicles will become plain.

1. The histories of the two kingdoms are given parallel with one another from 1 Kings 12 to 2 Kings 17, when Israel is taken captive.

2. The history of Judah alone is continued from 2 Kings 18 to Chapter 25.

3. The history of Israel - that is the ten tribes - is not given at all in the books of 1 and 2 Chronicles.

4. The great period from the death of Solomon to the captivity of Judah is recorded for us from three distinct points of view:

(a) The Royal point of view in the books of Kings;
(b) The Priestly point of view in the books of Chronicles;
(c) The Prophetic point of view in the books of the Prophets.

If these facts are remembered, and we read the books of Kings and Chronicles in the light of them, the Old Testament will become a new book to us.

1 Kings falls into 2 main sections:

1. The United Kingdom - Chapters 1 to 11
2. The Divided Kingdom - Chapters 12 to 22

However, I want to look at this book slightly different from that and notice:

(1) AN ERA OF ROYAL HISTORY: Chapters 1 to 11

These chapters tell the story of the united people of God before the division under Rehoboam of Judah and Jeroboam of Israel. Here there is brought before Israel:

(a) David: Their Finest King

The books of Kings open with King David and end with the King of Babylon. They open with the building of the temple and end with the burning of the temple. They open with David's first successor to the throne, Solomon, and end with one of his last successors to the throne, Jehoiachin. Before that happens, however, an important transition takes place that should have prepared the nation for future days of greatness. It was a transition of a godly king, David, to a great king, Solomon. 1 Kings opens as David lay on his deathbed. *"Now king David was old and stricken in years; and they covered him with clothes but he gat no heat"* (1 Kings 1:1). Can you identify with him? As you get older, you get colder.

King David is old. Adonijah assumes that he will be King, but the Lord has revealed that Solomon is His choice. (See 1 Chronicles 28:5) *"It was his from the Lord"* (1 Kings 2:15). So Solomon was crowned King before David died. (See Chapter 1:39) Indeed David charges him in Chapter 2 verses 1 to 9.

I cannot help but believe that part of David's charge was a reference to his own past mistakes. It is as if David is saying to his son: *"Son, don't make the mistake that I made by failing to always follow God. It was when I had a lapse in my walk that I made the biggest mistake of my life. Don't you do the same. If you follow God, you will succeed and prosper. Take it from me, the voice of experience."* Is it not interesting that David emphasized the spiritual before the political?

I wonder, what way will your children remember you? Will they remember you for your political passion or your spiritual power? Will they remember you as someone who would die for their country, but would not live for their Christ?

So passes from the scene David their Finest King and then:

(b) Solomon: Their Famous King

Solomon steps onto the stage of public history. Now he was very young when he came to the throne. His word is that he was *"but a little child"* (1 Kings 3:7). Eusebius says he was twelve. Josephus says he was fifteen. We may safely say that he was not more than twenty. *"Then sat Solomon upon the throne of David his father; and his kingdom was established greatly"* (Chapter 2:12).

The early years of Solomon's reign have been described as *"The Golden Age of Israel".* Solomon's reign began in a blaze of glory. Some of the greatest years of Israel's existence were during the reign of King Solomon. We can think of:

1. His Wisdom

"And God gave Solomon wisdom and understanding exceeding much, and largeness of heart, even as the sand that is on the sea shore. And Solomon's wisdom excelled the wisdom of all the children of the east country, and all the wisdom of Egypt. For he was wiser than all men ….. And there came of all people to hear the wisdom of Solomon, from all kings of the earth, which had heard of his wisdom." (Chapter 4:29-34)

When the Lord gave Solomon the privilege of asking for anything he wanted, he did not ask for wealth. He did not ask to be a warrior. He asked for wisdom and an understanding heart. (Chapter 3:9) God answered his prayer.

Is it not wonderful that we have access to the throne of Him who is *"greater than Solomon"* (Matthew 12:42) and who promises to give *"wisdom"* and meet every need.

Do you see here that God equips us for our calling? God made Solomon king and God supplied all that he needed to serve acceptably.

2. His Wealth

"And Solomon had forty thousand stalls of horses for his chariots, and twelve thousand horsemen" (Chapter 4:26). The Queen of Sheba testified: *"I believed not the words, until I came, and mine eyes had seen it: and, behold, the half was not told me: thy wisdom and prosperity exceedeth the fame which I heard"* (Chapter 10:7).

The immensity of Solomon's wealth is beyond description, but we can give it a try. Look at Chapter 10 verse 14: *"The weight of gold that came to Solomon in one year was six hundred threescore and six talents of gold"*. Do you know what that is worth? About $304 million in today's money. Do you think you could manage on that? But that is only the gold! The silver was so abundant that it was not even counted. (See Chapter 10:21) So we could safely round up $304 million to about $500 million a year. Solomon was the Bill Gates of his day. If ever there was a subject Solomon knew, it was money. He secured it, saved it, spent it, studied it, and shared it. It is possible for a person to enjoy material prosperity and still be spiritual, as in the case of Abraham, but most people cannot handle such wealth. How true is the saying: *"It takes a steady hand to carry a full cup!"*

Has God endowed you with wealth? Well, do you realise that you are only a steward of God's money? Do you see the house you have? Do you see the job you do? Do you see the money you make? Do you see the children you enjoy? Do you see the spiritual gift you exercise? Where does it all come from? The Lord! David, when speaking of preparing for the temple, said: *"For all things come of Thee, and of Thine own have we given Thee"* (1 Chronicles 29:14).

3. His Work

One of Solomon's greatest claims to fame and the greatest of his works was the building of the temple. Solomon finished the task that his father was not given permission to build.

It is interesting that the New Testament does not give us as much instruction as to the meaning of the temple as it does about the tabernacle. Some see the tabernacle as picture of Christ in His humility on the earth and the temple as a type of His present ministry in glory. It is too bad that the Jews trusted in the presence of their temple instead of in the promises of their Lord for, in less than 500 years, this temple was destroyed. The Jews then went into captivity for their sins.

Now, can see you something of the greatness of Solomon? Can you also see:

4. His Worship

At the dedication of the temple, King Solomon led the congregation in prayer and worship. What a prayer it was, for here Solomon acknowledged:

The Uniqueness of God: "_Lord God of Israel, there is no God like Thee_" (Chapter 8:23);
The Faithfulness of God: "_Who hast kept with Thy servant David my father that Thou promisedst him_" (Chapter 8:24);
The Greatness of God: "_Behold, the heaven and heaven of heavens cannot contain Thee_" (Chapter 8:27).

Do you ever hear anyone praying like that now? Prayers in a Christian assembly are often nothing more than coming to the Lord with a "_shopping list_" mentality, making one request after another without ever pausing to address the Lord in worship, praise and blessing. Do you recall the pattern the Lord Jesus gives us? "_After this manner therefore pray ye: Our Father which art in heaven, Hallowed be Thy name_" (Matthew 6:9). You see, true prayer begins by giving God His proper place. How do you approach God in prayer?

Dr. J. K. McClure tells about going to Lincoln Park in Chicago. As he sat there on a park bench he saw a splendid gentleman approach the statue of Abraham Lincoln. For a moment this man stood gazing into that rugged face so full of strength and tenderness, so marked with the deep lines of care. Then he reached up and removed his hat and allowed his white hair to be blown in the wind as he respectfully stood before the statue of this courageous statesman, Meanwhile, there was another man sitting at the base of this same statute, writing obscene verses and staining it with tobacco juice. _You see, the difference between these two men was great - and this story illustrates how different people approach God_. Some approach Him with reverence and respect. Others have no apparent regard for God at all. How do you approach God? As

Solomon did, do you appreciate Who it is that you are addressing?

When we think of Solomon we also think of:

5. His Words

"And he spake three thousand proverbs: and his songs were a thousand and five" (Chapter 4:32). According to Jewish tradition, Solomon wrote the *Song of Solomon* in his early years, expressing a young man's love. He wrote the book of *Proverbs* during his middle age years, revealing a mature wisdom. But, he wrote the book of *Ecclesiastes* in his declining, latter years, disclosing an old man's sorrow. Here is the record of Solomon's regret for his grave moral lapses: *"But king Solomon loved many strange women"* (Chapter 11:1). You see, while the Song of Solomon is a book of **sweet romance** and Proverbs is a book of **sacred regulations,** Ecclesiastes is a book of **sad retrospect.** Here is an old man who has come to the end of life having lived a wasted life and he preaches a sermon. Yet his wisdom, wealth, work and words define one of the greatest reigns of Israel's history. Those were years of greatness. But, to repeat the words of the Lord Jesus: *"A greater than Solomon is here"* (Matthew 12: 42).

The Lord Jesus is Greater than Solomon in Wisdom:

Solomon may have been wise, but Christ created everything Solomon knew about.

The Lord Jesus is Greater than Solomon in Wealth:

He can meet every need, physical, spiritual and material.

The Lord Jesus is Greater than Solomon in Work:

Solomon built houses of wood and stone, but Christ is building a household of faith.

The Lord Jesus is Greater than Solomon in Worship:

Solomon may have known how to go to the temple to make a sacrifice, but Christ knows how to take lost sinners and redeem them by the blood of His sacrifice.

The Lord Jesus is Greater than Solomon in Words:

Solomon spoke thousands of proverbs, but *"Never man spake like this man"* (John 7:46).

There is no-one like Christ! *"Behold a greater than Solomon is here!"*

Solomon's reign began in a blaze of glory, but it ended with a burden of grief.

There is an interesting comparison between 2 Samuel 11 and 1 Kings 11. In the first of these two chapters, *we have David's sinful decision.* In the second, *we have Solomon's spiritual decline.* Do you see:

6. His Weakness

Look at Chapter 11 verses 1 to 3. He had seven hundred wives and three hundred concubines. A thousand women! Can you imagine how it was when all the mothers-in-law came round to the palace at the weekend? The same writer who earlier rejoiced that *"Solomon loved the Lord"* (Chapter 3:3), now says: *"Solomon loved many strange (or foreign) women"* (Chapter 11:1). Like so many people, he had wisdom for everybody else, but not much for himself. His weakness was women. This was not just for sensual pleasure, but also for political power. In other words, he married these women to strengthen his kingdom. This was in direct violation of the law of God which said: *"Neither shalt thou make marriages with them"* (Deuteronomy 7:3) and: *"Neither shall he (the king) multiply wives to himself"* (Deuteronomy 17:17).

A person who does not believe, whether he be a religionist, a moralist, or an atheist, has no part with the child of God. Such a person is governed by different principles, passions and practices. This rules out forever the unequal yoke in marriage, in business, or in any other life-binding contract. God's Word is clear: *"Be ye not unequally yoked together with unbelievers"* (2 Corinthians 6:14). Are you embarking on a path forbidden by the Lord?

There was something else about Solomon:

7. His Worldliness

Look at Chapter 11 verse 4. His wives *"turned away his heart after other gods"*. The Lord wanted *"integrity of heart"* (Chapter 9:4) which means a united heart, single to the glory of God. But, Solomon had a divided heart, for he loved the world as he tried to serve the Lord. What a tragedy that the man who built the temple to the only true and living God should begin to worship at heathen altars. The wisest of all men had become the greatest of all fools. God was angry and the kingdom was going to be rent from Solomon's family, except for Judah. Thus Chapter 11 closes with the death of Solomon and that ends the first part of this book.

(2) AN ERA OF NATIONAL TRAGEDY - Chapters 12-22

These Chapters record *"the beginning of the end"*. With the death of Solomon, the nation's glory begins to fade. The writer, probably Jeremiah, presents us with:

(a) A DIVIDED NATION

Solomon reigned for 40 years. (See Chapter 11:42) Upon his death, civil unrest began to rise within the nation. Rehoboam, his son, threatened to levy heavier burdens upon the people. Had Rehoboam listened to the wisdom of the old leaders, he would have won the hearts of the people, but he was unwilling to be a servant to the people. The way to be a ruler is to be a servant! (See Mark 10:42-45) Rehoboam was a fool, and because of his foolish decisions, the once united kingdom was rent in two.

Look at Chapter 12 verses 16 to 19. So, what have we now?

1. The Northern Kingdom: the 10 tribes of Israel, with the capital in

Samaria.

2. The Southern Kingdom: the tribes of Judah and Benjamin, with the capital in Jerusalem.

The Northern Kingdom of Israel had 19 kings - and they were all bad. The Southern Kingdom had 19 kings and 1 Queen - some were good but most were bad.

It is interesting to see how the writer covers the events in the kingdoms of Judah and Israel simultaneously. One moment you could be reading about the king of Judah and the next moment you are reading about a king of Israel! These years of war and peace are marked by all the ups and downs to be expected when a wise king is followed by a weak king or by a wicked king or by a wishful king. Round and round the cycle goes, triumph and tragedy, victory and defeat, revival and relapse, glory and shame.

The nation is divided because of sin. Sin had taken what God had united and blessed and divided it and cursed it. God created order, unity, and peace but man created disorder, disunity and disturbance. The very same thing can happen in the local assembly. Sin and Satan can take what God has united – and they divide it and destroy it.

(b) A DEFILED NATION

This is what Israel, the Northern Kingdom, was. Note what Jeroboam instituted:

1. A New Object of Worship:

Afraid that the people of his kingdom would go up to Jerusalem for the annual feasts, he repeated Aaron's sin of Exodus 32 and made calves of gold and proclaimed: *"Behold thy gods, O Israel"* (Chapter 12:28).

2. A New Centre of Worship:

These golden calves were placed in Bethel – the extreme south - and Dan – the extreme north - (See Chapter 12:29), but Jerusalem was the place where God had chosen to place His name. (See Deuteronomy 12:11)

3. A New Order of Worship:

Jeroboam took those who were not of the tribe of Levi and placed them into the office of the priesthood. (See Chapter 12:31)

Twenty-one times during this period we read concerning the northern kings words like these: *"For he walked in all the way of Jeroboam the son of Nebat, and in his sin wherewith he made Israel to sin, to provoke the Lord God of Israel to anger with their vanities"* (See Chapter 16:26). Jeroboam's name became a synonym for all that is evil. He set God aside, then the subsequent kings set God aside - and God set them aside. Indeed this book presents us with not only a Divided Nation and a Defiled Nation, but:

(c) A DOOMED NATION

The Word of God says: *"Righteousness exalteth a nation: but sin is a reproach to any people"* (Proverbs 14:34). Remember, in the North all the kings were bad, in the South some were good but most were bad. When godly kings were ruling, God blessed His people, when ungodly men reigned, God sent judgment and defeat. Ultimately, both kingdoms were carried into captivity because of their sin.

In 722 B.C. Assyria came and captured Samaria and took the Northern Kingdom into captivity.
In 605, 597 and 586 B.C. Babylon came and captured Jerusalem and took the Southern Kingdom into captivity.

The temple was destroyed, the city was burned, the Hebrew monarchy had come to an end, the period of the kings was over and *"the times of the Gentiles"* had begun. From that day to this day Jerusalem has almost been entirely under Gentile control, and will remain so until the Lord Jesus comes to rule and reign.

(3) AN ERA OF SPIRITUAL MINISTRY - Chapters 17-22

We need to remember that when we are considering the Kings of Judah and Israel, the ministries of many of the prophets fall within this period. One such prophet was Elijah who ministered to the Northern Kingdom. Elijah appears on the stage of history during the reign of Israel's most wicked king. His name was Ahab (Chapter 16:30-33) and he hitched his wagon to a star - and what a dreadful star she was! As if all his other sins were not bad enough, he crowned them all by marrying Jezebel (See Deuteronomy 7:1-3). She was a pagan princess, who introduced the filthy cult of Baal worship into Israel, and she became the real power behind the throne. Satan has always sought to reverse God's order that the man is the head of the woman, that the woman is the heart of the man and that the children are the hub of the family.

It was at this time that Elijah appeared, God's prophet to challenge the apostasy of the nation. Keep in mind that the prophet had a dual role. He was not simply a *"fore-teller"* - he was also a *"forth-teller"* who announced God's judgment and exposed the sins of the people. Such a man was Elijah, *"a man subject to like passions as we are"* (James 5:17) yet a man with great courage and faith. E. A. Johnston says: *"But God has His 'man of the hour,' the prophet Elijah. Elijah was a bolt of fire God let loose upon wicked Ahab and idolatrous Israel".*

It is a principle with God that He never leaves Himself without a witness. Indeed the more degenerate the times, the more definite the testimony.

We could divide Elijah's ministry into two chapters and those are suggested by two little phrases that are found in relation to him. First of all we see:

(a) Elijah's Private Ministry: "Hide thyself".

Look at Chapter 17 verse 3. Having delivered his message to apostate Ahab, Elijah (whose name means: *"Jehovah is my God"*) now retires from public ministry for three years (see Luke 4:25) and during this time the Lord trains him, refines him, provides for him and gets him ready for public service.

"Hide thyself!"

"But Lord, I'm a prophet. I'm a palace man, I'm out here in public proclaiming Your Word. You seem to forget, Lord, I'm called to preach."

"No, not this time, Elijah, hide thyself."

The Hebrew expression suggests the idea of concealment. Here, in solitude, Elijah could wait on God, be alone with God, and talk to God.

Do you ever realise that ever before there can be a public ministry, there has to be a private ministry? Some believers are far too anxious to get onto the public stage. Moses spent one third of his life at the backside of the desert, Paul spent three years in Arabia (see Galatians 1:17-18) and the Lord Jesus Himself spent 30 years in obscurity before 3 years of ministry.

John Welch, the companion of John Knox, *"hid himself"* for he thought the day ill-spent if he did not spend 8 to 10 hours in close communion with the Lord. David Brainerd *"hid himself"* in the woods of North America. Christmas Evans *"hid himself"* in the long and lonely journeys amidst the hills of Wales.

Do you realise that if you would 'do much' for God you must 'be much' with God? Do you know the value of the hidden life? The most important part of our lives is the part that only God sees. He knows if we are real, if we are honest, if we are transparent.

(b) Elijah's Public Ministry: "Show thyself".

Look at Chapter 18 verse 1. *"Hide thyself"* was now to give way to *"show thyself"*. His private ministry was over and his public ministry was about to begin. Having been trained in private, the prophet can now be trusted in public. Do you recall what the apex of his ministry was? It was Mount Carmel. It was the showdown of the century! The competition between Ahab's god, Baal, and Elijah's God, Jehovah. What a challenge Elijah laid before the nation: *"The God that answereth by fire, let him be God"* (Chapter 18:24). The pagan prophets could not refuse Elijah's request because they said that Baal was the sun god. They tried to get the fire to come down, but they could not do so. What sarcasm Elijah uttered on these prophets! Then he repaired the altar of the Lord. Has the altar broken down in our home? Then he took the 12 stones to represent the oneness of the nation. It is only when we are united that the fire will fall. Then the fire fell.

Elijah prayed, and the rain stopped for 3½ years. He prayed again, and the "heaven gave rain" (James 5:18). He called down fire from Heaven and then went to Heaven in a ball of fire.

Elijah was not superhuman, but he obeyed, followed and served a God who is supernatural.

What we do with God in private is far more important than what He does for us in public. *Our hidden life prepares us for our public life.* Unless we are willing to go through the disciplines of the dry brook, the depleted barrel and the dead boy, we will never know the victories of Carmel.

Vance Havner says:

"Today, we do not need to ask: 'Where is the Lord God of Elijah?' But, what we need to ask is: 'Where are the Elijahs of the Lord God?'"

CHAPTER 13

2 Kings

Our journey through the Old Testament has shown us that we can divide it into 4 equal parts of roughly 500 years each.

1. From 2000 to 1500 B.C. - Israel (though they were not a nation at time) was led by **Patriarchs** - Abraham, Isaac, Jacob and Joseph.

2. From 1500 to 1000 B.C. - they were led by **Prophets:** from Moses to Samuel.

3. From 1000 B.C. to 500 B.C. - they were led by **Princes** or kings: from Saul and onwards.

4. From 500 B.C. and leading up to the time of Christ - they were led by **Priests:** from Joshua a priest who returned to Judah from exile under Zerubbabel's rule to Caiaphas in the time of Christ.

Now, we are looking at the third period when Israel were led by Princes or Kings. The reign of Solomon had a profound effect upon the nation of Israel. His rise to power meant prosperity, his fall opened the way for a major deterioration in the spiritual and moral life of the people. How far the nation had fallen under the reign of Solomon can be seen from the fact that only a short time after his death Jeroboam could introduce the worship of golden calves without creating a public outcry. The nation had divided. There was the Northern Kingdom with 10 tribes and the Southern Kingdom with 2 tribes.

The Northern Kingdom existed for just a little over 200 years from 930 B.C. to 722 B.C. and all of its kings were evil.

The Southern Kingdom, Judah, existed much longer - almost 350 years-and most of its kings were bad, but some were good.

At the close of the Second Book of Kings, the ten tribes of Israel are in exile in Assyria and the two tribes of Judah – Judah and Benjamin - are in exile in Babylon. Someone has said: *"It lay in the plan of divine providence to abandon them to oppression, to lead them to repentance through the school of misery."*

For centuries, Israel had been a theocracy, that is government was invested in God. There had been no visible head for the nation, though God had spoken through various men raised up from all walks of life, a Moses, a Joshua, a Gideon, a Samuel, a prophet, a priest and a king. But like anything else in which man has a part, the theocratic form of government failed. So God gave Israel a king. The two Books of Kings record the long, dismal failure of the monarchy as it was tried and tested over more than 500 years.

It is interesting to notice the contrast between 1 and 2 Kings:

1 Kings begins with the kingdom established in glory.
2 Kings ends with a kingdom divided in shame.

1 Kings begins with bright prospects for obedience (Chapter 3:3).
2 Kings ends with tragic judgments for disobedience (Chapter 17:8).

1 Kings begins with the dazzling splendour of the temple.
2 Kings ends with the smouldering ruins of the temple.

1 Kings opens with the translation of Elijah to Heaven.
2 Kings ends with the transportation of the Jews to Babylon.

1 Kings begins with Solomon in all his glory.
2 Kings ends with Zedekiah, broken, blinded and banished, bruised under the heel of a foreign, invading power.

We cannot read 2 Kings without thinking of Solomon's proverb: *"The way of transgressors is hard"* (Proverbs 13:15). Paul's word:

"The wages of sin is death" (Romans 6:23) is here demonstrated on a national scale.

When we look at the structure of this book, we discover that the first 10 chapters are wholly occupied with the northern kingdom, Israel, and here the ministry of Elisha to the Northern Kingdom is the predominant subject. Then, in the next group of chapters, from Chapter 11 to Chapter 17, the narrative alternates between both kingdoms, and it ends with the passing of Israel into Assyrian captivity. Finally, in Chapters 18 to 25, we have the history of Judah only and this last group of chapters ends with the passing of Judah into Babylonian captivity.

First of all, we are going to look at:

(1) THE DEFECTION OF THE NORTHERN KINGDOM - Chapters 1-10

At the opening of 2 Kings, Ahaziah rules Israel and Jehoshaphat rules Judah. There is a marked contrast between these two.

Of King Ahaziah of Israel, it says: *"And he did evil in the sight of the Lord, and walked in the way of his father, and in the way of his mother, and in the way of Jeroboam the son of Nebat, who made Israel to sin: for he served Baal, and worshipped him, and provoked to anger the Lord God of Israel, according to all that his father had done"* (1 Kings 22:52-53). By contrast, of King Jehoshaphat of Judah, it is written: *"And he walked in all the ways of Asa his father; he turned not aside from it, doing that which was right in the eyes of the Lord"* (1 Kings 22:43). You see, while Judah is experiencing the benefits of a good and godly king, Israel is ruled by a bad king.

When we look at Israel here, we are confronted with:

(a) THE DEGENERATE TIMES

Always remember that the appearance of a prophet was ever a mark of apostasy and rebellion in Israel. The prophets raised their voices in loud protest against the prevailing idolatry, corruption, and blindness of their times calling the nation back to God. The prophet was first of all a man with a message from God for his own generation, a *"forthteller"* rather than a *"foreteller"*.

What was the climate like in which Elisha lived? Well:

(1) POLITICALLY: The Nation was UNSTABLE

As we have seen, the two Books of Kings deal with the nation of Israel in three ways: (1) The United Kingdom; (2) The Divided kingdom; (3) The Surviving Kingdom.

It was to the Northern Kingdom that both Elijah and Elisha ministered. Elijah was raised up during the reign of one of the wicked kings of Israel. Do you recall Ahab? The Biblical record says: *"Ahab did evil in the sight of the Lord above all that were before him"* (1 Kings 16:30). Do you recall who Ahab's wife was? Jezebel. Ahab was one of the world's hen-pecked husbands! Here was a man who became the tool of a crafty, unscrupulous woman.

Elisha, who was Elijah's successor, began his ministry during the reign of Ahab's son and of Jehoram we read: *"And he wrought evil in the sight of the Lord; but not like his father, and like his mother"* (2 Kings 3:2).

So, politically, Elisha lived in an unstable climate. Locally, we have become more politically stable, but what about internationally? Does political instability not mark many of the nations in our western society?

(2) MORALLY: The Nation was UNCLEAN

When Jezebel came to Israel, she did not come alone. (See 1 Kings 16:31) She brought her gods with her and it was not long before Baal worship was established in the land. Now this was nothing new to Israel. Baal worship had been the religion of the Canaanites before Joshua conquered the land. Baal was the son of El who was thought to give increase to the family, to the flocks, to the crops. Fertility rites played a large part in Baal worship.

Chambers existed for male and female prostitutes. A main Baal altar was accompanied by an Asherah, a pole carried in honour of the goddess of that name. She was the consort of Baal. *Baal worship included prostitution, pornography and all kinds of sexual sin.* This was the day in which Elisha lived.

Is it not similar to our own day? Do we not live in a society without fixed standards? Do we not live in an age when everyone is doing that which is right in their own eyes? Christians have been seeking to oppose the new sexual-orientation laws and we have been blasted as old-fashioned, archaic and narrow-minded. We live in an hour when homosexuals are being ordained to the ministry, lesbians are demanding the right to have children, child abuse is on the increase, and our women cannot walk the streets of our cities at night for fear of being raped.

What an age we live in! Politically, unstable. Morally, unclean.

(3) RELIGIOUSLY: The Nation was UNSOUND

Although Jehoram did not go to the same extent of evil as his father and mother before him, yet of him we read: *"He cleaved unto the sins of Jeroboam the son of Nebat"* (2 Kings 3:3). What were these sins? Idolatry. It was Jeroboam who set up a golden calf in Bethel and in Dan. (See 1 Kings 12:28-29) He did so in an attempt to prevent the people going to Jerusalem to worship. The nation of Israel was overwhelmed with a floodtide of idolatry. What an age this was! Politically, it was unstable, Morally, it was unclean. Religiously, it was unsound. It was openly declared that Baal lived and Jehovah ceased to be.

Of course, an idol is any substitute for God. It may be anything that comes between your soul and God. Your house, your car, your children, your home, your job, your clothes, anything that comes between you and God. Are you guilty of idolatry? John closes his First Epistle with the exhortation: *"Little children, keep yourselves from idols. Amen"* (1 John 5:21).

Is it time for you to pray the words of William Cowper:

> *"The dearest idol I have known,*
> *Whate'er that idol be,*
> *Help me to tear it from Thy throne,*
> *And worship only Thee."*

Are we not living in similar times? Days of uncertainty, days when Biblical standards are thrown away, days when false prophets abound on every hand and various forms of idolatry even pervade our own lives. But look at:

(b) THE DEFINITE TESTIMONY

God never leaves Himself without a witness and so Elisha appears as Elijah's successor.

In the summer of 1993, the Atlanta Braves baseball team traded some of their minor league players for the All-Star first baseman of the San Diego Padres, Fred McGriff. He brought the Braves the firepower they needed to make a serious run for the championship. But what about the man McGriff replaced? Sid Bream, a believer in Christ, was the Braves' regular first baseman. He had helped Atlanta get to the World Series in 1992, but with McGriff coming he was headed for the bench. *"There's no doubt something like this hurts your pride and your ego"*, said Bream, *"But the one thing I'm counting on is that there's something better ahead."*

When we have done a job well for many years, it can be difficult to step aside for someone younger or better qualified. Elijah was in that kind of situation. His ministry was coming to an end. His attitude, however, revealed his trust in God. He said to Elisha, his successor: *"Ask what I shall do for thee, before I be taken away from thee"* (2 Kings 2:9). I wonder, has the time come for you to give up a position you have held for a long while? It could be at work or even a ministry at church. Will you ask God for the grace to accept His plan for you? Then, step aside gracefully.

Now there were scores of men in Israel who would have jumped at a chance to be Elijah's successor. Obadiah had a cave full of them. The school of the prophets had some more of them. The

Spirit of God, however, passed over all of them. *He already had his man in mind - Elisha, a man with no theological training or prophetic experience at all.*

It interesting to notice that:

1. Elisha's Ministry was Distinctive

It was in sharp contrast to that of his predecessor. God does something new in each generation. That is why it is not healthy for us to live in the past. We may learn from the past, but we must never live in the past. There is no better time for me being alive than now, no better place for me to be living than right here, for being alive in this time and in this place is God's will for me. Elisha's ministry was distinctive.

Now there is nowhere in Scripture that this is set forth more powerfully than in that great scene at Mount Horeb. (See 1 Kings 19:9-12) *You see, the ministry of Elijah was symbolized by the wind, the earthquake and the fire.* The wind rent the mountains, the earthquake caused Sinai to tremble, and the fire devoured everything that came within its reach. Now this tremendous upheaval was intended to mirror to Elijah the prophet, his own reforming methods. With the same turbulent energy Elijah had swept through the land as a messenger of judgment from the Lord of hosts, but now Elijah was gone and God chooses a different ministry, the ministry of Elisha, the ministry of the still, small voice to fulfil His purposes.

Elijah was the prophet of Judgment; Elisha was the prophet of Grace.

Elijah's ministry was mainly of a public character; Elisha's ministry was mainly of a private character.

Elijah's ministry was more with the masses; Elisha's ministry was more with the individual.

You see instead of Israel being driven by fear, they were now to be drawn by love.

Dr. J. Oswald Sanders states: *"The whispers from Calvary are infinitely more potent than the thunder of Sinai in bringing men to repentance"*.

Do you recall what Paul says to the Corinthian church? *"For the body is not one member, but many"* (1 Corinthians 12:14). There is diversity in unity. Now, unity and diversity must work together or one will destroy the other. Unity without diversity is uniformity, but diversity without unity is anarchy. The church needs both unity and diversity if it is to function in this world. God created us to be different from one another. Are you not glad about that? That there is not another you? That we are different from one another?

Paul poses the question: *"For who maketh thee to differ from another?"* (1 Corinthians 4:7). The answer is obvious! Now, if we let this truth sink down into our hearts we will be cured of jealousy for the rest of our lives. You see, the gifts that God has given to me, He has not given to you and the gifts God has given to you, He has withheld from me. Do you recognise that? Stephen Olford said: *"God does not make duplicates. He only makes originals"*. Your ministry is distinctive. Could it be that you are jealous of some Christian? Jealous of their ministry? Their gifts? Their talents? The truth is worth repeating: the gifts that God has given to me, He has not given to you and the gifts that He has given to you, He has withheld from me. Do you recognise that? Do you realise that your ministry is distinctive? It is unique.

2. Elisha's ministry was Effective

You see, the Lord was in the *"still small voice"* (1 Kings 19:12). God was there with Elisha. Elisha was justly called *"an holy man of God"* (2 Kings 4:9). Indeed, while Elijah performed eight miracles, Elisha performed sixteen. It was Elisha who:

1. Takes the mantle and divides the waters of Jordan (Chapter 2:14)
2. Heals the water (Chapter 2:22)
3. Curses those who mocked him (Chapter 2:24)
4. Provides water (Chapter 3:20)
5. Multiplies the widow's oil (Chapter 4:6)

6. Predicts the birth of a son (Chapter 4:16)
7. Raises the dead (Chapter 4:35)
8. Purifies a pot of stew (Chapter 4:41)
9. Feeds 100 men (Chapter 4:44)
10. Heals Naaman the leper (Chapter 5:14)
11. Gehazi smitten (Chapter 5:27)
12. Floats an axe head (Chapter 6:6)
13. Gives sight (Chapter 6:17)
14. Smites with blindness (Chapter 6:18)
15. Restores sight (Chapter 6:20)
16. His dead bones bring a man back to life (Chapter 13:21)

All this great work for God was done during a time when apostasy gripped the land with a vice-like grip. You see, Elisha illustrates for us what it means to live *"the abundant life"*. Is this not the greatest need of the hour? The Lord Jesus said: *"I am come that they might have life, and that they might have it more abundantly"* (John 10:10). Is that not genuine revival? Yet think of the fear and frustration, the defeat and depression, the bitterness and breakdown encountered increasingly in the churches and in the saints. Many are content to live below the standard set forth in the Scriptures (See Ephesians 4:17-32), hence their ministry is formal, futile and fruitless. What about your ministry? Is it effective? Is it fruitful? Is it characterised by blessing?

There were the degenerate times but, bless God, there was the definite testimony.

(2) THE DESCRIPTION OF THE TWO KINGDOMS - Chapters 11-17

These chapters tell the story of the two kingdoms down to the fall of Samaria, the capital of Israel. Now, it is a sad tale of chaos and disorder, culminating in the Assyrian conquest of the Northern Kingdom. I want you see here in this section:

(a) THE DIVERSITY OF THE KINGS

1. Consider their Number

In the Northern Kingdom there were 19 Kings; in the Southern Kingdom, there were 19 Kings and 1 Queen.

2. Consider their Names

In the Northern Kingdom there was:
1. Jeroboam
2. Nadab
3. Baasha
4. Elah
5. Zimri
6. Omri
7. Ahab
8. Ahaziah
9. Jehoram
10. Jehu
11. Jehoahaz
12. Jehoash
13. Jeroboam II
14. Zechariah
15. Shallum
16. Menahem
17. Pekahiah
18. Pekah
19. Hoshea

In the Southern Kingdom there was:
1. Rehoboam
2. Abijah
3. Asa
4. Jehoshaphat
5. Jehoram
6. Ahaziah
7. Athaliah, The Queen
8. Joash
9. Amaziah
10. Uzziah (Azariah)
11. Jotham
12. Ahaz

13. Hezekiah
14. Manasseh
15. Amon
16. Josiah
17. Jehoahaz
18. Jehoiakim
19. Jehoiachin
20. Zedekiah

Have you got them all?

3. Consider their Nature

The Northern Kingdom of Israel had 19 kings - and they were all bad. Of the 19 kings and one queen of the Southern Kingdom - most were bad and some were good. Now as the kings of Judah are measured against the yardstick of David, the man after God's own heart and the ideal king (See 1 Kings 11:4, 6, 33, 38 and 15:11), so the northern kings are measured by *"Jeroboam the son of Nebat who made Israel to sin"* (1 Kings 22:52). Time and again, Jeroboam is referred to as such. Indeed this wicked King projected his deadly shadow over the throne of Israel for 250 years until at last the people were taken into captivity by Assyria.

We would do well to reflect on the shadows cast by these two men, David and Jeroboam. You see, all of us are casting shadows as we go through this present life. The question is - What kind of shadow are we casting? When God calls us home, what kind of influence will we leave? What kind of shadows are we going to cast today and leave tomorrow? Will it be a shadow like that of Jeroboam or a shadow like that of David? You see, rulers have a powerful influence for good or bad upon a nation. Should this not give us cause for concern in our own day and in our own land? You see, it is still true that *"righteousness exalteth a nation: but sin is a reproach to any people"* (Proverbs 14:34). It is imperative, therefore, that we pray for those who have the rule over us. (See 1 Timothy 2:1-4)

(b) THE MINISTRY OF THE PROPHETS

The ministry of many of the prophets fall within this period. It is vitally important to understand the place the Hebrew prophets occupied in the Old Testament and where they fitted into the historical timescale. *You see, the prophets spoke to their own generation and their messages were relevant to the circumstances when they lived.* These men raised up by the Lord also spoke to an age far beyond their own day. Their function was twofold. It was to forthtell and to foretell, to describe and to prophesy. Thus, for example, Isaiah was the great prophet in Hezekiah's time, and Jeremiah the great prophet from Josiah's time.

There were the oral prophets and there were the written prophets and we have to see exactly where they fit into the historical picture.

(c) THE CAPTIVITY OF THE KINGDOM

In Chapter 17 of 2 Kings is the final indictment of the ten tribes and their deportation into Assyria, from which there would be no return. In these verses the Holy Spirit explains to us why Samaria fell.

1. The Nation Secretly Disobeyed (Chapter 17:8-9)

God had warned them not to mingle with the heathen nations in Canaan (see Deuteronomy 7:1), yet Israel secretly disobeyed and gradually yielded to heathen worship.

2. The Nation Openly Rebelled (Chapter 17:10-12)

What begins as secret sin ultimately becomes open sin. They set up images and groves.

3. The Nation Persistently Rejected (Chapter 17:13-15)

They heard God's call through the prophets, yet refused to bow the knee to the Lord. So, in 722 B.C., God judged them and sent them into captivity into Assyria.

Do you know something? These tragic events in the history of

Israel ought to cause us to fear for our country and pray for our leaders. Godless leaders produce godless generations of citizens and when the Word of the Lord is rejected there is no hope for a nation's future. (See Chapter 17:34-38) It used to be said: "The secret of Britain's greatness is the open Bible", but now our leaders repudiate the Word of God.

Will you learn the lesson? There is no cure for apostasy. Once a church, a denomination, a nation has turned away from the Lord, God must judge.

Did Judah learn from Israel? No!

(3) THE DOWNFALL OF THE SOUTHERN KINGDOM - Chapters 18-25

Judah's sins finally caught up with her and 135 years after Israel was carried into Assyria, Judah was carried into Babylon.

John Phillips divides these years into 5 periods.

(a) THE PERIOD OF REVIVAL - Chapter 18:1-20:21

Revival took place under Hezekiah. No king of Judah is more unreservedly commended than good king Hezekiah. His work included:

1. The Purification of the Temple

2. The Restoration of Worship

3. The Observance of the Passover

4. The Reformation of the People

Both Isaiah and Micah exercised their ministry during the reign of Hezekiah. Do you recall that Hezekiah had to face three enemies? He had to face *the Assyrian Invaders* (Chapters 18-19); he had to face *Death* (Chapter 20:1-11) and he had to face the *Babylonian*

Visitors (Chapter 20:12-21). It is interesting that in these different crises, the king resorted to prayer. Look at Chapter 19:14-19.

Have you ever received a poison pen letter? What have you done? Have you spread it before the Lord? Did you notice the real basis for prayer in verse 19? *"That all the kingdoms of the earth may know that Thou art the Lord God, even Thou only"*. You see, the glory of God was his chief concern. Maybe when we get past the *"self glory"*, *"church glory"* and *"denominational glory"* and get caught up with *"God's glory"*, we will see revival.

(b) THE PERIOD OF REBELLION - Chapter 21:1-26

There was rebellion under Manasseh and Amon. You see, Hezekiah was placed between a bad father, Ahaz, and an evil son, Manasseh, and by the time Hezekiah counteracted the evil of his father's reign, his son came to the throne and reversed all the reforms. Little is said about Manasseh's reign other than it was marked by injustice, idolatry and immorality. Taken to Babylon, Manasseh was put in prison. *"And when he was in affliction, he besought the Lord his God .... and He was intreated of him"* (2 Chronicles 33:12-13). Manasseh was a prodigal son and God saved him. *"Is any thing too hard for the Lord?"* (Genesis 18:14).

> *"Got any rivers you think are uncrossable?*
> *Got any mountains you can't tunnel through?*
> *God specialises in things thought impossible,*
> *He can do just what no other can do."*

(c) THE PERIOD OF REFORM – Chapter 22:1-23:30

There was reform under Josiah. It was during this period that Nahum, Zephaniah, Jeremiah and Habakkuk ministered. It was Josiah who embarked on a wide-ranging reformation. He cleansed the temple, then the city and then the country, putting an end to every form of false and cruel worship. Then the temple was repaired, the law of God was recovered and the Passover was reinstituted.

Josiah's godly life and ministry stayed the hand of judgment a few more years, but captivity was coming and nothing could prevent it.

(d) THE PERIOD OF REPUDIATION – Chapter 23:31-24:16

This soon followed. Jehoahaz (Chapter 23:31-35), Jehoiakim (Chapter 23:36-24:7) and Jehoiachin (Chapter 24:8-16) sought to cast off the authority of the Lord. The writing was on the wall, and then:

(e) THE PERIOD OF REMOVAL – Chapter 24:17-25:30

Judah was taken into captivity. Now keep in mind that the deportation took place in 3 stages. The first attack took place in *605 B.C.* at which time the first group of captives were taken, among whom were Daniel and his three friends. The second invasion took place in *597 B.C.* when a much larger number of people were taken, among whom was Ezekiel. (See Ezekiel 40:1) The third and final invasion took place in *586 B.C.* when the city was destroyed (See Chapter 25:1-12), the temple was disgraced (Chapter 25:13-17) and the land was left desolate (Chapter 25:18-30).

The judgment was long in coming, but when it came it was thorough, just and on time. Think of this: *Everything God had given the Jews was taken from them. They had no king on David's throne, nor do they have today. They had no temple for it had been burned and its sacred vessels confiscated – and today they have no temple. Their holy city was destroyed and ever since that time it has been the focal point for war and unrest. Their land was taken from them and they were scattered among the nations.*

Of course, this awful siege was but a forerunner of the terrible destruction in A.D. 70 when the nation lost its national character until May 1948. So here we see them, as one has put it: *"conquered, captive, and castaway"*. You see: *"Where there is no vision, the people perish"* (Proverbs 29:18). Where the vision of God is lost, there will certainly follow, as Dr. Campbell Morgan puts it, **"degraded ideals, deadened consciences, defeated purposes"**.

That is the human side, but on the divine side, the picture is one of ultimate triumph. For the greatest prophet of the era writes of the Lord: *"He shall not fail nor be discouraged"* (Isaiah 42:4). When the throne on earth falls to pieces, the throne in the heavens still stands. The **chosen people** may fail on earth, but the **chosen purpose** cannot fail. The Babylonian exile which came as a judgment on the Jews cured them for ever of their idolatry, and the Word of God became wonderfully precious to them.

They are still the chosen people. What a study they are! Scattered over the face of the earth, yet strangely one; ever persecuted, yet ever preserved; mixed in with all the races, yet the most distinct people in the world. Their history is a mystery - apart from God's Word. Other peoples have become extinct, yet they are still preserved and will be preserved until all human failure is completely eclipsed and David's greater Son, even the Lord Jesus, will sit on the throne in Jerusalem and will reign *"from shore to shore"*.

Treasure these words: **"He shall not fail nor be discouraged"**.

CHAPTER 14

1 Chronicles

When people try to read through the Bible, they tend to get stuck either in Leviticus or in Chronicles. Leviticus is difficult to read because there is no story-line and the rituals described seem to have no relevance to us in the 21st century. Chronicles is difficult because the first nine chapters are nothing more than genealogies with names that you cannot pronounce. The result of this is that 1 and 2 Chronicles are very little known in church circles today.

There is only one verse from these books that is widely quoted and that is from 2 Chronicles 7:14: *"If My people, which are called by My name, shall humble themselves, and pray, and seek My face, and turn from their wicked ways; then will I hear from heaven, and will forgive their sin, and will heal their land"*. No doubt, we can draw spiritual principles from that statement, but we need to appreciate that "their land" is not Britain, America or Ulster. The land in question was the land of Israel. But sadly apart from this verse and perhaps one or two others, people do not know Chronicles at all. So perhaps we could start by thinking about:

1. The Purpose of the Book

(a) There are Similarities

Similarities with other books.
1 Chronicles contains material found in 2 Samuel and 2 Chronicles contains material found in 1 and 2 Kings. There are similarities.

(b) There are Omissions

1. There is no mention of Samuel's part in choosing kings.
2. Saul barely gets a mention.
3. David is mentioned at some length, but even then it is interesting to notice what is omitted. His struggles with Saul are ignored; Absalom's rebellion is missed out, and the whole episode with Bathsheba, the turning point in David's reign, does not receive a single line.

(c) There are Additions

For example, 1 Chronicles starts with genealogies or *"family trees"*, but the author is only concerned with the royal line of David. Not one of the kings in the north was in the royal line - so they do not receive a mention. Chronicles is specifically a history of the royal house of David.

(d) There are Differences

Samuel and Kings are written from a prophetic viewpoint; Chronicles from a priestly.

Samuel and Kings are more negative; Chronicles is more positive.

Samuel and Kings are a record of both Israel and Judah; Chronicles is a record primarily of Judah.

Samuel and Kings is all about man's failings; Chronicles is all about God's faithfulness.

Samuel and Kings emphasise kings and prophets; Chronicles emphasises the temple and priests.

Samuel and Kings were written shortly after the beginning of Captivity in Babylon; Chronicles was written shortly after the return from the Captivity.

Now when you bring together the similarities, the omissions, the additions and the differences, you can see the purpose of the book. The books of Chronicles are given from a different viewpoint.

The books of Kings give us history from the viewpoint of the prophets; Chronicles from the viewpoint of the priests.

The books of Kings give us history from the human viewpoint; Chronicles from the divine standpoint.

The former show us man ruling; the latter show us God overruling. Chronicles, therefore, provides us with a more heavenly perspective.

(2) The Penman of the Book

It is because of the perspective given by the books that the penman is thought to be Ezra. Remember that 'a chronicle' is a record of events. Have you ever heard of *"The Banbridge Chronicle"*? Does it not sound a lot more impressive than *"The Lurgan Mail"*? 1 & 2 Chronicles were originally one book. The original title in the Hebrew Bible read: *"The annals (i.e. events or happenings) of the days"*. When they were divided into two books in around 200 B.C. the title changed to: *"The things omitted"*, reflecting material not found in Samuel and Kings. The English title *"Chronicles"* originated with Jerome's Latin Vulgate translation around 400 A.D. which used the fuller title: *"The Chronicles of the Entire Sacred History"*.

There is a very clear resemblance in style and language between the two books of Chronicles and those of Ezra and Nehemiah. As a result 1 & 2 Chronicles are generally credited to Ezra the priest who was a skilled scholar and teacher of the Jewish law. (See Ezra 7:6) Now that brings us to:

(3) The Period of the Book

When you speak about Ezra, you are talking about the post-exilic period, that is the period after the exile. Actually, 1 and 2 Chronicles cover the longest period of any of the books of the Bible, beginning with Adam and ending with the decree of Cyrus, King of Persia, in 536 B.C. authorizing the Jews to go back to Jerusalem to rebuild the Temple. Now that is the scope of Chronicles. As John Phillips says: *"It represents a period of time not less than thirty five hundred years".*

Do you know what the last book in the Hebrew Old Testament is? It is Chronicles! In our English Old Testament it is Malachi, but in the Hebrew Bible it is Chronicles. This might lead us to believe that its connection with Kings is not as great as we may think. This brings us to consider:

(4) The People of the Book

The Chronicles were compiled after the Babylonian exile, when the remnant had returned from Babylon to Judaea under Ezra and Zerubbabel. (See 1 Chronicles 6:15 and 9:1) The very last words of 2 Chronicles make even the edict of Cyrus (2 Chronicles 36:22-23), which officially ended the exile, a thing of the past. Thus the Chronicles were specially written for these repatriated Jews as a chronicle of God's intention of future blessing in spite of the nation's past moral and spiritual failure. You see, here were the Jews back in the land of promise with a monumental task before them. Their cities were heaps of rubble, their temple was gone, the land was desolate and in ruins. Ancient enemies were hostile still and many Jewish people were indifferent to their emancipation, preferring a life of luxury in Babylon and Persia to the rigours of pioneering work in Jerusalem. Most devastating of all, the throne of David was gone, and the returning remnant under Zerubbabel had a commission to build a temple not a throne. So these books of Chronicles were written to interpret to the people the meaning of their history and to encourage them to rebuild the temple - for God had not forgotten His promises to His people. As Wilkinson & Boa put it, it is as though these books were saying: *"All is not lost. Though the glory has departed and the people are under the control of Gentile powers, God still has a future for them. The throne of David is gone, but the line of David is still intact."*

1 Chronicles falls into two parts: the genealogies from Adam to David (Chapter 1:1-9:44) and then the reign of David (Chapter 10:1-29:30). So, first of all we are struck with:

(1) THEIR IMPRESSIVE ANCESTRY - Chapters 1-9

This is a series of genealogical tables. Sidlow Baxter says:

"Nine chapters of genealogical tables. What waste of space! Nay, rather, what blindness to think so! No part of the Chronicles is more important. Such lines of descent were of sacred importance to all godly Jews, and rightly so, for they knew that their nation, besides being the repository of a special Divine revelation was the possessor of wonderful Divine promises reaching on to unborn generations. The chronicler himself knew well enough that these genealogies reveal the selective process of Divine election from Adam downwards, and that the covenant line of redemptive purpose was to culminate in the Messiah."

I want you to notice here that there is no interest whatsoever in the northern tribes. The breakaway under Jeroboam is to be reckoned to be a serious spiritual, as well as national, disaster, and the returned exiles among whom Chronicles was circulated are not interested in the story of disloyal Israel. Only Judah is in their thoughts.

So, in this impressive ancestry we see:

(a) A CERTAIN PEOPLE

Now, when you are having your daily devotions, what do you do when you come to the genealogies? Is getting a blessing out of a genealogy like expecting to find a marriage proposal in a telephone directory? Now Chronicles begins with a list of names. So what? Who cares? What is the point and purpose of all these names?

An old Scottish preacher was reading the opening chapter of Matthew 1. He read: *"Abraham begat Isaac; and Isaac begat Jacob; and Jacob begat Judah and his brethren"*. Then he paused and said: *"And they kept on begetting one another all the way down this side of the page and clear on to the other side"*.

Put yourself in Ezra's shoes. He had a ministry especially to a little remnant of hardy souls who had come back from Babylon in order to raise a new nation from the rubble of the past. His first aim was to show that although the throne was gone, the royal line of David was still intact. Hence the genealogies. Now, the point has already been made that in the Hebrew Bible, the book of Chronicles is not found in the historical section. It does not follow in sequence after the book of Kings. Rather it concludes the Old Testament.

You see, the genealogies in Chronicles lead up to the genealogy in Matthew 1 which opens the New Testament. The Jew reading his Bible comes to this register which is not complete, but when he turns to Matthew 1, he finds it completed there.

Do you recall that the earliest prophecy of the Messiah simply promised a Saviour from the human race? Do you recall what God said to the serpent? *"I will put enmity between thee and the woman, and between thy seed and her seed; it shall bruise thy head, and thou shalt bruise his heel"* (Genesis 3:15).

But then, over time, the specific race and then the particular family from which the Messiah would come were identified. He was to come of Abraham (Genesis 12:3); of Judah (Genesis 49:10); and of David (2 Samuel 7:12-16) You see, when these exiles returned home, the temple was gone, and the throne was gone, but the line of David was still intact - from *"Adam"* to *"Zedekiah"* (1 Chronicles 3:15). The Chronicles proved God had preserved the line of David to execute His sovereign purpose of bringing the Lord Jesus into this world.

The Companion Bible offers an insightful commentary to 1 and 2 Chronicles:

"These books belong to quite another part of the Old Testament, and do not follow in sequence to the books of Kings. They are, according to the Hebrew Canon, the conclusion of the Old Testament; and, the genealogies here lead up to that of Matthew 1:1 and the commencement of the New Testament. They end with the ending of the kingdom; and the question of Cyrus: 'Who is there?' (2 Chronicles 36:23) is followed by the answer: 'Where is he?' (Matthew 2:2), and the proclamation of the kingdom by the rightful King and His forerunner. It begins

with the first Adam and leads on to the 'last' Adam. It deals with the kingdom of Judah because Christ was proclaimed as the successor of David."

During the period of the Hebrew history of the Old Testament, Israel came into conflict with 4 world powers.

In relation to Egypt: Israel **Grew** Up;
In relation to Assyria: Israel **Gave** Up;
In relation to Babylon: Israel **Girded** Up;
In relation to Persia: Israel **Got** Up.

Against this changing panorama of world empires, the Lord wrote Hebrew history. Through it all, God was working His eternal and sovereign purpose to bring the Lord Jesus into a lost and dying world for Jews and Gentiles. From the Creation to the Flood to Egyptian bondage through the Red Sea, in the Wilderness, to the Land of Promise, through the times of the Judges, Kings, Prophets, and through 70 years of captivity, where man ruled, God overruled.

John Phillips says:

"He overruled the passions and powers of men, immutable in His counsels, invincible in His purposes, from generation to generation, pursuing His eternal purpose to prove that He cannot be impeached, He cannot be overtaken, and He cannot be dethroned".

What a comfort to know that He knows what we do not know. His eye is on the clock; His hand is on the compass; He doeth all things well, and He maketh no mistakes. Hallelujah, *"God is still on the throne"*.

(b) A CERTAIN PRAYER

There are some marvellous *"gems among the genealogies"* that you have to look for when reading through them. One is found in Chapter 4 verses 9 and 10. It concerns Jabez. Now, this story may have been have been included to encourage the dispirited returning exiles. You see, 'Jabez' means *"pain"*. So, the pain felt by the returning exiles can be changed to blessing by the God who answers our prayers, enlarges our borders, dispels our loneliness and conquers our enemies.

Do you see this is a prayer for:

1. Divine Enrichment

"Oh that Thou wouldest bless me indeed".

What is a blessing? Well, *"to bless" in the Biblical sense, means to ask for or to impart supernatural favour. When we ask for God's favour, we are not asking for more of what we could get for ourselves. We are crying out for the wonderful, unlimited goodness that only God has the power to know about or give to us.* The Bible tells us: *"The blessing of the Lord, it maketh rich, and He addeth no sorrow with it"* (Proverbs 10:22). Now, a blessing has three characteristics. It comes:

• **From God for His glory;**
• **To you for your good;**
• **It is channeled through you for the good of others.**

Do not forget that. *"O that Thou wouldest bless me indeed!"* I do not want a substitute blessing, or a false blessing. I want it to come from God for His glory. I want it to come for me for my good. But, if you stop there, you are selfish. I want it to come to me to touch the lives of others. You see, God blesses us that we might be a blessing to others (See Genesis 12:3). Is this your desire? *"Oh that Thou wouldest bless me indeed."*

2. Divine Enlargement

"And enlarge my coast" (Chapter 4:10).

In that day, a person's border or territory would mark the limit of his influence. Jabez was asking God to give him greater responsibility, more influence, larger opportunities to do something for Him. His was a God-sanctioned ambition for his underlying motive was the glory of God. You see, here is a man who asks God for increase. He wants God to expand his opportunities for service. The last phrase in verse 10 confirms this: *"And God granted him that which he requested"*.

The more faithful you are, the more God will bless you; the more God blesses you, the more enlargement there is; the more enlargement there is, the more work you have to do. Do you recall what was said to the good servant? *"Thou hast been faithful in a very little, have thou authority over ten cities"* (Luke 19:17). It is an unchanging principle in the Word of God. Faithfulness in little things is God's appointed way to bigger things. *"O that Thou wouldest.... enlarge my coast."* It was Hudson Taylor that used to pray: *"Oh God, give me wider usefulness"*.

Is it not sad that there are Christians who are looking for retirement so that they can do less? Jabez was not looking to do less. He was looking to do more. He was not looking to slow up. He was looking to speed up. In effect, what he was saying was: *"Oh God, expand my opportunities and my impact in such a way that I can touch more lives for Your glory"*. Is this your desire?

3. Divine Enablement

"And that Thine hand might be with me" (Chapter 4:10).

You see, enlarged territory involves increased responsibilities and imposes greater demands. Jabez knew that he required a power greater than his own to possess and develop his new land for God. God's hand represents His mighty power. When God wants to get something done, He gets His hand upon you. Ezra says: *"I was strengthened as the hand of the Lord my God was upon me"* (Ezra 7:28). Nehemiah testifies: *"I told them of the hand of my God which was good upon me"* (Nehemiah 2:18) and John the Baptist moved Israel so mightily because *"the hand of the Lord was with him"* (Luke 1:66). That is what Jabez wanted: *"Oh, that ... that Thine hand might be with me"*, pushing me, holding me, sustaining me.

You see, Jabez realised something very important. *The Blesser is more important than the blessing.* When you start seeking the blessings of God, you have to remember that with them you must seek God in the blessing. Why? Otherwise, you will not be able to handle the blessings that God gives you. *Do you know that success is far more dangerous than failure?* Failure never went to anyone's head. You see, it finally hit Jabez - if God answers my prayer and God blesses me and God enlarges my territory and God gives me more responsibility and more opportunity, His hand had better be on my life or I will not be able to handle it all. Independence says: *"Keep your hands off me".* Dependence says: *"Keep your hands on me".* There is no problem you cannot solve, no circumstance you cannot face, no enemy you cannot defeat, if the hand of the Lord is with you. What a prayer this was! But Jabez was not finished yet:

4. Divine Environment

"And that Thou wouldest keep me from evil, that it may not grieve me!" (Chapter 4:10).

Jabez knew well the inevitable peril of an enlarged coast - increased activity on the part of his enemies. He knew that the more you do for God, and the more God does through you, the higher ambition you have, and the more advancement that comes your way, the more you are being exposed for the devil to tempt you, trip you, and trap you. Does this not show how mature and godly Jabez really was? He was saying: *"God bless me, enlarge me, lead me, empower me, but keep me humble and keep me holy".* Do you remember what Christ taught us to pray? *"And forgive us our sins; for we also forgive every one that is indebted to us. And lead us not into temptation; but deliver us from evil"* (Luke 11:4). How many of you have ever committed a sin? How many of you have ever committed the same sin a second time, a third time, ten times? Why is that? We keep committing sin, and then come to the Lord and say: *"Lord, forgive me; I have messed up again".* Now, He does forgive us of our sins – and how thankful we are for that - but Christ taught us to not only pray: *"forgive us our sins",* but also: *"deliver us from evil".* We need protection from sin.

One day Coach Jordan of Auborn University in the USA said to Mike Kolen who played for the Miami Dolphins: *"Mike, I want you to do some scouting for me".* Mike said: *"Sure, coach, what kind of man do you need?"* Coach Jordan said: *"Well, Mike, you know there's a man who when he is knocked down, he just stays there".* Mike said: *"We don't want him, do we coach?" "No, sir, we don't want him."* Then the Coach said: *"You know, Mike, there's a man who when he is knocked down, he gets back up, and when he's knocked back down, he stays there." "I don't think we want him either, coach."* The Coach then said: *"Mike, there's a man who when he gets knocked down, he gets up, he gets down again and he gets up, he gets knocked down again and he gets up. In fact, every time he keeps getting up." "Yes, coach, that's the kind of man we want, isn't it?"*

"No, Mike, I want you to find the man who keeps knocking every one else down!"

There are times when we get knocked down and we are grateful that the Lord Jesus will pick us up. But God wants us to do a little knocking down for a change. He wants us to be victorious in our battles with sin. That is why Jabez prayed for God to protect him from evil: evil communications (1 Corinthians 15:33); evil speaking (Ephesians 4:31) and an evil heart (Hebrews 3:12). You see, the one thing that can reverse the process and take you from the extraordinary to the ordinary is sin. For example, from the time Samson was born, he was intended by God to be extraordinary, but sin took away his supernatural strength and made him just like any other man.

When you measure your praying by this man's praying, how do you feel? *Mind you, it was not a long prayer, but prayer is not measured by its length but by its strength.*

Did God respond? *"And God granted him that which he requested."*

(c) A CERTAIN PRINCIPLE

The principle, running through the first nine chapters of this book, is this - God's work deserves the best!

1.That is why Saul was Rejected

In 1 Samuel 31, it is simply recorded that King Saul met his death in battle with the Philistines. But do you see how the chronicler reports it in Chapter 10 verses 13 and 14? *"Saul died for his transgression which he committed against the Lord."* Who slew him? The Lord slew him. The Philistines were merely the executioners acting out God's justice. Do you know what God wants from His people in this 21st century? The same thing that He wanted from His people in every century. Obedience. John says: *"And hereby we do know that we know Him, if we keep His commandments"* (1 John 2:3). Does God's work not deserve the best?

2. That is why the Priests were Rewarded

Details are given in these opening chapters about the Levites and their appointment *"unto all manner of service of the tabernacle of the house of God"* (Chapter 6:48). They have seemed to have responded enthusiastically to their duties and responsibilities. Later, some of the priests are described as *"very able men for the work of the service of the house of God"* (Chapter 9:13). You see, only the best is good enough for the service of God. Does this not rebuke our half-heartedness? When it comes to the work of God, what kind of attitude do you have? Apathy? Lethargy? The kind of attitude that says that anything will do for the work of God? Are you giving of your best?

(2) THEIR IDEAL KING - Chapters 10-29

The remaining chapters focus on David, the national hero. Now, David was the yardstick by which God measured the behaviour of each successive king of Judah, which is why the book of Chronicles spends so much time on him. (See 1 Kings 11:4, 6 and 15:11) David was Israel's ideal king. He was a shepherd at heart, but he was also a soldier, a psalmist, a statesman, and a saint. He loved the Lord and not even his glaring sins could obscure that fact. You see, the great burden of this book seems to be: *"Oh, if only we could go back to David. If only the golden days of David could be restored. If only the kings of Judah not only sat on David's throne but ruled with David's heart."* In these concluding chapters we see:

(a) DAVID THE SOVEREIGN

In 1 Chronicles, David is presented in all his strength and, with the exception of the census in Chapter 21, David is presented in his best light. He personifies the hopes of the nation. He is the one to whom the Israelites look for a type of their Messiah, their Saviour and their Deliverer. So David was crowned. Then we see:

(b) DAVID THE SOLDIER

Although David's agonizing years with King Saul are omitted in Chronicles, David's leadership skills as a soldier are not. When David hit rock-bottom, God gave him a ministry helping 600 men (1 Samuel 23:13) who had been weakened by despair to become strong warriors. (See 1 Chronicles 12:8) Do you recall the motley band that came to him when he was in the cave at Adullam? (See 1 Samuel 22:1-2) The despised, the distressed, the debtors, and the discontented. (Sounds like a local church!) But, under his leadership, these men became a disciplined, highly competent fighting unity. (Chapter 12:2 & 8)

Is this not one of the responsibilities of leadership? To train new leaders. Do you recall what Paul says to Timothy? *"And the things that thou hast heard of me among many witnesses, the same commit thou to faithful men, who shall be able to teach others also"* (2 Timothy 2:2). There ought to be a legacy of spiritual truth passed from one generation to the next. May the principles that we have always embraced prevail – never sell the truth!

(c) DAVID THE SERVANT

He brings up *"the ark of God the Lord"* (Chapter 13:6) to Jerusalem. Now, what was the ark? Well, the ark was the sacred chest which stood in the Holy of Holies in the tabernacle. It was the most important piece of furniture in the tabernacle, for God said: *"There I will meet with thee, and I will commune with thee from above the mercy seat, from between the two cherubims"* (Exodus 25:22).

Here was an available place of meeting with God, an opportunity for constant communion with Him. Do you see the desire David possessed? What a passion he had for God! He says in one of his Psalms: *"Surely ... I will not give sleep to mine eyes, or slumber to mine eyelids, until I find out a place for the Lord, an habitation for the mighty God of Jacob"* (Psalm 132:3-5). Do you have this passion for God? Do you long to know God through His Word? Do you long to meet with God in public and private? Do you desire His presence above all else?

(d) DAVID THE SCRIBE

We read: *"Then on that day David delivered first this psalm to thank the Lord into the hand of Asaph and his brethren"* (Chapter 16:7). David writes over half of the Psalms in the Word of God. Then:

(e) DAVID THE STEWARD

David longs for a more permanent home for the ark. He says: *"Nathan, I'm troubled that I have a nicer house than the ark does, than the Lord does"* (See Chapter 17:1). I wonder, are we as spiritual in heart as David was? Is there a striking contrast between what we spend on ourselves and what we offer to the Lord? Someone has said: *"To do less for God than you do for yourself shows where your heart is"*. David is here expressing his love for the Lord. He wants to build the temple. God informs him that this will not be possible. The house of peace could not be built by a man of war. However, Solomon, David's son, would build it. Then, in Chapter 21, we see:

(f) DAVID THE STATISTICIAN

David was tempted by Satan to conduct a census of Israel's fighting men. What was it that lay behind David's desire for a national census? Probably it was pride. He had won a number of great victories (see 1 Chronicles 18-20) and perhaps wanted to bask in the glory of success. The book ends with:

(g) DAVID THE SPONSOR

David, with a great attitude, says: *"If I can't build the temple, then I will buy it, I will raise the money for it"*. Someone has calculated that in USA dollars the value of David's gift was that in silver he gave $450 million and in gold he gave $17 billion. (Chapter 29:3-4) You say: *"David had plenty of money!"* Yes! but he realised that it was not his. Look at Chapter 29 verse 14: *"All things come of Thee, and of Thine own have we given Thee"*. David says: *"Look at everything you have and remember this: (1) God owns it. It belongs to Him. (2) God gave it. It came from Him"* (See Deuteronomy 8:18).

We are simply the stewards of God's money. The Lord is simply asking us to give back to Him what He has given us. Look at Chapter 29 verse 15: *"We are as strangers before Thee, and sojourners, as were all our fathers: our days on the earth are as a shadow, and there is none abiding"*. Shadow speaks of the brevity and swiftness of life.

Here is an old warrior about to leave this scene, passing the baton of responsibility on to Solomon, an inexperienced son, encouraging him in relation to God's Work, God's Word and God's Will.

David finished very well! Paul says: *"For David, after he had served his own generation by the will of God, fell on sleep"* (Acts 13:36).

We need to learn this lesson. Every believer should desire to finish well. How will you finish?

"Who then is willing to consecrate his service this day unto the Lord?" (1 Chronicles 29:5)

CHAPTER 15

2 Chronicles

Around the year 1952, General Dwight D. Eisenhower was thinking about running for the presidency of the United States. An oil baron in Fort Worth, Texas named Sid Richardson wanted him to run, and Sid talked to Billy Graham about it. Billy was a young man who had just become a popular national figure in America. So Billy Graham wrote a letter to Dwight Eisenhower. *In his letter, Billy Graham quoted a politician who had said to him: "If Washington is not cleaned out in the next two or three years, we are going to enter a period of chaos that could bring about our downfall".* Billy quoted that statement to Eisenhower and then added: *"Sometimes I wonder who is going to win the battle first, the barbarians beating at our gates from without, or the termites of immorality from within".* Well, when Eisenhower read the letter he was taken back and said: *"Who is this young man?"*

Eisenhower *did* run for the White House, and when he won the election he called Billy Graham and asked to meet him at the Commodore Hotel in New York.

It was five days before the inauguration and Eisenhower told Billy that he was concerned about the spiritual condition of America. He asked the preacher to give him a Scripture verse he could claim as his own as he prepared to take the oath of office. Billy Graham suggested this verse: 2 Chronicles 7:14. When Eisenhower took the oath of office, his hand rested on a Bible that was opened to this passage.

If the President of the United States and if the United States of America needed that verse when I was a baby in my mother's arms, we need it a hundred times more today. When I think of growing up in the 1950s, I think of it as a time of relative innocence. Ulster was by and large a church-attending country. In primary school, we opened each day with devotions. There was an atmosphere where God was feared. Yet, in that same decade, Dwight Eisenhower was worried about the spiritual condition of the U.S.A. and as he took the oath of office his hand rested on a Bible that was opened to 2 Chronicles 7 verse 14.

The 1950s are long gone and things have never been as bad as they are today. Yet, the formula for revival is still the same:

"If My people, which are called by My name, shall humble themselves, and pray, and seek My face, and turn from their wicked ways; then will I hear from heaven, and will forgive their sin, and will heal their land".

Bible scholars tell us there are sixteen different revivals described for us in the Bible, and the greatest book in the Bible on the subject of revival is 2 Chronicles. This Old Testament record gives us the biblical formula for revival, and then describes for us five different revivals under five different Old Testament kings.

Now before we get there let us refresh our minds with the background to these books.

(a) There are Similarities

There are similarities with other books. 1 Chronicles contains material found in 2 Samuel and 2 Chronicles contains material found in 1 and 2 Kings. There are similarities. Of course, the books of Chronicles and Kings are not the only parts of the Bible where the same period is covered twice. There are four accounts of the life of Christ in the New Testament. Even though the books seem the same, each comes from a different angle, because each Gospel was written for a different kind of person. The same is true about 1 and 2 Chronicles.

(b) There are Omissions

Saul barely gets a mention. David is mentioned at some length, but even then it is interesting to notice what is omitted. His struggles with Saul are ignored; Absalom's rebellion is missed out and the whole episode with Bathsheba - the turning point in David's reign - does not receive a single line.

(c) There are Additions

For example, 1 Chronicles starts with genealogies or *"family trees"*, but the author is only concerned with the royal line of David. Not one of the kings in the North was in the royal line so they do not receive a mention. Chronicles is specifically a history of the royal house of David and nothing more.

(d) There are Differences

Samuel and Kings are written from a prophetic viewpoint; Chronicles from a priestly viewpoint.

Samuel and Kings are more negative; Chronicles is more positive.

Samuel and Kings are a record of both Israel and Judah; Chronicles is a record of Judah.

Samuel and Kings are all about man's failings; Chronicles is all about God's faithfulness.

Samuel and Kings emphasise kings and prophets; Chronicles emphasises the temple and priests.

Samuel and Kings were written shortly after the beginning of captivity in Babylon; Chronicles was written shortly after the return from the captivity.

Now when you bring together the similarities, the omissions, the additions and the differences you can see the purpose of the book.

The books of Chronicles are given from a different viewpoint. The books of Kings give us history from the viewpoint of the prophets;

Chronicles from the viewpoint of the priests.

The books of Kings give us history from the human standpoint; Chronicles from the divine standpoint.

The former show us man ruling; the latter show us God overruling. Chronicles therefore provides us with a more heavenly perspective.

It is because of this that many believe the books were written by Ezra. They were written after the Babylonian captivity to demonstrate the significance of their history. You see, in Kings the people needed an explanation for why they had been sent into exile, but in Chronicles they knew why they had been there. They just needed to be encouraged and sent back to the land to re-establish the walls of the city and rebuild the temple. *So Chronicles was a sermon for a returning remnant to encourage them to persevere amidst the difficult times.*

Now when they got back to Jerusalem, it was not very exciting. They had to struggle to make a living. They were very poor and building the temple was slow work. It needed two prophets, Haggai and Zechariah, to urge them to keep going. The author of this book had to get the truth instilled in them that God must come first in their life as a people. **Is this not why the emphasis is on the temple?** You see, even before Nehemiah is sent to rebuild the city, Ezra and Zerubbabel are sent to rebuild the temple. As Sidlow Baxter says: *"In any national reconstruction, we must begin there with the temple, that is with God. Our politicians will not learn. They persist in the worldly-wise idea that the city must be built before the temple. Well, they are wrong".*

So these books of Chronicles were written to explain to the people the meaning of their history and to encourage them to rebuild the temple - for God had not forgotten His promises to His people.

Chronicles contains material found in other books. 2 Chronicles contains material found in 1 and 2 Kings so this book opens where 1 Chronicles left off. 1 Chronicles closes with the death of David, 2 Chronicles opens with:

(1) THE REIGN OF SOLOMON - Chapters 1 to 9

Solomon's reign is Israel's *"golden age"* of peace and prosperity. The glory and grandeur of Solomon's kingdom spanned from the border of Egypt to the east and south to the River Euphrates to the east and north. (See 1 Kings 4:21) Solomon's reign began in a blaze of glory. Some of the greatest years of Israel's existence were during the reign of Solomon. Consider:

(a) SOLOMON'S WISDOM

When the Lord gave to Solomon a blank cheque and said to him: *"Ask what I shall give thee"* (Chapter 1:7), Solomon reminded the Lord of the circumstances and responsibilities of his life and prayed: *"Give me now wisdom and knowledge"* (Chapter 1:10). God answered his prayer.

Are you, like Solomon, involved in the work of God? Maybe, like him, you are in a position of leadership and you feel your need of wisdom. Perhaps it is soul- winning or outreach or evangelism among the children or working with the youth, do you not need this wisdom? John Blanchard defined wisdom as: *"The ability to discern God's hand in human circumstances and apply heavenly judgments to earthly situations"*. How we stand in need of this heavenly wisdom! Human reasoning is deficient!

(b) SOLOMON'S WEALTH

Look at verses 15 to 17 of Chapter 1. Solomon was the Bill Gates of his day. If ever there was a subject Solomon knew, it was money. He secured it, saved it, spent it, studied it and shared it.

Has God endowed you with wealth? Well, do you realise that you are only a steward of God's money? There is an interesting verse in the book of Deuteromony that says: *"But thou shalt remember the Lord thy God: for it is He that giveth thee power to get wealth"* (Deuteronomy 8:18). Who gives you the power to get wealth? Who gives you the mental capacity to make money? Where does it all come from? The Lord. (See 1 Chronicles 29:14) Do you realise that you are only a steward of God's money?

(c) SOLOMON'S WORK

This book gives the history of what is known as Solomon's temple. In the opening chapters, it is **built**, but by the final chapters, it is **burnt**. The concluding verses, however, hold out hope that a further temple would replace it. This was later built by Zerubbabel. *You see, if David gave Judah a sceptre, Solomon gave Judah a sanctuary.* Tenderly the writer of Chronicles keeps in mind the fortunes of the temple. *Conceived* in the mind of David, *constructed* under the guidance of Solomon, *contaminated* by some of the kings, *cleansed* by others, and at last *consumed* in the fires that demolished Jerusalem, the temple is never far from the centre of the story. Commenced in the fourth year of Solomon's reign, it was completed seven years later. (See 1 Kings 6:38 and 2 Chronicles 3:2) God originally dwelt in the tabernacle (Exodus 40:34); then in Solomon's temple (2 Chronicles 6:18 and 7:1); then the glory of God came to earth in the person of the Lord Jesus (See John 1:14). Today, the church corporately (Ephesians 2:21) and the Christian individually (1 Corinthians 6:19-20) is the temple of God.

Do you recall Paul's words? *"What? Know ye not that your body is the temple of the Holy Ghost which is in you, which ye have of God, and ye are not your own?"* (1 Corinthians 6:19). Do you realise that what you do to your body, you are doing to the temple of God? When you overeat, smoke or engage in sexual sin, do you know what you are doing? You are defiling the temple of God. (Someone says: *"Smoking won't take you to hell!"* No, it only makes you smell as if you have already been there!) Now can you see something of the greatness of Solomon?

(d) SOLOMON'S WORSHIP

At the dedication of the temple, King Solomon led the congregation in prayer and worship. It is interesting that Solomon makes it clear in his prayer that the condition of Israel's heart is more important than the presence of the temple. He knew that sin would bring chastening, but that repentance would bring blessing. It was far more important to dedicate the people than the building. I wonder if we were to assemble to worship correctly, reverently, and submissively if the *"glory of the Lord would fill the house"* (Chapter 7:1).

The remaining chapters in this opening section are taken up with:

(e) SOLOMON'S WAYS

In 1 Chronicles, David's sins in relation to Bathsheba and Uriah are omitted, so in 2 Chronicles the sins of Solomon are not recorded. 1 Kings 11 recorded those sins and they are presented as the reason for the division of the kingdom. Do you see the focus again? You see, a prophet would concentrate on the bad things the kings did which brought judgment on the land. But the priest is pleased to record the building of the temple, the arrangement of the choirs and the establishment of worship. David and Solomon are seen in a different light in Chronicles from that in Kings.

(2) THE REVIVAL IN JUDAH - Chapters 10 to 36

Let us not forget where we exactly are in this book. The first nine chapters are given over to the reign of Solomon. Then, in Chapter 10, we have the division of the kingdom but after that only the account of the southern kingdom of Judah is given. The spotlight is on the kings who followed in the line of David. Remember the times of the Kings generally were some of the darkest days of Israel's illustrious history. Idolatry, immorality, apostasy and apathy filled the land. *The worship of the preeminent God had been replaced with the worship of many pagan gods.* The Northern Kingdom of Israel had 19 kings and they were all bad. Of the 19 Kings and 1 Queen of the Southern Kingdom, most were bad but some were good. It is interesting to note that although there were more bad kings ruling Judah, the sum total of their years on the throne amounts to considerably less than that of the combined reigns of the good kings.

Given special prominence are five of these kings in whose reigns were periods of revival, renewal, and reformation. These kings were:

1. Asa (Chapters 14 - 16)

2. Jehoshaphat (Chapters 17 - 20)

3. Joash (Chapters 23 – 24)

4. Hezekiah (Chapters 29 – 32)

5. Josiah (Chapters 34 – 35)

What is revival?

James MacDonald said: *"Revival is renewed interest after a period of indifference or decline"*. Martyn Lloyd-Jones said: *"A revival means days of Heaven on earth"*. Stephen Olford said: *"Revival is an invasion from Heaven that brings a conscious awareness of God"*. Vance Havner said: *"Revival is the church falling in love with Jesus all over again"*. Perhaps the best definition is found in Acts 3:19: *"Times of refreshing from the presence of the Lord"*.

During this time of degradation, God sent five periods of revival. With each of these five kings, a different aspect of revival is emphasised:

(a) King Asa: We have the Social Aspect of Revival

Revival impacts society. You see, the first revival was during the reign of Asa. Of him we read: *"For he took away the altars of the strange gods, and the high places, and brake down the images, and cut down the groves: And commanded Judah to seek the Lord God of their fathers, and to do the law and the commandment. Also he took away out of all the cities of Judah the high places and the images: and the kingdom was quiet before him"* (2 Chronicles 14:3-5). Asa tore down idolatry, he took up idolatry, he threw away idolatry. Asa even took away the throne from his own mother, Maachah, because she *"had made an idol in a grove"* (Chapter 15:16). When the Ethiopians attack with an army twice the size of Judah's, King Asa turns in total reliance upon the Lord and experiences a great and overwhelming victory.

The Lord gives him a promise with a condition: *"The Lord is with you, while ye be with Him; and if ye seek Him, He will be found of you; but if ye forsake Him, He will forsake you"* (Chapter 15:2). Asa responded whole-heartedly to that prophecy and dealt ruthlessly with idolatry in the land.

Do you remember the words of the Psalmist after he had prayed for revival? He says: *"Truth shall spring out of the earth; and righteousness shall look down from heaven. Yea, the Lord shall give that which is good; and our land shall yield her increase"* (Psalm 85:11-12). Did you know that every major social and political reform that ever came about came as a result of revival? The abolition of slavery was a result of revival. The end of the 90-hour week came because of revival. The removal of child labour resulted from revival in the days of John Wesley, The Y.M.C.A., the Salvation Army and the Sunday School movement - all of those movements came as a result of revival.

(b) King Jehoshaphat: We have the Supernatural Aspect of Revival

Jehoshaphat was Asa's son who sent the Levites to teach the Law of God in every city. This strategy had such an effect that the nations around Judah were gripped by the fear of the Lord. (See Chapter 17:10) So much so, that none of them attempted to make war with Judah. However, some years later the Ammonites, with the Moabites and the inhabitants of Mount Seir come up against Judah. When news of this mighty invasion reaches the King of Judah, he reacts as only the godly can do. Can you see here:

<u>1. The Prayer to the Lord</u>

Look at Chapter 20 verses 6 to 12. Jehoshaphat prays. What a prayer! Prayer is the key that opens the door to revival.

George Müller was born in 1805 and he lived until 1898. He was born in Germany, and as a young man he got himself into a lot of trouble. In fact, he was just wild, doing whatever he felt like doing. By the age of 16, he was in prison. When he got out of prison, he started where he had left off and he lived a thoroughly immoral life. But in his early 20s, he began getting tired of it. One day a friend invited him to go with him to a Bible study group, and instantly Müller knew that he wanted to go. He did go that evening and it was the turning-point in his life. Müller went on to become a man of incredible faith and prayer. He started evangelistic works, missionary enterprises and orphanages, and ran them all by faith and prayer. He would pray and specific, virtually miraculous, answers would come down from Heaven. He published an account of this in a book called *"Answers to Prayer"*. Copies of this book made it to Ireland and in January 1857, a young man named James McQuilkin read that book. McQuilkin was deeply moved by Müller's record and he went out and found a prayer partner, and, in time, they recruited a handful of prayer partners, four of them as far as we know. Every Friday night, these four men gathered in the old schoolhouse in Kells and prayed for revival.

McQuilkin and his very small group prayed for about a year, and on 1st January 1858, the Lord gave them their first remarkable answer to prayer, *the conversion of a farm worker.* Encouraged by this, the group continued meeting in earnest prayer as more people came to faith in Christ. Another year passed, and in February of 1859, a spirit of revival broke out in a nearby church as McQuilkin preached. So many people came and crammed themselves into the church that fears arose that the balconies and galleries would collapse. The revival overflowed into the streets. It spread to other churches and towns. The new believers carried the spiritual fire to other places and a revival spread throughout this country.

It is estimated that as many as a thousand people a day gave themselves to Christ. Businesses came to a complete standstill for a brief period of time as people could not do anything else until they got themselves right with God. People were unable to sleep at night. They were under such conviction that they wept and prayed through the night in their homes. And, it all began with prayer!

2. The Praise of the Lord

Look at Chapter 20 verses 21 and 22. Can you imagine - putting singers into the battle at the head of the army!

3. The Power from the Lord

"The Lord sent ambushments against the children of Ammon, Moab, and Mount Seir, which were come against Judah; and they were smitten" (Chapter 20:22). Do you see the supernatural aspect here? The Lord had to do it. God was the source of this blessing.

Do you recall the prayer of the Psalmist in Psalm 85 verse 6: *"Wilt Thou not revive us again?"* The book of Habakkuk has a prayer like this: *"O Lord, revive Thy work in the midst of the years"* (Habakkuk 3:2). Isaiah prayed: *"Oh that Thou wouldest rend the heavens, that Thou wouldest come down, that the mountains might flow down at Thy presence"* (Isaiah 64:1) When revival comes, it is something which God has to do. *We* are not able to bring revival. Sure, we can do the human thing that God expects of us, but we must recognise that we cannot work up revival. David Matthews stated the truth well: *"Revival movements have their birthplace in the heart of Deity"*.

(c) King Joash: We have the Sacrificial Aspect of Revival

It was Joash who set about repairing the house of the Lord after the reign of wicked Queen Athaliah. Joash devised a rather unique way to get the offerings of the people to repair the house of the Lord. He had a chest built. (Chapter 24:8-14) I want you to notice how these Israelites gave:

1. They gave Obediently

It says that they were *"to bring in to the Lord the collection that Moses the servant of God laid upon Israel in the wilderness"* (Chapter 24:9). In other words, they gave because the Bible says to give. Have you started to give to the work of the Lord? The question that we need to answer is this: *"How much owest thou unto my Lord?"* (Luke 16:5). Yes, unto the Lord who has given you life, breath, and all things to enjoy. To the Lord who has loved you eternally, redeemed you sacrificially and indwells you permanently. *"How much owest thou unto my Lord?"*

2. They gave Joyfully

Do you notice Chapter 24 verse 10? *"And all the people rejoiced."* Paul says: *"God loveth a cheerful giver"* (2 Corinthians 9:7). Did you know that the word *"cheerful"* literally means *"hilarious"*? The Lord loves a hilarious giver. Is that how you give?

3. They gave Abundantly

It says they gave *"much money"* (Chapter 24:11). In the last part of verse 11, it says they *"gathered money in abundance"*.

What did they do with all that money? Well, look at Chapter 24 verse 12: *"Gave it to such as did the work of the service of the house of the Lord"*. In other words, they took the money and put it in the hands of those who would do the work of the Lord. Now, there are a lot of believers who talk about revival but they are robbing God. Do you recall how God charged the people of Malachi's day? *"Will a man rob God? Yet ye have robbed Me. But ye say, Wherein have we robbed Thee? In tithes and offerings ... Bring ye all the tithes into the storehouse .... and prove Me now herewith, saith the Lord of hosts, if I will not open you the windows of heaven, and pour you out a blessing, that there shall not be room enough to receive it"* (Malachi 3:8-10). Do you long to see revival? Well, what about your giving?

(d) King Hezekiah: We have the Spiritual Aspect of Revival

No king of Judah is more unreservedly commended than good king Hezekiah.

He was marked by *holiness*. He said to the Levites: *"Hear me, ye Levites, sanctify now yourselves, and sanctify the house of the Lord God of your fathers, and carry forth the filthiness out of the holy place"* (Chapter 29:5). By the time Hezekiah came to power, the temple had become filled with filth, rubbish and garbage all throughout the courts. It took the workers 16 days to remove all of the refuse. There are sinful habits and practices in the lives of believers that are spoiling their testimony and they need to be removed. He was marked by *thankfulness*. He celebrated the first Passover feast that had been kept in the kingdom for many a year. (See Chapter 30:26) He was marked by *boldness*. It was Hezekiah who defied the Assyrians. (See Chapter 32:8) He was marked by *prayerfulness*. Each crisis in his life drove him to the place of prayer. (See Chapter 32:24 and Isaiah 37:16-20)

It was a time of revival but sadly the changes were only on the surface. It never touched the rank and file of the common people and once their sponsors were dead, the people went back to their old evil ways. Finally in:

(e) King Josiah: We have the Scriptural Aspect of Revival

Josiah was the boy King (Chapter 34:1) who, during a spring-cleaning of the temple, found the book of the law. What an effect the Word of God had on him. Look at Chapter 34 verses 23 to 28. Josiah had a tender heart. He responded with a sincere commitment to follow the Lord and he called the people to join him. (See verse 29) The rediscovery of the book of the law sparked an awakening that changed the course of a nation.

Is this not what happened in the 16th century Protestant Reformation? The Bible was rediscovered. It had been hid under the cloak of Romanism for many a year. Then Martin Luther discovered that wonderful, liberating truth: *"The just shall live by faith". Then its great truths were unveiled to the millions in Europe and the fires of revival began to spread.*

Do I have a tender heart? When God's Word is being preached, I want to tremble, not sleep. This is the Word of the living God and today we have almost lost respect for it.

Central to any real movement of the Spirit of God will be the Word of God. People often speak about witnessing revival, but so often they are content with the emotional, the exotic, the exciting and the charismatic. The question is, where does the Word of God feature? Is it central? Is it fundamental? Is it predominant?

Sadly, after five revivals, Ezra underscored the increasing rebellion of Judah. The people refused to repent and went into Babylonian captivity. (See Chapter 36:14-21) But the book ends on a bright note with:

(3) THE RETURN FROM CAPTIVITY

Notice Chapter 36 verses 22 and 23. These closing words of 2 Chronicles are identical to the opening words of Ezra. This is why scholars tell us that Ezra was the author of this book. Do you know what the Lord was doing here?

(a) GOD WAS FULFILLING HIS WORD

Do you see that phrase: *"That the Word of the Lord spoken by the mouth of Jeremiah might be accomplished"* (Chapter 36:22)? You see, Jeremiah had prophesied not only the fact of the Babylonian captivity but the duration of it. He said: *"For thus saith the Lord, That after seventy years be accomplished at Babylon I will visit you, and perform My good word toward you, in causing you to return to this place"* (Jeremiah 29:10). The seventy year captivity began in 605 B.C. and in 536 B.C. Cyrus issues this amazing proclamation, allowing the Jews to go back to their homeland to rebuild the temple. *The decree of Cyrus was the fulfilment of prophecy.* No doubt, during the long night of the exile, God's people must have wondered at times if they would ever see Jerusalem again, but God was faithful to His Word and did not forget His people.

Is this not an amazing book we hold in our hands? In spite of their sins, these exiles were God's chosen people and children of the covenant He had made with Abraham, Isaac and Jacob. (See Genesis 12:1-3) God was faithful to His promises and He did not forget His people. *But then, He never does.* Are you finding that difficult to believe? Are you going through some kind of personal exile? Is your situation dark and gloomy? Is Satan whispering in your ear that God has forgotten you? Is he tempting you to look at your circumstances rather than God?

The truth is that at such a time, when everything else has failed, the only thing we have left to rely on is the faithfulness of God and His Word.

(b) GOD WAS ORDERING HIS WORLD

God is in control of the nations. God is governing global affairs in accordance with His blueprint for mankind. God is still on the throne. History is simply His story! As we see the world in all its restlessness, its rebelliousness, its perverseness, its shaky foundations, we can become fearful, but remember: *"The most High ruleth in the kingdom of men, and giveth it to whomsoever He will"* (Daniel 4:17). It was the Lord who raised up Nebuchadnezzar: *"My servant"* (Jeremiah 25:9; 27:6 and 43:10) to chasten the people of Judah, and then He raised up Cyrus to defeat the Babylonians and establish the Persian Empire. Cyrus is described as: *"My shepherd"* (Isaiah 44:28) and *"His anointed"* (Isaiah 45:1). The Lord said: *"He shall build My city, and he shall let go My captives"* (Isaiah 45:13). This is all the more remarkable when we realise that Cyrus did not know God. (See Isaiah 45:5) But, God knew Cyrus! Whatever political motives lay behind Cyrus' decree, God was working out His own plans.

What a Bible we have! What a God we have!

"The king's heart is in the hand of the Lord, as the rivers of water: He turneth it whithersoever He will" (Proverbs 21:1). People do not have to be Christian believers for God to use them. It does not matter whether it is a president or a prime minister or a mayor or a governor, God can exercise His sovereign power to accomplish His purposes for His people. Puritan John Watson said: **"God can make a straight stroke with a crooked stick"** and that is what He did with Cyrus.

Chronicles is not such a dry book after all! It is **the book** on revival - and do we not desperately need it?

David Dodge was in conversation with a devout Quaker who like Dodge was eager to see a fresh movement of the Spirit of God. The Quaker agreed with Dodge concerning the need of more zeal, more prayer and more consecration. Finally, the Quaker broke in with these words: *"Friend Dodge, suppose thee and I make a beginning"*. That is it. Suppose *"thee and I"* make a beginning, remembering that **'I'** is central to the word 'revival'.

Is our prayer:

> *Lord, do it again,*
> *Lord, do it again,*
> *Send us a great revival,*
> *Lord, do it again.*

CHAPTER 16

Ezra

Late one night, in 1914, Thomas Edison's facilities in West Orange, New Jersey were heavily damaged by fire. Edison lost about $1,000,000 worth of equipment, along with a lot of paperwork containing the details of his inventions. Walking about the charred embers of his hopes and dreams the following morning, the 67 year old inventor said: *"There is value in disaster. God has worked it out so that all of our mistakes are burned up. Now, we can start anew."*

The books of Ezra and Nehemiah, which originally were probably one book, present to us the people of God beginning afresh and starting anew.

In introducing this book, there are several things we need to keep in mind. The first is:

1. The Captivity of Judah

(a) The Captivity Commenced

The Captivity commenced with three deportations of Judah. In 605 B.C. Nebuchadnezzar first invaded the land and took away Jehoiakim and the leading nobles. If you take away the cream of the nation, people like Daniel, it is easier to keep things under control. Then, in 597 B.C., Babylon came a second time and took away all the craftsmen and merchants in the hope that if they removed the people who made the money they could impoverish the people and finally bring them under control. Among those who were taken was a man called Ezekiel. Then, in 586 B.C., the final destruction of Jerusalem took place. The temple was razed to the ground and the Babylonians destroyed everything. The land began to make up for its neglected Sabbaths. (See 2 Chronicles 36:21) So, the Captivity commenced with three deportations and:

(b) The Captivity Concluded

The Captivity concluded with three returns. About the year 538 B.C. Cyrus the Persian issued a decree that gave the Jews liberty to return to Jerusalem and rebuild the temple. Led by Zerubbabel about 50,000 people responded. Then, in 458 B.C., a further group returned the leadership of Ezra. This return was a whole generation later than the first. Then, in the year 445 B.C., Nehemiah a high official in the Persian court was given permission to return to rebuild the walls of Jerusalem. So in the three returns there is the rebuilding of the spiritual life under Zerubbabel, the social life under Ezra and the physical life under Nehemiah.

2. The History of the Old Testament

Do you see now that there were two *"exodus"* movements in Old Testament history? The first was from Egypt to Canaan and the second was from Babylon to Canaan - with almost a millennium lying between the two events. Both these exiles and returns were the subject of prophecy, the first in Genesis 15 verses 13 and 14 and the second in Jeremiah 25 verses 11 and 12 and Chapter 29 verses 10 and 11.

3. The Chronology of the Period

A brief chronology of the period would look like this:

In 605, 597 and 586 B.C., Babylon begins invading and deporting people from the city of Jerusalem.
In 539 B.C., Babylon falls to Cyrus and the Media-Persian Empire begins.
In 538 or 536 B.C., Cyrus permits the Jews to return, about 50,000 return.
In 535 B.C., the Jews begin to rebuild the temple, but the work stops.
In 520 B.C., after fifteen years, the work begins again.

In 515 B.C., the temple is completed and dedicated.
In 476 B.C., Esther becomes Queen of Persia.
In 458 B.C., Ezra travels to Jerusalem with a further group.
In 445 B.C., Nehemiah comes to Jerusalem to rebuild the walls.

So the whole subject-matter of Ezra and Nehemiah has to do with: the return to the land and city; the rebuilding of the temple; the reforming of the people, and the rebuilding of the walls.

4. The Variety of the Leaders

Ezra is presented to us as a godly and patriotic Jew who was a priest and a scribe. (See Ezra 7:1-6) He was a devoted student of the Scriptures and helped to restore the Law to the nation. He was also a man of prayer (See Chapter 8:21-23) and a man who was greatly burdened for the spiritual welfare of his people (Chapter 9:3-4). His name means *"help"*. Now please note that Ezra did not lead the first group of Jews back to Jerusalem. This was done by Zerubbabel and Joshua.

Zerubbabel was also called 'Sheshbazzar' (Chapter 1:8 & 11 and Chapter 5:16). His official title was *"Tirshatha"* (Chapter 2:63) which means *"governor"*. 1 Chronicles indicates that Zerubbabel was in the royal line of David. (See 1 Chronicles 3:17-19) Joshua was the high priest at this time (Ezra 3:2; Haggai 1:1, 12 & 14, and Zechariah 3:1-10). Nehemiah was an officer in the king's court when God called him to return to Jerusalem and rebuild the walls. The two prophets were Haggai and Zechariah.

Now, with that by way of background, I want us to look at this book in three ways. First of all we see the people:

(1) RETURNING - CHAPTERS 1-2

Did you notice that it all begins with God? (Ezra 1:1) The Lord moves the heart of the king, the hands of the people (Chapter 1:5) and even their neighbours who reach for their purses (Chapter 1:4 & 6). Now Cyrus was the Persian ruler who had conquered Babylon and he was the ruler of the Number One world power at this time, but he seems to have been a very benevolent man with a policy of kindness towards conquered peoples. His attitude to prisoners of war was opposite to that of Babylon. He encouraged the Jews to return to their own land. Yet, beyond all that, we see the hand of God, for the Jews are returning:

(a) IN GOD'S PURPOSE

These opening verses in Ezra are almost identical to the closing verses in 2 Chronicles 36 verses 22 and 23. This leads many to believe that the same author was responsible for 1 & 2 Chronicles and Ezra and Nehemiah. Ezra was a careful man who was able to keep records and it appears that he wrote these books. No doubt Cyrus had been influenced by Daniel (See Daniel 6:28), who was at this time Prime Minister in Babylon. It could well have been that his last official duty was to prepare the papers authorizing the Jews to return to their land. Behind all of this return was *"the hand of God"* (Chapter 7:6). They were returning in God's purpose. Do you recall what Jeremiah prophesied concerning them? (see Jeremiah 29:10-14) The decree of Cyrus was the fulfilment of prophecy. No doubt, during the long night of the exile, God's people must have wondered at times if they would ever see Jerusalem again. But God was faithful to His Word and did not forget His people. You see, it was the Lord who had raised up Nebuchadnezzar *"My servant"* (Jeremiah 25:9; 27:6 and 43:10) to chasten the people of Judah and then God raised up Cyrus to defeat the Babylonians and re-establish the Persian Empire.

Do you know what the Lord called Cyrus? He calls him: *"My shepherd"* (Isaiah 44:28) and he is described as: *"His anointed"* (Isaiah 45:1). The Lord said: *"He shall build My city and he shall let go My captives"* (Isaiah 45:13). Is that not amazing? Many scholars cannot believe that Isaiah could possibly have known the name 'Cyrus', and insist that the text was written after the event. But God did know the name of the man! Two hundred years before Cyrus issued his decree, Isaiah told us the name of the man who would set the Jews free. Is it not wonderful to stand back and see the heart of God planning and the hand of God shaping? God is still on the throne.

(b) AS GOD'S PEOPLE

Look at Chapter 1 verse 3: *"Who is there among you of all His people?"* Although only three tribes are mentioned here in this first chapter, we know from other passages that there were representatives from all twelve tribes who returned. For example, in 2 Chronicles 11 verses 13 to 17, we are told at the time of Israel's civil war that various individuals from all twelve tribes moved to Jerusalem. Paul speaks of *"our twelve tribes"* (Acts 26:7). (Do these verses alone not challenge the doctrine of British Israelism which teaches the *"ten lost tribes"* are really the British and the Americans?) Now the actual number who responded to Cyrus' decree was very small, in all about fifty thousand people. One reason the number was small related to the journey itself. It involved a four to five month journey and a distance of almost 1,000 miles.

Moreover, all were not ready to leave Babylon. Jerusalem and its temple lay in ruins, but that did not matter to them. The majority of Jews preferred the land of plenty to the land of promise. Babylon looked good to them and they preferred to stay. You see, revival is disturbing, upsetting and life-changing!

Is that why history records that so few returned? Do you see what happened here? *"Then rose up .... all them whose spirit God had raised"* (Chapter 1:5). Is this not what revival is all about? God stirring the hearts of His people! Revival is not something on the outside that works in – it is something that God does on the inside that works out. Revival is a heart matter. It is something that begins to take place in the human heart.

There is <u>*Divine Sovereignty*</u> in revival as God stirs the heart, but there is <u>*Human Responsibility*</u> in revival as we meet the challenge.

"Who is there among you of all His people?...let him go up...and build" (Chapter 1:3). We cannot create the wind but we can set the sails. Is your cry this?

> *Oh, for the floods on a thirsty land,*
> *Oh for a mighty revival,*

> *Oh for a sanctified fearless band,*
> *Ready to hail its arrival.*

(c) WITH GOD'S PROVISION

The Lord had called them back to do a difficult job - to rebuild the temple, restore the city and reform the people. Who would meet the need? God! Who would provide the materials? God! Who would give the manpower? God! The people of Babylon gave gifts towards the rebuilding programme. (See Chapter 1:6) King Cyrus also restored the treasures captured from the temple (verse 7). But, behind it all was God. Do you know what one of the great names for God in the Bible is? *Jehovah-Jireh, the Lord will provide.* (See Genesis 22:14) You see, those whom God calls, He equips.

One night, George Müller of Bristol made known his intention at a public meeting to start an orphanage. He made it clear that no-one would ever be asked for money or materials, there would be no charge for admission and no restriction on entry because of class or creed. *All those employed as masters, matrons and assistants would be unpaid and had to be believers.* At the end of the meeting no collection was made, but a lady gave him ten shillings and volunteered for the work. The next day, a husband and wife volunteered their help, and also promised to give all their furniture for use in the orphanage. From that point on Müller never looked back and never lacked support for the work. *For God's work done in God's way will never lack God's supply.*

(d) UNDER GOD'S PRESERVATION

Now, be honest. What do you do when you come to a chapter in God's Word like Chapter 2? Do you say: *"Why? this is only a list of names!"* and so you hurry on? Well, the Holy Spirit would never have moved Ezra to write it unless it had a purpose. This same list is cited in Nehemiah 7 verses 6 to 73 and it shows that the returning exiles were the legitimate descendants of the Jews who occupied Israel prior to their deportation to Babylon. Such lists are meant to show that God has preserved the chosen people and the promised line of Messiah from generation to generation.

Israel is a remarkable nation. Israel, not Ulster, is God's covenant people. Throughout the history of this tiny nation an invisible hand has been upon her and it is the hand of God. Israel is the nation that will not go away. She is an indestructible people. (See Jeremiah 31:35-37)

Judah in the exile was preserved by God. Dr. Ironside says: *"Most of the names are for us only names, but God has not forgotten one of the persons once called by these names on earth"*. Think of the pains the children of Israel took to keep a strict record of their families while in captivity, and here God uses His servant Ezra under the inspiration of the Spirit of God to pen their names. You see, they were preserved by God because they were precious to God. They did not feel like that. Do you know something? These same people down in Babylon felt that the Lord had forgotten them. *"But Zion said, The Lord hath forsaken me, and my Lord hath forgotten me"* (Isaiah 49:14).

Is that exactly how you feel? Do you feel that because that trial has crossed your pathway that God does not care? Do you recall what the Lord Jesus said to His disciples? *"Are not two sparrows sold for a farthing? And one of them shall not fall on the ground without your Father. But the very hairs of your head are all numbered. Fear ye not therefore, ye are of more value than many sparrows."* (Matthew 10:29-31)

At the very time you are saying: *"My Lord has forgotten me"*, God is saying: *"Behold, I have graven thee upon the palms of My hands"* (Isaiah 49:16). The palms are the tenderest part of our hands and the place on which we always look. The thought in Isaiah 49 is that our remembrance of God is intermittent. We may remember the Lord in the morning or in the middle of the day or before we go to bed, but God's remembrance of us is continual, is eternal and is remedial.

So here they were going up to Jerusalem in God's purpose, as God's people, with God's provision and under God's preservation. The first phase is all about **Returning.**

(2) REBUILDING – CHAPTERS 3-6

Here they are, at the end of the journey and they are back in the land. Can you imagine the depth of feeling they experienced? Can you try and enter into the very thoughts that must have coursed through their minds? As they stood in a ruined city, in a desecrated temple, in the very place that God had chosen to reveal His glory, but now there was a new beginning, a glorious opportunity to start over again.

Is that what you need to do? As a believer have you lived carelessly, failed miserably, and disobeyed continually? In the goodness of God, you can start again. Failure is not final. Look at these chapters and notice:

(a) WORSHIP WAS RESTORED

Look at Chapter 3 verses 2 and 3. The altar was built. The altar was the place of worship. Of Abraham, we read: *"And Abram went up out of Egypt .... unto the place of the altar, which he had made there at the first: and there Abram called on the name of the Lord"* (Genesis 13:1 & 4). What was the first thing that Elijah did as he challenged the prophets of Baal on Mount Carmel? The Bible says: *"And he repaired the altar of the Lord that was broken down"* (1 Kings 18:30). You see, the people had to get back to a right relationship with God through worship and prayer. Of course, revival always results in worship. When there is a *"stirring"* of the people of God, the result is they will return to the place of worship. One of the sad things in our land is that so many people whose names are on church rolls seldom, if ever, darken the door of those churches. However, here were a people who were determined to set their worship and lives on a right footing from the beginning.

We read: *"They offered burnt offerings thereon unto the Lord"* (Chapter 3:3). You see, the burnt offering was the one that spoke specifically of worship. The burnt offering was all for God. There was no sharing here. All for God - for God must come first. What a lovely picture of our Lord's dedication of Himself to God: *"Lo, I come: in the volume of the book it is written of Me, I delight to do Thy will, O My*

God: yea Thy law is within My heart" (Psalm 40:7-8).

Is your devotion to the Lord full? Have you presented your body as *"a living sacrifice, holy, acceptable unto God"*?

(b) WORK WAS RESUMED

"Now in the second year of their coming unto the house of God at Jerusalem, in the second month, began Zerubbabel .... and Joshua .... to set forward the work of the house of the Lord" (Chapter 3:8).

Worship is always followed by service. God's work goes forward. The house of the Lord was beginning to be rebuilt. We read: *"And all the people shouted with a great shout, when they praised the Lord, because the foundation of the house of the Lord was laid"* (Chapter 3:11). When the building got under way, there was a division of labour and a commitment to see the job done. *"Facing a task unfinished"* - is that not where we are today?

How thankful we are for those who have gifts and talents to bring into the service of the Lord, but then the Holy Spirit has not left one single believer without some gift to enable him or her to serve God. He has divided *to "every man severally as He will"* (1 Corinthians 12:11). But, the real question is seldom one of gift or even of opportunity, but rather one of faithfulness and commitment. Does the fervour of these Old Testament saints not put us to shame? Are you still enthusiastic about the Lord's work? Or are you saying: *"I have given enough, I have done my bit!"*

We can learn from David Livingstone, the pioneer missionary to Africa, who walked over 29,000 miles. His wife died early in their ministry and he faced stiff opposition from his Scottish brethren. However, the words in his diary ought to challenge us: *"Lord, send me anywhere, only go with me. Lay any burden on me, only sustain me. Sever me from any tie, but the tie that binds me to Your service and heart"*. How does that leave you? It leaves me feeling ashamed! Then:

(c) WARFARE WAS RESISTED

This revival among the people of God soon ran into opposition. It is a repeated truism that where God is at work, then Satan will be at work as well. God's purpose is to build up and edify; Satan's purpose is to tear down and destroy. So every time God begins to build, you can be sure that the devil will begin to battle. Opportunity and opposition usually go together, and the greater the opportunity, the greater the opposition. Do you recall Paul's words: *"For a great door and effectual is opened unto me, and there are many adversaries"* (1 Corinthians 16:9)? Opportunity and opposition always go together, and that is exactly what we find here from the people around them. These Samaritans were half-Jewish and half-Gentile and they had a false religion. The Bible says: *"They feared the Lord, and served their own gods"* (2 Kings 17:33).

1. Their First Approach was very Subtle

"Let us build with you: for we seek your God, as ye do" (Chapter 4:2). Why was it so subtle and dangerous? Because they would have led the Jews back into idolatry again. (See Deuteronomy 7:1-11 and 12:1-3) Is this not the offer of the ecumenical movement? *"Let us co-operate. Let us sink our differences. We may differ slightly, but let us compromise for the sake of the common good."* Is this not what we are being told on a church level? *"Let us sink our differences. Forget about our principles. Join together on a common platform."* Are you not glad that Zerubbabel was not like so many church leaders? He was not a compromiser, or a ditherer: *"Ye have nothing to do with us to build an house unto our God; but we ourselves together will build"* (Chapter 4:3).

Do you see what then happened when God's people stood their ground and said: "No!"?

2. Their Further Approach was very Strong

Literally, 'all hell broke loose'. Do you see Chapter 4 verse 4? *"The people of the land weakened the hands of the people of Judah, and troubled them."* Sometimes Satan comes as the serpent to deceive (see Chapter 4:2) and when that fails he comes as the lion to devour (see Chapter 4:4). He will use friends and family, times of joy and sadness, times when things are going well with us and times when circumstances are against us. But always his aim is the same - to undermine the work of God and to crush the people of God. Here it looked as if Satan was successful. Notice that:

(d) WEARINESS WAS REVEALED

"Then ceased the work of the house of God which is at Jerusalem" (Chapter 4:24). The constant opposition had taken its toll. The work ceased. The immediate cause was opposition from without, but the secondary cause was discouragement from within. Haggai, who was a contemporary, tells us in his book that the people of God had lost heart. They were thinking only of themselves and their own houses. They were saying: *"The time is not come, the time that the Lord's house should be built"* (Haggai 1:2).

1. They lost Heart: the battle was too much.
2. They lost Vision: they put materialism before the things of God.
3. They lost Sight of God: For 15 years they had an altar, but the freshness of their first love was gone.

Is this you? Are you on the brink of resigning from some Christian ministry through discouragement? Are you ready to call it a day? To call it quits? Some years ago, someone gave me a little plaque that said: *"It's always too soon to quit"*. Why would you quit? You have the Word of God before you, the Christ of God beside you, the Spirit of God within you, the people of God around you, the glory of God before you. *"Let us not be weary in well doing: for in due season we shall reap, if we faint not (if we do not lose heart)"* (Galatians 6:9). Do you know what you need? You need to hear the Word of God again, for we see here:

(e) WITNESSING WAS RENEWED

"Then the prophets, Haggai ... and Zechariah ... prophesied unto the Jews that were in Judah and Jerusalem in the name of the God of Israel ... Then rose up Zerubbabel ... and Jeshua ... and began to build the house of God ... And they builded, and finished it, according to the commandment of the God of Israel (Chapter 5:1-2 and 6:14).

Now the opposition did not stop. Indeed it became more vocal and vehement than ever, but God's people simply left the opposition to God and went on with the work. Within five years, the temple was completed. Is it not amazing how the Word of God can transform people? These discouraged and fearful people were changed into warriors who wielded trowels in the battle to build for the glory of God.

The temple was completed in 515 B.C. (See Chapter 6:15) It started about 535 B.C. (See Chapter 3:10) So, it was over 20 years in building. In:

Chapter 3: The Building Commenced;
Chapter 4: The Building Ceased;
Chapter 5: The Building Continued;
Chapter 6: The Building Completed.

Human nature, however, remains human nature. Even such a great revival as this could not last. No revival has ever lasted. Within a generation was needed a fresh visitation of the Spirit of God. Someone has said that a movement that ceases to move becomes a monument! So we move on from Ezra 6 to Chapter 7, remembering as we do that we pass over fifty-seven years and to this interim period belongs the story of Esther. Now we have come to the final phase of the book:

(3) REFORMING - CHAPTERS 7-10

The word *"reform"* means *"correction of abuses or malpractices"* or *"to improve by correcting abuses"*. Was this not exactly what happened here in Ezra's day? You see, Ezra was only back there for four months (See Chapter 7:9 and Chapter 10:9) when he learned that all was not well with the people of God. *There was sin in the camp.* God's own people were marrying their non-Jewish, idol-worshipping neighbours. This was a continual problem with the Jews. It is a sad fact that frequently the same sin seems to come back to haunt us. Can you imagine the grief and disappointment of the man of God?

If the first section of the book is all about *national restoration* (Chapters 1-6), then the last section of the book has to do with *spiritual reformation* (Chapters 7-10). *You see, if revival comes from above, then reformation comes from below.* In *revival,* the supernatural element is uppermost as the Spirit of God works in the hearts of the people of God. But in *reformation,* the human element is largely at work in taking the initiative to plan and bring about change for the better. Ezra as a teacher of the Word of God could see that the people needed to be taught afresh the doctrine of separation. This was a reforming process and it was done with great thoroughness and prayer. Do you know what this tells us? *It tells us that while we long for revival in the church, but cannot make it happen, we can nevertheless bring about a reformation where it is needed.*

Leaders, members, believers can reform the structures of their local church so as to make its witness more effective in the community. Is this not vital if the Gospel is to meet the challenges of today, and the church is to remain relevant in this age? *What about our personal lives? Do we not need from time to time to take a long, hard look at ourselves and ask ourselves if we need reforming? What about your prayer life? What about your faithfulness at the services? Your input into the local church?* Are these not areas that need reforming in order to give a sharper edge to our Christian experience and witness?

Notice that this reformation:

(a) Commences on a Scriptural Level

Remember that almost sixty years had elapsed since Zerubbabel had finished the temple. Sixty years is a long time in human history. A generation passes away, another generation takes its place and waxes old and prepares to hand over to the grandchildren. It is not often that the third generation has the fervour and fire of the first for spiritual truth or for a spiritual awakening. Well, in Israel, in the Promised Land spiritual truth had worn thin. The Scriptures had been neglected and the people were occupied with material things. So God found a man, Ezra by name, who was addicted to the Word of God. Look at Chapter 7 verse 10: *"For Ezra had prepared his heart to seek the law of the Lord, and to do it, and to teach in Israel statutes and judgments"*. You see, Ezra had prepared his heart for the day that he would return to his own land. He knew it was coming because he had faith in God, so he inwardly determined to make three things the chief objective of his life. He was determined:

1. To Ponder God's Word

Do you see how he puts it? *"To seek the law of the Lord"*. He would have agreed with the Psalmist who wrote: *"O how I love Thy law! it is my meditation all the day"* (Psalm 119:97). What time do you give to the reading and meditation of God's Word?

2. To Practise God's Word

"And to do it." Martin Luther speaking of a pastor by the name of Nicholas Hussman said: *"What we preach, he lives"*. Could that be said of you?

3. To Preach God's Word

"And to teach in Israel statutes and judgments." Ezra was a man of the book. He wanted to know it, obey it and teach it. It is believed he wrote Chronicles, Ezra and Nehemiah, organized the sacred writings into the Old Testament canon, wrote Psalm 119 as well as Psalm 1 as a preface to the book of Psalms and promoted the *"synagogue"* as the local place to teach God's Word. No wonder Ezra was able to bring about reform. He knew God's Word.

(b) Continues on a Spiritual Level

1. Ezra had a Heart for God

He was a man of prayer. Before he left for the Promised Land, he and his group sought the Lord: *"That we might afflict ourselves before our God, to seek of Him a right way for us, and for our little ones, and for all our substance"* (Chapter 8:21). They brought the matter of *their footsteps, their families and their finances* before the Lord. When he got back to Jerusalem and discovered that God's people were marrying outside of the people of God (see Deuteronomy 7:1-3 and Exodus 34:15-17), he was broken. Hear him as he cries: *"O my God, I am ashamed and blush to lift up my face to Thee"* (Chapter 9:6). Is sin still shocking to you? Do the sins of God's people move you to tears?

2. Ezra knew the Hand of God

Indeed, was this not the secret of his ministry? The hand of God is:

1. A Giving Hand: *"The king granted him all his request, according to the hand of the Lord his God upon him"* (Chapter 7:6).

2. A Sustaining Hand: for they kept safe on their long journey of 4 months *"according to the good hand of his God upon him"* (Chapter 7:9).

3. An Enabling Hand: *"And I was strengthened as the hand of the Lord my God was upon me"* (Chapter 7:28).

4. A Protecting Hand: *"And the hand of our God was upon us, and He delivered us from the hand of the enemy"* (Chapter 8:31).

When God wants something done, He gets His hand upon a man.

This reformation:

(c) Culminates on a Social Level

The people who had been born in the land after the first revival soon lost sight of a basic spiritual truth. They lost sight of the truth of separation from the world. Do you see what happened when Ezra came? See Chapter 9 verses 1 to 3. Do you see what was needed? Things needed to be put right socially, domestically and personally. Do you know what the last verse in the book says? *"Some of them had wives by whom they had children"* (Chapter 10:44). Can you imagine the pain when they had to put away their foreign wives and children? But this was the price of continuing reformation!

God's desire for Israel then is God's desire for you now. *"Be ye holy; for I am holy"* (1 Peter 1:16 and Leviticus 11:44). That is the standard of separation. Are you violating it? Are there aspects of your life that need reforming? Has the Lord been placing His finger on those things? How will you respond? Will you say with God's people of old: *"As Thou hast said, so must we do"* (Chapter 10:12)?

> *Lord, take my life and make it wholly Thine,*
> *Fill my poor heart with Thy great love Divine,*
> *Take all my will, my passion, self and pride,*
> *I now surrender, Lord, in me abide.*

CHAPTER 17

Nehemiah

Many years ago, in a certain kingdom there was a large boulder in the middle of the roadway. Traveller after traveller walked past the boulder, veering off to the side of the road to get around it. All the time, they were shaking their head and muttering: *"Can you believe that? Someone should get that big thing out of the way! What an inconvenience!"* Finally, a man came along and seeing the boulder took a strong branch from a tree and prised the boulder enough to get it rolling, and it rolled off to the side of the road. Lying underneath the boulder he found a note. It read as follows:

"Thank you for being a true servant of the kingdom. Many have passed this way and complained because of the state of the problem, but you have taken the responsibility upon yourself to serve the kingdom instead. You are the type of citizen we need more of in the kingdom. Please accept this bag of gold that traveller after traveller has walked by, because they did not care enough about the kingdom to serve."

I wonder what *"bags of gold"* we are missing each day, simply because we do not bother enough to get involved in serving the King of Kings and Lord of Lords? Does anyone really care about the state of the work of God?

Nehemiah, whose name means *"Jehovah comforts"*, was the kind of person who cared. He cared about the traditions of the past; the needs of the present, and the hopes of the future. Nehemiah cared about his heritage, his ancestral city and the glory of his God. Although he had a highly responsible job, in a secure environment in a fine Persian city, noted for its opulence and prosperity, magnificent buildings, and spacious gardens, Nehemiah was not preoccupied with himself. *Rather he was concerned with the people of God, and the work of God at Jerusalem.* Nehemiah cared. *Do you care?* Do you care that the cause of God in this land is at a lower ebb than ever before? Do you care that souls are not being saved in the numbers they used to be? Do you care about the walls that are broken down in the life of your local church and in your own life? Before we embark on an analysis of this book let us see where we are:

1. Historically

In 538 B.C., 50,000 Jews returned to the land of Israel under the leadership of Zerubbabel. Eventually, after opposition from the Samaritans and great encouragement from the prophets Haggai and Zechariah, the temple was completed in 515 B.C. In 458 B.C., Ezra travels to Jerusalem with a further group and now 13 years later in 445 B.C. Nehemiah comes to Jerusalem to rebuild the walls. That is where we are historically.

2. Biblically

After the Pentateuch, the historical books of the Old Testament begin with Joshua and end with Nehemiah and Esther and span a period of about one thousand years.

Both the Greek Septuagint and the Latin Vulgate originally named this book: *"Second Ezra"*. Even though the two books of Ezra and Nehemiah are now separate in most English Bibles, they may have once been joined together in one single unit - as they are currently in the Hebrew texts.

When we come to Nehemiah, we come to the end of Old Testament history. With the exception of Malachi, who was a contemporary of Nehemiah, all the other books precede Nehemiah in terms of chronology. 400 years are now to pass in prophetic silence until the coming of the forerunner of the Lord Jesus, John the Baptist. In the rebuilding of the walls, Malachi was to Nehemiah what Haggai and Zechariah had been to Ezra.

3. Spirituality

In the years between Ezra's return to the Promised Land and the arrival of Nehemiah in Jerusalem, great changes have taken place. Ezra seems to be no longer Governor; the people were in great affliction and under constant reproach. The Arabs, Israel's enemies then as now, had moved their hostile camps close to Jerusalem. Sanballat and his enemies seemed to be all-powerful. Priests and people alike had gone back to their foreign wives. Some of the poorer Jews had been forced to mortgage themselves to their wealthier compatriots. The temple had been rebuilt but already neglect of the Sabbath was a common thing. One glimpse at the book of Malachi will tell us that things were bad spiritually.

4. Biographically

Nehemiah himself is a really first-rank character. He stands out conspicuously as a man of prayer, a man of faith, a man of vision, a man of courage and a man of action. Some people are so heavenly minded that they are no earthly use, but not this man. He did not mind putting his hand to cementing. He could organize well, he studied the gates and the walls and assessed the needs of the people. His head was not up in the clouds. He was a practical man. *Is it not wonderful when you get a combination of a practical man and a prayerful man?*

Samuel Chadwick, beloved by all sound Methodists, once used the following words in a prayer at a service which he was conducting in Manchester: *"O Lord, make us intensely spiritual, but keep us perfectly natural and thoroughly practical"*. Does Nehemiah not illustrate those three expressions? Intensely spiritual, perfectly natural and thoroughly practical. There is such a balance in his character.

This book falls into three parts. Notice the first section has to do with:

(1) REBUILDING THEIR WALLS - CHAPTERS 1-6

Right away we are introduced to Nehemiah. Now who was he? Zerubbabel was a prince of the house of Judah, Ezra was a priest of the family of Aaron and a scribe, but Nehemiah was a nobody – in the sense that his ancestry is unknown. All we know is: he was the son of Hachaliah; the brother of Hanani, and he was the king's cupbearer. The king was Artaxerxes Longimanus who reigned over the Persian Empire for forty years.

How did Nehemiah, a Jew, become the king's cupbearer? Well, the fact that Esther was the king's stepmother may have had something to do with it. It was not an especially pleasant job to drink the wine, literally wondering if your next drink would be your last, but it was a responsible position. It made him a confidant of the king and he would share things in the relaxed atmosphere of that relationship. It was while Nehemiah was doing his job that he learned about the sad condition of the people of God. Can you see:

(a) THE BURDEN THAT NEHEMIAH CAUGHT

Probably Hanani had been sent up to the Persian capital by Ezra to bring information about the condition of the Jews in Jerusalem. Do you see Chapter 1 verses 2 to 4? Nehemiah was burdened enough:

1. To Ask

Here is man looking out in compassion at the needs of others. Do you notice that he asked about the _People_: *"the Jews"* and then he asked about the _Place_: *"and concerning Jerusalem"*? Can you sense the burden of his heart? Nehemiah cared enough to ask. When missionaries come home from the field of service, do you ask how they are getting on? What about evangelists? What about pastors/ teachers? Do you ever lift the phone and say: *"How are the meetings going?"*

2. To Weep

On hearing of his people's needs, Nehemiah, *"sat down and wept, and mourned certain days, and fasted"* (verse 4).

Jerusalem's plight was a 1000 miles from Shushan the palace, but because he loved them, the anguish of his people reduced everything else in his life to lesser importance. He wept. He was not the last person to weep over Jerusalem's troubles. During the last week of His earthly ministry, the Lord Jesus looked over the rebellious city and found it impossible to hold back the tears. *"And when He was come near, He beheld the city, and wept over it"* (Luke 19:41). Nehemiah was called to build the wall, but first he had to weep over the ruins. He cared enough to weep.

Is my ministry marked by tears? Not silly tears, shallow tears, crocodile tears, but sincere tears for the state of God's cause and the salvation of men's souls? Does the thought of Christless feet on the way to Hell break your heart? Do you know what it is to come before the Lord and mourn over your own coldness, indifference and apathy?

Samuel Hadley was a great soul-winner in New York. One night he was overheard as he prayed: *"O God, the sin of this city is breaking my heart"*. Have you ever thought about the sin and citizens of your community? Have you a real burden for the work of God in this place? Does that burden find expression at the throne of grace?

3. To Pray

Do you see Chapter 1 verse 4? He *"prayed before the God of heaven"*. Nehemiah's first act did not involve rushing off to the king and trading on his position as the king's cupbearer. That might have been the *"sensible"* thing to do, but it was not the *"spiritual"* thing to do. Nehemiah did the spiritual thing. He had the ear of the king, but more importantly he had the ear of God so he *"fasted, and prayed before the God of heaven"*. Does your burden find expression at the throne of grace? Like Nehemiah have you caught the burden?

(b) THE BLESSING THAT NEHEMIAH SOUGHT

Nehemiah was a man of prayer. There are twelve instances of prayer recorded in this book: Chapters 1:4; 2:4; 4:4 & 9; 5:19; 6:9 &

14; 9:4; 13:14, 22, 29 & 31. The book of Nehemiah opens and closes with prayer. This man is never out of touch with God. Nehemiah mastered the art of prolonged prayer. He also shot up to Heaven the arrow of intercession when necessary. Nehemiah succeeded because he depended on God. Speaking about the church's ministry today, Alan Redpath said: *"There is too much working before men and too little waiting before God"*.

What was the blessing that Nehemiah sought? Come to Chapter 2. Four months have now passed. Four months of fasting and prayer have left their mark on Nehemiah's face. One day as he was in the presence of the king, the king suddenly noticed: *"Nehemiah, what's the matter. You look sad"*. This was the opening for which Nehemiah had been praying and so he says: *"Let the king live forever: why should not my countenance be sad, when the city, the place of my fathers' sepulchres, lieth waste, and the gates thereof are consumed with fire?"* (Chapter 2:3) Then the king said to him: *"For what dost thou make request?"* Nehemiah records his response: *"So I prayed to the God of heaven"* (Chapter 2:4). This is what Guy King calls *"a sky telegram"*, but remember the sky telegram was backed by four solid months of persistent prayer. It was like an arrow out of a bow. *"So I prayed to the God of heaven."* Hudson Taylor said: *"It's possible to move men through God by prayer alone"*. Nehemiah petitioned a heavenly throne and then he petitioned an earthly throne. You see, Nehemiah wanted to:

1. Be Sent: He wanted Royal Permission

Do you see the two words in verse 5 of Chapter 2: *"Send me"*? Nehemiah was answering his own prayer and putting his own life on the line. Is this not to be the dominating factor in all our service for God? Not the needs of others, but the command of the Lord, His absolute sovereignty to send His people anywhere. Is this not the only thing that will keep your hand to the plough when the going gets tough? To know that you are sent by the Lord.

2. Be Safe: He wanted Royal Protection

Do you see the two words in verse 7 of Chapter 2: *"Convey me"*?

What a surprise Nehemiah must have got the day he left for Jerusalem, for we read in verse 9: *"Now the king had sent captains of the army and horsemen with me"*. Does this not teach us that we must never embark on any service for the Lord alone? Do you realise that you might be the means in God's hands for keeping some servant of God safe spiritually because of your prayers?

3. Be Supplied: He wanted Royal Provision

Do you see the two words in verse 8 of Chapter 2: *"Give me"*? Nehemiah wanted the materials to do the job. Was he asking too much? Artaxerxes did not think so, for we read: *"And the king granted me, according to the good hand of my God upon me"* (Chapter 2:8). Is it not interesting that Nehemiah was not just an agoniser but an organiser, for there was:

(c) THE BRILLIANCE THAT NEHEMIAH BROUGHT

This book shows us how to plan our work and work our plan and at the same time rely on the Lord. Nehemiah was a capable organizer and he divided the wall into sections, each section running from one gate to the next. John Phillips says: *"There were forty-two work parties and each worked on the section on the wall nearest to where they lived. This was good psychology and it worked"*. Indeed, there is a phrase that appears at least 4 times in Chapter 3: *"Even over against his house"* (Chapter 3:10, 23, 28 & 30). Is this not where every real work for God must begin? We can complement and implement the work of God if we will do our homework. Have you begun at your Jerusalem? *"Over against his house."* (See Mark 5:19 and Luke 8:39) Are you doing the work that lies nearest to your home? Are you starting with your own family?

This book is a rebuke to those who tell us that any kind of organization in God's work is wrong. Spirituality plus organization plus hard work all played a part in Nehemiah's success - and successful he was! The work was finished in fifty-two days, but not without a battle, for consider:

(d) THE BATTLE THAT NEHEMIAH FOUGHT

It was inevitable that once the man of God said: "Let us arise and build", the enemy said: "Let us arise and stop him". The door of opportunity swings on the hinges of opposition. There was:

1. Opposition from Without

Sanballat was governor of Samaria, Tobiah of the region east of the Jordan and Geshem, an Arab chief. This was the *"3 A Society"*: Apollyon's Aggravation Association. Do you see the tactics that they used?

SCORN: (Chapter 4:1-6)

British author Thomas Carlyle called ridicule the *"language of the devil"*. Is it not an amazing thing that that which is precious to God, His work, is an object of scorn for the devil: *"What do these feeble Jews?"*

When we say that the only hope for the world is the Gospel of Christ, the world rises up and says: *"You with your feeble prayer meetings, your silly plans of getting folk saved, you have no intellect, no status and no resources"*. How did Nehemiah meet the scorn of the enemy? He just kept on praying and kept on building.

FORCE: (Chapter 4:7-23)

Taunts became threats and sneers became plots. Things certainly looked pretty serious. The opposition had developed into a formidable alliance. (See verse 7) Is it not amazing that mutual enemies become mutual friends to oppose the work of God. Do you recall that prior to the crucifixion Pilate sent the Saviour to Herod? We read: *"And the same day Pilate and Herod were made friends together: for before they were at enmity between themselves"* (Luke 23:12). Is there not a word of encouragement for us here? You see, whatever scorn, derision, threat has ever been directed against you has first of all been poured out upon your precious Lord and *"the servant is not greater than his Lord"* (John 15:20). Scorn, then force and now:

GUILE: (Chapter 6:1-19)

They were secretly plotting. They said: *"Come, let us meet together in some one of the villages in the plain of Ono"* (Chapter 6:2). *"Nehemiah, come down; let's talk; be friends; don't be so extreme or narrow."* Have you heard that language? Are these words familiar to your ears? *"Come down, compromise. Be a Christian if you like, but don't be so fanatical about it. Let go of your principles. Drop your standards. A visit to the dance-hall or having a drink will do you no harm!"* Is that what Satan has been whispering in your ear? *'Come into the parlour'*, said the spider to the fly!

"Come to the plains of Ono", they say to Nehemiah. What do you think Nehemiah said? "Ono!" If they had said to Nehemiah: *"Let's meet in the little town of Oyes"*, Nehemiah would still have said "Ono!"

Do you see how Nehemiah responds? With a mind to work (Chapter 6:3); an eye to watch (Chapter 4:9) and a heart to pray (Chapter 4:9). But Nehemiah had not only to battle with Opposition from Without, he also had to face:

2. Hindrances from Within

There was Debris

"And Judah said, The strength of the bearers of burdens is decayed, and there is much rubbish: so that we are not able to build the wall" (Chapter 4:10). The sheer massiveness of the task discouraged them. Does it trouble you? When you think of the souls that have to be saved, the resources that have to be found, the decline that has to be halted, do you say: *"We can't!"*? Does the work discourage you?

There was Fear

Look at verses 11 to 14 of Chapter 4. Jews from outlying districts brought repeated warning that a surprise attack was being planned by Nehemiah's enemies. This spread fear among the workers. Nothing is more paralysing than fear. How often it

A Journey Through the Bible

paralyses Christian service today. Do you know what the antidote to fear is? The Lord! I wonder, do you need to get your eye off the circumstances and onto the Lord? *"Remember the Lord, which is great and terrible"*, cries Nehemiah in Chapter 4 verse 14.

There was Greed
================

Look at verses 1 to 13 of Chapter 5. Jews the world over are known for their business acumen. Some of the rich Jews were making profit at the expense of their poorer brethren by forcing them into slavery and acquiring their properties.

If Satan cannot ruin a work for Christ from without, he will seek to ruin it from within. If he cannot do it by discouragement, by fear, he will try to do it through self-seeking and other wrong motives between Christian and Christian.

Satan does not care what tactic is used as long as the work stops. But is it not encouraging to read in Chapter 6 verse 15: *"So the wall was finished"*. It was finished in less than two months. The cause of God was victorious.

Martin Luther was told that he could not build a wall to withstand the pressures of the Roman Catholic hierarchy, but he placed his great heart and mind into the Herculean task and *"so the wall was finished"*.

What did Winston Churchill say to the pupils of the Harrow school? *"Never give in, never, never, never, never, never, never give in."*

(2) RENEWING THEIR FAITH - CHAPTERS 7-10

A revival is only as strong, after all, as the work it accomplishes in the hearts of men and women. We can do all the building we want, but if the heart is not right, then nothing will last. So Nehemiah joined forced forces with Ezra the scribe to ensure that a real work would be done in the hearts of the people.

How do you renew your faith? How do you rekindle your love for the Lord? Well it needs to be done:

(a) IN THE CONGREGATION OF SAINTS

Nehemiah faced an anomaly. There was a city without citizens. So, in order to re-populate the city, Nehemiah needed to know how many really belonged to the community of God's people. So Nehemiah 7 is Ezra 2 all over again. It simply shows that the returning exiles were the legitimate descendants of the Jews who occupied Israel prior to their deportation to Babylon. Here the names of God's people are written into God's book.

God's chief concern is His people. His people rather than buildings. *Here were a people who were important to the Lord, a people who were precious to Him.* Do you realise that you may not be important in the eyes of the world, but you are precious in the eyes of God? We must never get so taken up with the programme that we overlook the people. Faith needs to be renewed in the company of the saints.

(b) BY THE COMPREHENSION OF SCRIPTURE

Do you know what we have in Chapter 8? A *"Back to the Bible"* movement. Having finished <u>the work of reconstruction</u> (Chapters 1-6), Nehemiah and Ezra begin the <u>work of reinstruction</u> (Chapters 7-13). This meant instructing the people of God in the Word of God. Surely the test of any movement or mission that claims to be doing the work of God is the place given to the Word of God. Any revival not solidly based on the Bible is suspect from the start. Revival is usually an emotional time. Hearts are stirred, consciences are ripped open, sins are confessed, tears are shed, and wrongs are righted. There is a great deal of emotion, but emotionalism is no solid basis for a continuing work. Unless that work is undergirded by the Word of God, it will soon lead to unscriptural excess. So Nehemiah brought in the Bible teacher.

Do you see Chapter 8 verse 5? Ezra opened the book – and all the people stood up. What a respect they had for the Word of God! But look at verse 8. There was:

1. The Reading of the Text of God's Word: *"They read in the book in the law of God distinctly"*.

2. The Revealing of the Truth of God's Word: *"They gave the sense"*.

3. The Relating of the Thrust of God's Word: *"And caused them to understand the reading"*.

Is that not a very good definition or statement of expository preaching? Exposition is the opening up of the Scriptures so people can understand them, so they will know what the Book has to say. Ezra is a Bible expositor. He is expounding the Scriptures. He is explaining the Word of God. His ministry is Bible-centred. Do you recall what was said of the Early Church? *"They spake the word of God with boldness"* (Acts 4:31). *"They .... went every where preaching the word"* (Acts 8:4). Is our ministry Bible-centred? What about your ministry in the Sunday School, among the young people, the seniors, on the doors, with your neighbours? It is so easy to become entangled in politics and philosophies instead of the Word of God. *"Preach the Word!"*

When Charles Spurgeon came to London, he found that the people were *"so starved that a morsel of the Gospel was a treat to them"*. A remarkable work for the Lord then took place. People were saved week by week. Years later when Spurgeon died, it was said that the people in his congregation knew more of their Bibles than the theologians. Why? Because he expounded the Word of God. Do you want your faith to be renewed? Do you want your love for the Lord to be rekindled? Then the cry of your heart will need to be: *"Bring the book."*

For them it was the Pentateuch, for us it is the complete canon of Scripture. *"Bring the book"*, Sir Walter Scott pleaded as he lay a-dying. *"What book?"* asked his servant. *"There is only one book - the Bible"* was his famous response. I wonder - is this the cry of your heart? *"Bring the book!"* Do you have a hunger for the Word? Do you feel like Job when he said: *"I have esteemed the words of His mouth more than my necessary food"* (Job 23:12)?

(c) UNTO THE CONFESSION OF SIN

Martin Luther said: *"The Bible is alive - it speaks to me; it has feet - it runs after me; it has hands - it lays hold of me"*.

One thing is sure, when Ezra and the Levites read the Word and gave the sense the people were moved. The Spirit of God through the Word of God had touched the hearts of the people of God. In Chapter 9, we have the longest prayer recorded in the Bible. A prayer that takes us from the *creation* of the universe (verse 6) to the *condition* of God's people (verse 33). You see, as they reviewed God's goodness and their faithlessness, they were brought to the place of confession before the Lord. Look at verse 38. They pledged that from then onwards they would order their lives according to the demands and dictates of God's Word. First of all, they dedicated themselves to God (See Chapter 9:38-12:26) and then they dedicated the newly-constructed wall (See Chapter 12:27-47). Is this not revival? Revival is not thrills and chills and babbling and boasting. Revival is getting right with God.

> *Back to the Bible the true living Word,*
> *Sweetest old story that ever was heard,*
> *Back to the giving of money and time,*
> *Back to the life of contentment sublime,*
> *Back to the beautiful path I once trod,*
> *Back to the church and the people of God.*

(3) REFORMING THEIR CONDUCT - CHAPTERS 11-13

In Chapter 13 verse 6, we are told that Nehemiah's leave of absence ran out and that he returned to the palace at Shushan. This was about 433 B.C. We are not sure how long he stayed, perhaps until 424 B.C., but in that interval conditions got worse. *Is it not so true that we often go back to the same old sins that we have committed before?* When Nehemiah returned to Jerusalem:

(a) THE SANCTUARY NEEDED TO BE RECLAIMED

Tobiah, the very man who had been a thorn in Nehemiah's side, had infiltrated and was now living in the House of God like a lord. (See Chapter 13:7) Do you see, in verses 8 and 9, what Nehemiah did? In this respect, Nehemiah typifies the Lord Jesus who drove out of the temple *"those that sold oxen and sheep and doves, and the changers of money"* (John 2:14). Nehemiah cleansed the temple. Is that where we need to start? Paul says: *"What? know ye not that your body is the temple of the Holy Ghost which is in you, which ye have of God, and ye are not your own?"* (1 Corinthians 6:19). Is your body, the temple, filled with sinful clutter, practices, or habits? What is there in your life or home that needs to be put on the street?

(b) THE SUPPORT NEEDED TO BE RENEWED

Do you see what Nehemiah says? *"Why is the house of God forsaken?"* (Chapter 13:11) A foolish high priest had been taken in by a deceptive enemy and the Levites had been deprived of their proper support. (See Chapter 10:36-37) Is it not tragic when we, the people of God, fail in our stewardship? I wonder - are there missionaries unable to continue due to a lack of support? Servants who have had to moon-light because a church has starved them out? Could it be that it is time for us to renew our stewardship?

(c) THE SABBATH NEEEDED TO BE RESTORED

Do you see verse 15 of Chapter 13? Nehemiah found Jews desecrating the Sabbath, turning God's day of rest into another day of business, and he put a speedy end to that. (See Chapter 13:18-22) Of course, we know that the Sabbath as a law is a distinctly Jewish institution (Deuteronomy 5:12-15). Does that mean that there is no day of rest and worship for us as New Testament believers? *Not at all.* You see, God has set His seal on the first day of the week. *"And upon the first day of the week, when the disciples came together to break bread"* (Acts 20:7). *"Upon the first day of the week let every one of you lay by him in store, as God hath prospered him"* (1 Corinthians 16:2). The church meets on the first day of the week, the Lord's Day, and we meet on resurrection ground and set aside this day for worship and witness. What are you doing with the Lord's Day? Are you keeping Sunday special?

(d) THE SOCIETY NEEDED TO BE REBUKED

Despite all that they had promised (Chapter 10:30), they had once again contracted marriages with the ungodly. Nehemiah rebuked them.

The difference between Ezra and Nehemiah is that Ezra pulled out his own hair (Ezra 9:3), *but Nehemiah pulled out other people's* (Nehemiah 13:25)!

Note how this great book of Nehemiah ends: *"Remember me, O my God, for good"* (Chapter 13:14, 22, 29 & 31). Earlier he has said *"Think upon me, my God, for good, according to all that I have done for this people"* (Chapter 5:19). Could you make a similar appeal to God for recognition, for remembrance and reward?

Many years ago John Williams, the missionary, while speaking in Edinburgh held an audience spell-bound with thrilling accounts of God's work among the tribes of the New Hebrides Islands. His address was followed by a brief report from a missionary who had also been asked to tell of his work. In a low trembling voice he said: *"I have no remarkable success to relate like Mr. Williams. I have laboured for Christ in a far-off land for many years and have seen only small results but I have this comfort. When the Master comes to reckon with His servants, He will not say: 'Well done, good and successful servant', but 'Well done, good and faithful servant'* (See Matthew 25:21) *and I have tried to be faithful".*

As I reflect on this classic book on Christian service, I see a man who was faithful to the very end. Are you such a person? I wonder, even now is the devil tempting you to quit? Will you say with Nehemiah: *"I am doing a great work ... I cannot come down"* (Chapter 6:3). In his faithfulness, he was a picture of the Lord Jesus. As the crowd gathered around the Cross, they cried: *"Come down!"*

How glad we should be that He refused: *"I am doing a great work ... I cannot come down".*

CHAPTER 18
Esther

It was an hour of crisis. A situation had arisen in which the destiny of the United Kingdom was in the balance. The morning of 10th May 1940 dawned in London with the news of a German offensive. Holland and Belgium had been invaded, and France was soon to be trodden under by the rapidly advancing Nazi boot. At six o'clock that morning a message summoned Churchill to Buckingham Palace. There the King asked him to mobilise the government against Hitler. By the end of the day, Churchill had accepted a position he would hold for the duration of the war, one that would secure him a place of honour in history. His journal records his feelings of that fateful night:

"During these crowded days of the political crisis, my pulse had not quickened at any moment. I took it all as it came. But I cannot conceal from the reader of this truthful account that as I went to bed at about 3 am I was conscious of a profound sense of relief. At last I had the authority to give directions over the whole scene. I felt as if I were walking with destiny, and that all my past life had been but a preparation for this hour and for this trial."

It was an hour of crisis. A situation had arisen in which the destiny of the Jewish nation was in the balance. Ahasuerus, or Xerxes, the King of Persia (Esther 3:1) had consented to sign a decree at the request of the wicked Haman (verse 10), the wicked and implacable enemy of God's people, that on the thirteenth day of the twelfth month (verse 13) all Jews, somewhere in the region of 15 million, throughout his vast empire should be slain. It seemed that certain judgment was about to overwhelm God's people, and that the lamp of Israel would be put out for ever.

God in His purposes had decreed that the Jewish people would be indestructible. In fact, God had promised that the Jewish nation would be as lasting as the sun, moon and stars. (See Jeremiah 31:35) God had said: *"No weapon that is formed against thee shall prosper"* (Isaiah 54:17). Yet now, in this book of Esther, we find the purpose of God and the plan of man on a collision course. The atmosphere is one of bewilderment. The capital city is thrown into a state of confusion.

Can this really be true? Can there be no appeal? Can there be anyone who could change the plan? Amend it? Delay it? Abolish it?

For the Jews, the sky was falling in upon them and there was no place to hide. But then, God is always standing somewhere in the shadows, ruling and overruling. In the wondrous providence of God, a Hebrew orphan girl had been brought into a unique relationship with the king. Ahasuerus had chosen Esther as his bride. He had set the royal crown on her head and made her Queen. (See Chapter 2:17) God had so ordained that she should come to the kingdom for such a time, that out of desperate weakness His people might be made strong, that in an hour of impending judgment, there might arise deliverance to the Jewish people.

It is such an hour of crisis today. Satan, *"the Haman"* of the people of God, knows that his time is short. From within and without he is making a last desperate bid to overwhelm the church. Surely it is obvious to every thoughtful mind that the situation is desperate. Time is running out. World events are moving fast. The nations are lining up for the last great conflagration. Only a last great sweep of the Spirit of God can meet the need. This is indeed the hour of crisis and: *"Who knoweth whether thou art come to the kingdom for such a time as this?"* (Esther 4:14)

The book of Esther is one of two books in the Bible named after women. Ruth was a Gentile woman who married a Jew; Esther was a Jewish woman who married a Gentile.

1. The Place of this Story

The story is set in Shushan. This was located 150 miles east of Babylon, in modern Iran not far from the Iraqi border.

2. The Period of this Story

The events of Esther occur between the first return of the Jews under Zerubbabel in 538 B.C., and the second return led by Ezra in 458 B.C. Ahasuerus ruled from 486 B.C. to 465 B.C. and Esther covers the 483 – 473 B.C. portion of his reign. *Now this story takes place among the Jews who decided to remain in Babylon.* They felt that life was too good in Babylon and so they decided they would remain there and not be part of the remnant that went back to the land of promise. Of course, you can see from the opening verse that it is no longer Babylon but Persia that is now in control. The Persian Empire was the largest the world had ever seen. It covered modern day Turkey, Iraq, Iran, Pakistan, Jordan, Lebanon, Israel and parts of Egypt, Sudan, Libya and Arabia. Millions of people, speaking a multitude of languages, all owed allegiance to their sovereign lord the king. Ahasuerus was known as: *"The Great King, the King of kings"*.

3. The People of this Story

There are several main characters in this book. There is Ahasuerus the king. His Greek name is Xerxes. There is Vashti his Queen in Chapter 1. Her name means *"beautiful"*. We also find Haman. He hated the Jews. We find Mordecai, the Jewish cousin of Esther. Then we find Esther herself. This was her Persian name and the name means *"Star"*. But what is:

4. The Purpose of this Story

The purpose is to show us that though God is invisible, He is invincible. Here is a story about how God preserved the nation of Israel from annihilation. It is a story that was not new to Esther. Indeed it is a story that has continued to this very day. It started in the land of Egypt when Pharaoh set out to destroy the Jewish people. It continued in modern history when Hitler gassed six million Jews. *Indeed, is this story not continuing to this very day?* But,

God is in control!

Though the name of God appears nowhere in this book, the hand of God appears everywhere. Now for some there is:

5. The Problem of this Story

The problem is this very thing. God's name nowhere appears and this has made some question whether this book should be included in the divinely-inspired Scriptures. *Martin Luther is reputed to have disliked the book and wished that it did not exist.* But if the name of God is not mentioned in the book of Esther, His finger certainly is. But why is God never mentioned? Well, here is the biggest surprise. **God *is* mentioned.** God is actually mentioned five times, but few are able to spot it. The secret hiding of God's name is not evident in the English Bible, but scholars tell us in the Hebrew Bible the name of God (Jehovah) does appear in acrostic form. (Chapter 1:20; 5:4; 5:13; 7:5 and 7:7)

One thing is certain - the key to understanding the book of Esther is one word. Do you know what it is? **Providence.** That word providence comes from two words, the word *"pro"* meaning *"before"* and the word *"video"* meaning *"to see".* Providence simply means "to see beforehand and to provide for what is seen".

Do you hear that word *"provide"* in the word "providence"? The providence of God simply means that God sees every event before it occurs and provides for that event and makes sure that it fits into His plan for your life.

Louis Berkhof says: *"Providence is that work of God in which He preserves all His creatures, is active in all that happens in the world and directs all things to their appointed end".* Providence has also been defined as: *"The hand of God in the glove of history".* Now keeping that in mind, we can divide this book into three sections which show us three aspects of God's providence.

(1) THE PREPARATION FOR GOD'S PROVIDENCE - Chapter 1:1-2:20

It all begins with Queen Vashti's refusal to obey King Ahasuerus. Who can blame her? Her sense of purity and dignity in refusing to attend this drunken orgy is used by God to cause the king to look for another Queen. Esther, a Jewess, is chosen. You see, it is essential for the Lord's purposes that one of His own people should have the ear of this pagan monarch.

The book of Esther begins with a feast. Actually there are three feasts in this book:

1. The Feast of the King: Chapters 1-2
2. The Feast of the Queen: Chapters 3-7
3. The Feast of Purim: Chapters 8-10

Now what is the purpose behind this banquet in Chapter 1? Scripture does not tell us, but secular history does. Herodotus, the ancient Greek historian, mentions a great gathering of officials in Shushan in the year 483 BC to consider the war against Greece. Greece had soundly defeated the Persians at Marathon in 490 BC when Darius I, Ahasuerus' father, attacked them, and Darius had died several years later when preparing to return to Greece to get revenge for the loss. *So now his son feels compelled to avenge his father and expand his empire at the same time.* To help gain the support of the rulers of the various provinces, Ahasuerus wined and dined these officials with much feasting to break down any resistance they had to his wishes. It was a bit like the salesman who takes you out to an exclusive restaurant for an expensive dinner to try to seal a business contract. Ahasuerus is simply using his prosperity and luxury to soften them up. He hoped they would agree to go to battle. Here was a man who had trouble with wine. He liked to drink (Chapter 3:15) and he drank too much. Indeed Chapter 1 verse 10 says: *"When the heart of the king was merry with wine"*, he called on his wife to display herself.

Do you see here:

(a) THE QUEEN THAT IS DETHRONED: Exit Vashti

Look at Chapter 1 verses 11 and 12. Here is an old boy that wants his wife to show off her beautiful body to the lustful, drunken men at his feast. *Some Jewish scholars believe the text of Scripture meant that Vashti was to come nude with only her royal crown on.* But Vashti was a Queen who preferred to lose her crown of royalty to retain her crown of integrity. She said *"No!"* to something wrong knowing that she risked her crown. *Do you not admire Queen Vashti? She set her modesty above the goal of career advancement.*

Is it not sad that we have lost modesty *in the nation*? We are living in a culture when people take their clothes off and pose for magazines and become instant celebrities. **"Oh, be careful little eyes what you see"** on the television, in the magazine, on Facebook, the internet, the film.

Is it not sad that we have lost modesty *in the church?* Yet the Word of God says: *"In like manner also, that women adorn themselves in modest apparel"* (1 Timothy 2:9). The Greek word for *"Adorn"* means to *" arrange", "to put in order"* or *"to make ready".* A woman is to arrange herself appropriately for the worship service. This includes wearing decent clothing which reflects a properly-adorned chaste heart. I am all for the covering of a Christian lady's head, for I believe the head covering is Scriptural, but what about the covering of a Christian lady's body? *Ladies, when you dress for a worship service so as to attract attention to yourself, you have violated the purpose of worship.* You need to examine your motives and goals for the way you dress. Is your intent to show the grace and beauty of womanhood? Is it to show your love and devotion to your husband? Is it to reveal a humble heart devoted to worshipping God? Or is it to call attention to yourself and flaunt your shape, your wealth, your beauty? Like Vashti, is your conduct modest? Are you prepared to take a stand for decency, purity and modesty? Vashti, a heathen woman, was prepared to say: "No!" to these drunken, lustful men.

Can you see these old boys now? One woman has said *"No!"* and they are in real trouble. So what do they do? They reward good with evil. The King and his counsellors make a decision: *"That Vashti come no more before King Ahasuerus; and let the king give her royal estate unto another that is better than she"* (Chapter 1:19) In other words, you see here a Queen that is dethroned and then:

(b) THE QUEEN THAT IS ENTHRONED: Enter Esther

What you have to keep in mind is that Esther does not have any idea of what is going on. She knows nothing of the events that are taking place in the royal palace. She knows nothing about this *"royal edict"* which will set events in motion that will totally change her life.

Now who was Esther? Well, she was a cousin of Mordecai whose family had been taken into captivity in 597 B.C. Her own parents were dead, so he took her into his own home and reared her as his own daughter. Her Hebrew name 'Hadassah' means *"myrtle"*, while her Persian name 'Esther' means *"star"*. Can you see:

1. Her External Beauty

The Bible says she was fair and beautiful. The Hebrew means she had a pretty face and figure. Josephus says: *"She surpassed all women in beauty"* in the entire habitable world. Satan is always using beautiful bodies to promote his work, but Satan is here outmanoeuvred by God in the beautiful body business. God uses a beautiful body to defeat one of Satan's major plans for destroying the Jewish race. Esther won the Miss Persia beauty contest. Look at Chapter 2 verse 17. But Esther not only had external beauty, for there was:

2. Her Internal Beauty

She captured the attention of the king's servant Hegai and he promoted her (Chapter 2:9). Moreover, she was a woman of self-control (verse 10). She could keep a secret. Do you see what God is doing here? He is putting the right people in the right places to accomplish His sovereign purpose.

(2) THE DEMONSTRATION OF GOD'S PROVIDENCE - Chapter 2:21-7:10

Through seemingly coincidental circumstances, the Jews are delivered from certain annihilation. Now it seems that there are four strands to this displaying of God's providence. Notice it begins with:

(a) AHASUERUS' PRESERVATION

A plot to assassinate the king was foiled. Mordecai, in a place of position and honour (See Chapter 2:21), gets hold of the information. He goes to Esther, his adopted daughter. She, in turns, informs the king. They put the S.A.S. on the job. They discover it is true and the two conspirators are hanged on a tree. Now something was recorded: *"And it was written in the book of the chronicles before the king"* (Chapter 2:23). These chronicles were a historical diary of important government happenings – and the record was then stored away.

Later on when King Ahasuerus could not sleep, he had some of these chronicles read to him. This brought his attention to Mordecai at a most opportune time. (Chapter 6:1–3) Mordecai had revealed the plot against the King. Through his intervention, the King's life had been saved.

Does that not seem incidental? What has this got to do with God? What has it do with Esther? What has it do with us? Well, for the believer nothing is unimportant. The little things in life are just as important as the big things in life. Someone has said: *"God swings big doors on little hinges"*. Your whole life can change on one little thing. One little phone call. One little visit. One little text message. One little email. One little word - and your whole life can change.

Will you put it into your memory? *"And it was written in the book of the chronicles before the king."*

(b) HAMAN'S PLOT

Everything about Haman is hateful. He is the villain, the *"baddie"* in the story. Because of his lineage from Agag, Haman carried deep hostility toward the Jews. (See Deuteronomy 25:18 and 1 Samuel

15:32-33) The flash-point here came when Mordecai refused to offer Haman the reverence and adoration which was due to God alone. (See Exodus 20:3-4) Everyone else was bowing down in worship to Haman, but Mordecai was standing up. Now that is not easy. It is not easy to go against the crowd. It is not easy to be a non-conformist. But here was one man who would not bow. The world said to him: *"Bow down, you stupid fool"*, but he said: *"I will not bow"*. So Haman asks that all Jews should be slain. Here is the ultimate in anti-Semitic action in the Old Testament. Here is the Old Testament Adolf Hitler. Here is a picture of *"the man of sin"* who will one day appear and ruthlessly reign over humanity. (See 2 Thessalonians 2:4 and Revelation 13:7) Do you see Haman as he goes in to make a proposal to the king? He talks to the king about:

1. A People

A people and *"their laws are diverse from all people"* (Chapter 3:8). Their laws were different because they were God's chosen people. They alone received God's law from His hand.

2. A Price

Haman offers to pay the king 10,000 talents of silver for the privilege of getting rid of the Jews.

3. A Permission

"If it please the king, let it be written that they may be destroyed" (Chapter 3:9). A nation is about to be eradicated, yet no question is asked!

4. A Proclamation

"Death to the Jews!" Can you imagine the grief, the anguish as the royal couriers take this message to every part of the empire? Can you see the Jews now? Haman not only wants to destroy this people, but he wants to terrorise them for a whole year. (See Chapter 3:12-13)

Why is Satan so opposed to the Jews? Satan is determined to destroy the Jews because salvation is of the Jews. Satan was behind the slaughter of the boys in Egypt. He was behind the slaughter of the babies in Bethlehem. There is something demonic about Anti-Semitism. Pharaoh tried to drown the Jews. Haman tried to destroy the Jews. Herod tried to murder the Jews. Hitler tried to gas the Jews. *"Death to the Jews!"* keeps popping up in history because salvation is of the Jews. We ought to be very grateful to the Jewish people. We owe them a great debt. Everything we know about God came through them and our Saviour was and is a Jew. Without the Jews we would not have a Bible at all. No wonder they are hated more than any other people. Yet, as J. Vernon McGee used to say: *"The Jew has attended the funeral of every one of the nations that has tried to exterminate him"*. Do you see:

(c) MORDECAI'S PLAN

He calls:

1. Esther to Utilize Her Special Position

He cries: *"Go in unto the king"* (Chapter 4:8). She was to use her unique position with the king for the deliverance of her people. He says: *"Esther, be active, be decisive, go into the king"*. For far too long Christians have been indecisive and inactive in a worsening world situation and in a deteriorating church situation. What we need is to be awakened to the perils of the hour and to the possibilities of revival. This is not a time for sitting back. There is a call from God to intervene, to get involved, to do something for Him before He calls you home.

2. Esther to Recognize God's Sovereign Purpose

"Who knoweth whether thou art come to the kingdom for such a time as this?" (Chapter 4:14) *"Esther, can you see God in all of this? Can you see His hand in your appointment and elevation to the palace? Do you see that God is behind all of this?"*

Do we always discern God's hand in the "ordinary" affairs of everyday life? *"Who knoweth whether thou art come to the kingdom for such a time as this?"* What a choice Esther had to make! I wonder, have you ever thought about the choice that is facing you today? You see, there is a sense in which God's servants have all been born *"for such a time as this".* We should all be asking, whether we are younger like Esther or older like Mordecai: *"What work has the Lord especially for me to do because He has allowed me to be alive at this particular time?"* Do you realise that this is your time?

In such a time as this - what are you standing against and what are you standing for? Does the Lord want you to stand against pornography? Does He want you to speak a word in opposition to abortion? Does the Lord want you to help the alcoholic or the abused children? What about the disabled? What are you doing to stand up, to stand alone, to answer the call of God in this hour?

Are you ready to be salt and light in this world in such an hour? Esther was! Do you see what she said: *"So will I go in unto the king …. and if I perish, I perish"* (verse 16). *"Enough of the easy life in the palace",* says Esther. *"It is time to put my name on the line. I am Jewish and I believe in the living God. I am ready to stand alone for my people and if I perish, I perish".*

(d) ESTHER'S PLEA

Will you notice how carefully, calmly and skilfully Esther approaches this problem. Although the days are precious, she does not rush into the matter. You see, God is at work in it all and He gives the Queen favour (Chapter 5:2) and the King insomnia (Chapter 6:1). As a possible cure for his sleeplessness he orders that the state records be read. Surely they will send anyone off to sleep! He is made aware of Mordecai's kindness and realizes that the loyal Jew has never been rewarded. Events move swiftly after this. At the banquet Haman is exposed as the originator of the plot against the Jews (Chapter 7:3-6) and the judgment is reversed so that Haman is hanged from the very gallows he had hoped to use for Mordecai. Now I want to see here:

1. The Sleeplessness of the King

"On that night could not the king sleep" (Chapter 6:1). It was the night before the day that Haman planned to hang Mordecai. What kept the king awake? Does the perfect timing of God not take your breath away? On no other night was Mordecai in such danger as this night. I love the first three words of this chapter: *"On that night"*.

Richard Sibbes, in the sixteenth century, says this:

"Nothing so high, that is above His providence; nothing so low that is beneath it; nothing so large but it is bounded by it; nothing so confused but God can order it; nothing so bad but He can draw good out of it; nothing so wisely plotted but God can disappoint it."

Can you see the king now? He sits up in bed and says: *"Have we rewarded this man?"* "What man?" "Mordecai." Do you see what God is doing? He is preparing the heart of the king for the request of Esther, for we see here not only the Sleeplessness of the King but also:

2. The Brokenness of the Queen

Look at Chapter 7 verses 1 to 4. Esther describes what lies ahead for her people: *"We are to be sold, I and my people, to be destroyed, to be slain, and to perish"*. Do you see Chapter 8 verse 6? Haman has been killed, but Esther still pleads with the King: *"How can I endure to see the evil that shall come unto my people?"* Do you feel like that? Esther approaches the King selflessly, with a burden for others.

Is this how we approach the King of Kings and Lord of Lords? Weighed down with a burden, for the salvation of others. Do you recall Paul's passion for the lost? He says: *"I have great heaviness and continual sorrow in my heart. For I could wish that myself were accursed from Christ for my brethren, my kinsmen according to the flesh"* (Romans 9:2-3). Sheer heaviness of spirit brought Paul to tears, real tears. On another occasion, he could remind his brethren: *"By the space of three years"* he *"ceased not warn every one night and day with tears"* (Acts 20:31). What about the Saviour Himself? Do we

A Journey Through the Bible

not read that He was a Man of *"strong crying and tears"* (Hebrews 5:7)? He was *"a man of sorrows, and acquainted with grief"* (Isaiah 53:3).

Are you like the Saviour? Do you have a heart of concern for the lost? When was the last time that we had such a concern for lost friends that we actually shed real tears of concern that they might be saved?

William Burns as a lad of 17 years, visiting Glasgow for the first time, was overwhelmed by so many sad faces. He got separated from his mother, but eventually she found him weeping bitterly: *"What ails you, lad? Are you ill?"* she asked. *"Oh, mother, mother",* he sobbed: *"The thud of those many Christless feet on their way to Hell breaks my heart".* Do Christless feet on the way to Hell break your heart? Like Esther, are you concerned for your fellow men and women?

Is this not interesting? Haman had been furious because a Jewish man would not bow down to him. Now Haman was prostrate before a Jewish woman begging for his life. It was all over for Haman. In the end God always wins.

(3) THE CELEBRATION ABOUT GOD'S PROVIDENCE - Chapters 8-10

Through a grateful Gentile king, Israel receives a perpetual memorial of their miraculous existence. Once Haman is out of the way, peace reigns in the palace.

(a) A NEW DECREE IS COMMUNICATED

This gave the Jews the right to defend themselves. (See Chapter 8:11) Do you know what the first edict of the king was all about? Condemnation. Do you know what the second edict of the king was all about? Salvation. You see, the law of the Medes and Persians was like some churches. It never changed! (Daniel 6:8) King Ahasuerus could not legally revoke his edict, but he could issue a new decree that would favour the Jews.

This was good news and you will notice they wanted to get the *"good news"* out urgently. *"The posts . . . . being hastened and pressed on by the king's commandment"* (Chapter 8:14). If only the church today were like those couriers. How we need to tell the peoples of the world in their own language the good news of salvation through faith in Jesus Christ! But for some reason we linger, we hesitate, we procrastinate. We say *"the time is not come, the time that the Lord's house should be built"* (Haggai 1:2).

(b) A NEW DAY IS COMMEMORATED

The feast of Purim was ordained by the Jews rather than by God. (Chapter 9:27) To this very day, the Jews keep the feast of Purim. It is the plural of the word *"pur"* which means *"lots"* (See Chapter 9:24 and 3:7). Each year the Jews celebrate this deliverance in the festival of Purim. For Jews and their family it is very much a day of celebration. Every time Haman's name is mentioned, there is hissing and booing and every time Mordecai's name is mentioned, it is greeted with cheers. Children take gifts of food to the elderly, and the day is spent in a party atmosphere. One of the purposes of the book of Esther is to explain how this non-Mosaic feast of Purim became part of the Jewish calendar. Over the Feast of Purim we can write one word. Do you know what it is? *"Remember!"*

Over the Lord's Supper, we can write one word: *"Remember"*. The Lord Jesus said: *"This do in remembrance of Me"* (Luke 22:19).

Is it not astonishing that we who are redeemed need a reminder? Yet such is the Lord's understanding of our weakness and the treachery of our own hearts that He has made provision for us to be reminded in this "forget Me not feast". He wants us to keep the centrality of His death ever before our minds.

> *Remember Thee and all Thy pains,*
> *And all Thy love to me,*
> *Yea, while a breath, a pulse remains,*
> *Will I remember Thee.*

(c) A NEW DIGNITY IS CIRCULATED

Who would have guessed that the one-time gate keeper would be promoted to Prime Minister? *"For Mordecai the Jew was next unto King Ahasuerus, and great among the Jews, and accepted of the multitude of his brethren, seeking the wealth of his people and speaking peace to all his seed"* (Chapter 10:3).

Can you imagine the headlines of the 'Susa Daily Sun'? ***"Gentile King chooses new Prime Minister ...... a Jew."*** How unchanging is the principle: *"Them that honour Me, I will honour"* (1 Samuel 2:30).

So the book ends and so this first volume of our *"A Journey Through the Bible"* ends. But what a way to end! In the end, God wins.

God will always win, for He is in control. The name of God is not mentioned here, but the hand of God used this woman of God to spare the people of God so that the Son of God might come to demonstrate the love of God. God took the Wrong man out so He could ultimately bring the Right man in.

Amy Carmichael as a little brown-eyed girl prayed that God would give her blue eyes. She even asked her mother to pray with her that God would give her blue eyes. Her mother said: *"But honey, God gave you brown eyes. He wanted you to have brown eyes and He gave you brown eyes for a reason"*. Years later, while a missionary in India, Amy Carmichael realized the truth of her mother's words. When persecution broke out, the Christians were some of the first that were arrested. Amy Carmichael overheard a group of soldiers talking: *"Get all the Christians, especially the Carmichael woman"*. One soldier asked: *"How will we know her?"* He was answered: *"She is a foreigner. All foreigners have blue eyes. Look for everyone with blue eyes"*. Amy Carmichael finally understood why God had given her brown eyes.

The book of Esther reminds us that even when we cannot see God's hand, we can trust God's heart. Even if we cannot hear His name, we will not forget His nature.

Truth forever on the scaffold, wrong forever on the throne,

Yet that scaffold sways the future and behind the dim unknown,
Standeth God within the shadows, keeping watch above His own.

He was God all day yesterday, He is God all day today and He will be God all day tomorrow.

He is the God of history, of prophecy, of destiny, of eternity. He is still on the throne, still in control, still in charge.

Trust Him!

Also available by Denis Lyle:

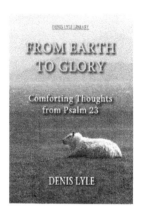

From Earth to Glory - Psalm 23
ISBN 9781872734484

Denis Lyle has taken a very fresh and inspiring approach to Psalm 23. *From Earth to Glory* focuses on the Lord as the Shepherd. The illustrations throughout the narrative are fascinating and the spiritual lessons from them give value to the book.

The reading and studying of *From Earth to Glory* will most certainly be of spiritual help and blessing.

Norrie Emerson

Available from:

www.ritchiechristianmedia.co.uk